Ride the White Horse
A Checkered Jockey's Story
Of
Racing, Rage and Redemption

By Eddie Donnally

D1496459

Ride the White Horse
A Checkered Jockey's Story
Of
Racing, Rage and Redemption

"Donnally can flat out write. He relates a wrenching, no-holds barred tale with the masterful strokes of one entirely at ease with words. . . (The) title provides a good hint at where this is going and what a wild and bumpy ride it will be. He was a good rider, but he's a great writer."
Mary Simon, two-time Eclipse Award winning writer for the "Daily Racing Form."

"Years ago, Eddie Donnally and I shared a prestigious turf-writing award. Now Eddie's sharing a riveting, brass-knuckles story that not even some of his closest friends knew. Hollywood, pay attention. And don't worry about the inspirational happy ending getting in the way."
Bill Christine: Eclipse Award winning former writer for the "Los Angeles Times."

"A fallen jockey's raw ride to redemption; beautifully written and straight from the heart" -- Sasscer Hill, Agatha and Macavity nominated author of THE SEA HORSE TRADE

"Your inspirational story should be a must read for those who are suffering from some form of addiction and believe salvation is impossible. This book is one for the ages." Dan Mearns: Former Managing Editor, Blood-Horse Magazine and Thoroughbred Times and author, "Seattle Slew: Racing's Only Undefeated Triple Crown Winner."

"It takes guts to ride an animal that weighs a half ton and can run up to 40 mph! It takes probably even more courage to write a candid and transparent autobiography, baring one's soul to a wide and mostly unknown audience. Of course, Reverend Eddie Donnally has done both! And in Ride the White Horse, he tells of the awesome and loving God that carried him all along the way!" Steve Jeck, Online Program Director, Knox Theological Seminary and author: "The Stone Builder: How Obstacles Lead to Your Destiny"

"Ride the White Horse" is enormously entertaining. It is a well written treatment of a fascinating subject, touching on all the highs and not avoiding any of the lows. Eddie Donnally is clearly a man who can talk the talk. That's because he has definitely walked the walk. W. Cothran "Cot" Campbell: President Dogwood Stables, Thoroughbred racing partnership pioneer and author, "Memoirs of a Longshot, Lightning in a Bottle," and "Rascals and Racehorses."

"Donnally depicts a dark and sometimes frightening journey that leads ultimately to an affirmation of life. Paul Moran: Former journalist for Newsday and two time winner of the Eclipse Award.

Ride the White Horse
A Checkered Jockey's Story
Of
Racing, Rage and Redemption

By Eddie Donnally

Eddie with his wife, Sandi

Eddie Donnally is the only professional jockey to win an Eclipse Award for Newspaper Writing and one who has been a television show producer and host, certified fund raiser and minister and chaplain.

A jockey for 19 years, he rode 10,2790 races at 54 tracks, winning nearly 1,177. He was indicted for sports bribery in 1978 and in 1996 left the Los Angeles Twin Towers jail to begin his ministry at the Los Angeles Dream Center, where in four years he became a licensed Foursquare Minister.

A former sportswriter for the "Dallas Morning News," he published over 100 other articles in other newspapers and magazines, was an Associate Pastor at two Los Angeles Foursquare Churches and recently led a team of 15 to provide spiritual care to victims of Hurricane Sandy. He served as the Race Track Chaplaincy of America's Director of Development for eight years. There, he founded the "White Horse Award," given each year during Breeders' Cup week to an underserved racing hero. He holds a Certificate in Fund Raising from UCLA and a Doctorate of Ministry from Summit Bible College.

His story has been published in magazines and books, discussed on radio shows and featured on "The 700 Club" and Christian Television Network's "Herman and Sharron Show." A frequent speaker in churches, recovery conferences and rehab centers, he shares his checkered career as a jockey, sibling sexual trauma, suicide attempt, two stays in psyche wards and battles with addictions to sex and crack cocaine. In 1996, God's Shekinah Glory lit up a holding cell housing him and a dozen other inmates. The event healed him and put him in full time ministry since. He and his wife, Sandi, live in Clearwater Florida where he is a hospital and hospice chaplain.

Ride the White Horse, an autobiography by Eddie Donnally.
Copyright Dr. Edward C. Donnally DMIN. Library of Congress
Registration Number
TXu-1-850-811, January 20, 2013

LIBRARY OF CONGRESS CATALOGING-IN PUBLICATION DATA
Dr. Edward C. Donnally DMIN: Sole Author
Ride the White Horse
p.cm
LCCN
ISBN # **0989136604**

Published by Shine Publishing Co.
P/O Box 354
Safety Harbor Fl. 34695-0354
Ridethewhitehorse1@gmail.com

All Biblical quotes are from the New Kings James Version

I would like to profusely thank my wife, Sandi who not only gave me the space and time to write this book but listened when I needed to talk about it. She also trusted me enough to write details about past relationships, something that required true generosity of heart. She is the love of my life.

I would like to acknowledge the significant contribution made to this book by my editor and advisor, Amy Owens of Lexington, KY. I am convinced her input made this a much better read.

I thank Brian D. Greene, Mary Simon and Suncoast hospice chaplain Virginia "Ginny" Bishop for their final proofing and editing.

I also want to thank Jan and Mark Robbins at California's Shadow Mountain Stables for the use of the cover photo, which I happened to take, of their rare white Thoroughbred stallion, Arctic White.

For updated news on the book, Eddie's book signings, speaking engagements and more, go to www.ridethewhitehorse.org. Check him out on Face Book, email him at: *ridethewhitehorse1@gmail.com* or follow him a #chaplaineddie.

TABLE OF CONTENTS

9: Covington Virginia May 1960
(A) CHILDHOOD TO ARREST
RAGING WITH MY FATHER

10: Richardson Texas, Spring 1991
(B) BATTLING ATTRACTIONS AND ADDICTIONS
A BIPOLAR LIFE

11: Philippe Park on Tampa Bay, March 17, 1974
(C) LIFE AS A JOCKEY
SHAKEN DOWN/DERBY DISASTER

12: Chatsworth High School near Los Angeles, September 13, 2008
(D) LIFE TODAY
METROLINK MINISTER

13: Low Moor Virginia, August 1960
(A) CHILDHOOD TO ARREST: LEARNING TO RIDE
LEAVING MY HOME, NOT MY PAIN

14: Richardson Texas, December 21, 1992
(B) BATTLING ATTRACTIONS AND ADDICTIONS
A BANNER DAY/ LEAVING AGAIN AND GOING NOWHERE

15: Suffolk Downs, East Boston Massachusetts, October 16, 1974
(C) LIFE AS A JOCKEY
A LIFE CHANGING RACE

16: Time and Place Anonymous
(D) LIFE TODAY
AN ABUSED CHAPLAIN/ A NEW DIRECTION; MAYBE

17: Patchen Wilkes Farm, Lexington Kentucky, August 1960
(A) CHILDHOOD TO ARREST: STILL LEARNING
PAIN ON A HORSE / HURT IN MY HEART

18: Sam Houston Race Park, Houston Texas, April 24, 1994
(B) BATTLING ATTRACTIONS AND ADDICTIONS
A NEW CITY / A NEW ADDICTION

19: Salem New Hampshire, Evening, October 16, 1974
(C) LIFE AS A JOCKEY
A BOTCHED FIX / WHAT NOW?

20: Lexington Kentucky, October 2006
(D) LIFE TODAY
WHITE HORSE BATTLES / WHITE HORSE WINS

21: Bowie Race Course, Bowie Maryland, March 1963
(A) CHILDHOOD TO ARREST: RACING BEGINS
CHEATING: RISKY BUT PROFITABLE

22: Houston Texas, Summer 1994
(B) BATTLING ATTRACTIONS AND ADDICTIONS
HOOKED

23: Somerville Massachusetts, October 17, 1974
(C) LIFE AS A JOCKEY
GETTING COZY WITH KILLERS

24: Venice Beach California, August 2009
(D) LIFE TODAY
PREACHING OR HELPING?

25: Baltimore Maryland, Fall 1969
(A) CHILDHOOD TO ARREST: RACING AND REALITY
EGGS AND TOUTS/TALES OF THE TOUGH

26: Inglewood California, November 1994
(B) BATTLING ATTRACTIONS AND ADDICTIONS
ONE DAWN IN MY DARK NIGHT OF THE SOUL

27: Churchill Downs, Louisville Kentucky, Spring 1975
(C) LIFE AS A JOCKEY
MAKING NICE WITH THE MOB

28: Humboldt County Fair, Ferndale California, August 2006
(D) LIFE TODAY
OH BOY, I'M A REAL CHAPLAIN NOW

29: Latonia Racetrack, Florence Kentucky, March 31, 1973
(A) CHILDHOOD TO ARREST
STUPID IS HARD/ELECTRIC JOCKEY WITH A JUICE MACHINE

30: Hollywood Park, Inglewood California, Winter 1994-95
(B) BATTLINGS ATTRACTIONS AND ADDICTIONS
RUBBING GRETA AND GLORY

31: Rockingham Park, Salem New Hampshire, July 1, 1978
(C) LIFE AS A JOCKEY
HELLO U.S. MARSHALS/TAKEN FOR A RIDE

32: Santa Anita, Arcadia California, October 23, 2008
(D) LIFE TODAY
TURNING THE PAGE. . . OUCH!

33: Oaklawn Park, Hot Springs Arkansas, Valentine's Day 1979
(A) CHILDHOOD TO ARREST
A VALENTINE FROM THE FEDS

34: Hollywood Park, Inglewood California, Spring 1995
(B) ATTRACTIONS AND ADDICTIONS
JACK THE TRAINER MEET JACK THE DOG

35: Rochester New York, May 1979
(C) LIFE AS A JOCKEY
LIVING ON THE Q-TEE

36: Time and Place Anonymous
(D) LIFE TODAY
SACRED SPACE/ WHAT IS GOD SAYING

37: Boston Massachusetts, July 1979
LIFE AS JOCKEY
BACK TO BOSTON

38: Hollywood Park, Inglewood California, Summer 1995
BATTLING ATTRACTIONS AND ADDICTIONS
BYE BYE BACKSTRETCH

39: Hollywood Park, Inglewood California, November 9, 1984
LIFE AS A SPORTSWRITER
HANGING WITH THE HEAVIES

40: Methodist Hospital, Arcadia California, December 9, 2010
LIFE TODAY
GOODBYE, OLD FRIEND

INTRODUCTION

Bossier City Louisiana, Fall 1986

I look up from my well-bitten toenails dangling from a decades-old hospital bed, time and place returning to my mind like a paralysis nightmare. I sit in a backless gurney and stare through a twilight window. It's quiet, far too quiet, and six stories below in a driving rain cars move silently across the Red River. Everybody's going home except me. Last night I swallowed 36 tranquilizers.

Unlike most of the commuters, no one waits at home for me. My white brick ranch home lies on a pine forest hilltop on the other side of the river from this Shreveport, Louisiana, psychiatric hospital. It's less than a mile from Louisiana Downs racetrack, where I work as the Turf writer for The Dallas Morning News. Like my heart, the house is empty, silent in darkness. Here, there are bars on the windows to prevent jumping. I can't remember if I checked myself in or if someone just brought me here. I know the hallway door is locked and manned by orderlies around the clock. I'm 42 and for the first time in my life, I'm captured.

Beyond the window, grayness is settling over the land. Mercifully, inside the dim room my mind is also fading to black. Thinking is like sandpaper scratching across my exposed brain. Had I known what lay before me in the next seven years, I would have worked at unbolting the bars and jumping. Before me is a descent into the darkness of self destruction in which the only light reveals a path leading to deeper shades of blackness. Yet at the end is redemption at a level that at the time I could not envision.

Writing a memoir about any of the three, my racing career, rage born in childhood or my much later redemption would be more commercially palatable. Yet the three are intertwined beyond separation. Still, it's one thing to ask God to forgive me, and it's another to ask the horse racing world and all those I've hurt to forgive me. The former came in a blue metallic haze inside a San Pedro, California, jail cell in 1996. The latter, I hope will come in this book. It would be hypocritical for me to condemn horse racing. The persons in it are no better or worse than people anywhere else. That I was at times a bad actor in no way condemns the hundreds of thousands in the sport who are not.

I don't blame my actions on anyone mentioned here. God has given me the power to forgive and that is the most liberating power on earth. I take responsibility for all the things I did, right or wrong. I wish no one harm, yet I must remain true to the actual events. I left out or changed some names and left a few times, places and persons anonymous for the sake of confidentiality. All the scenes I describe actually took place, are factually accurate and are retold to the best of my memory and others I interviewed. All of the conversations for which I use dialogue took place. Their tone and setting are accurate. However, remembering the exact wording is impossible and thus was recreated to the best of my memory. Let it be known to all that my memory is exactly that: my memory. It can conflict with the memories of others and if so, I make no claim to my memory being better than theirs.

The book's formatting is like nothing I have encountered. I didn't want to spend two-thirds of the book on my struggles and failings before I finally related the jail cell miracle and the changes it brought. Because my redemption is the diamond laid on the black pillow of my past, I make it part of the ongoing story.

The book has four tracks with each in sequence, and it is important to read the dates in the sub-headings.

Track A: Childhood to Arrest relives the period from my first memory, a violent one, to the pain of losing my mother, my grandmother who raised me at 12, stepbrother sexual trauma, leaving home at 16 to become a jockey and my early days as a race rider. It merges with Track C after I was arrested for sports bribery in 1978.

Track B: Battling Attractions and Addictions chronicles the period from my divorce, remarriage, fall into bisexuality, being bipolar, stays in two psyche wards, a suicide attempt and going from hosting my own TV show and writing for a major newspaper to rubbing horses for trainer Jack Van Berg within seven months because of an addiction to crack cocaine. The battles continue until my jailhouse miracle.

Track C: Life as a Jockey records the period I rode races, starting when I met my first wife Debbie at Finger Lakes Racetrack when I was 27, winning a race after taking a bribe from Boston's Winter Hill Gang to lose, being asked by the FBI to testify against its members in an infamous race-fixing trial, my life on the run and the race-fixing trial in Boston.

Track D: Life Today is samplings of my life as a minster and chaplain that hopefully relates to the first three chapters in that particular sequence.

The first three tracks converge late in the book. Feel free to read from front to back, one track at a time or even skip around. Many of the chapters are self contained. I hate writers who build suspense and set the hook only to put the reader somewhere else in the next chapter. My only hope is that you put the period of my life after salvation in context. Racing and rage are my life's shadows. Redemption is its bones and flesh. I think you will find those chapters a welcome respite.

17

In the book of Joshua, the Israelite priests carrying the Ark of the Covenant stepped out on their faith and into a flood-swollen Jordan River. It immediately receded, allowing Joshua, his army of thousands and the entire Hebrew people who had departed Egypt 40 years earlier to cross over to the Promised Land. In honor of the miracle, each of the 12 tribes' leaders picked up a rock and used the stones to erect an altar to God. That is the intention of this book: to commemorate a series of God's supernatural miracles and to record one cheating jockey's true story of racing, rage and redemption.

I rode the "pale" horse of hell in Revelation Six and I am convinced I will one day ride the white horse of heaven in Revelation 19. I'll ride back to earth on a white horse, following Jesus, who leads the battle against evil aboard his white stallion. One day this guy who rode over 10,000 races will literally get to gallop across heaven aboard a white horse.

(A) CHILDHOOD TO ARREST

LOVE LOST EARLY

1: Low Moor Virginia, Summer 1947

My father is running through my grandmother's grape arbor, chasing my mother. I'm crying, knowing for sure that if he catches her, she'll get hurt.

We live at the edge of the village of Low Moor in southwestern Virginia and for 40 miles behind my house is wilderness. The grape arbor sits at the end of our jumbo garden near our eight-room house in the foothills of the Allegheny Mountains. I'm four, and it's my first memory.

The walk started well. Mabel, my mother, and Westwood, my father walk through rows of corn and tomatoes in our garden, then move on to the grassy arbor to look at the grapes. It's dog-day hot. Flies and bees buzz around the plants. I can smell the ripe tomatoes and sweet corn still in their husks.

The mood is light, the conversation happy. The garden is doing well. Yet the talk becomes an argument. They exchange threats, him to break her neck; her to kick him out of the house. My mother screams at my father. He moves toward her. She runs. I'm sure now. He wants to hurt her. I'm screaming my lungs out.

But she's fast, more agile than my father and on her side is fear. She's ducking in and out of the black arbor poles, and his feet are sliding in the loose dirt. He's getting closer. She screams. I scream louder.

The back screen door slams shut. My grandmother, drying her flour-covered hands on her apron descends the porch steps in an awkward waddle as her Sherman tank frame makes for the arbor. Matronly and stern, she scoops me up with one of her flabby arms. With me clinging to her neck, she moves to stand between her railroad-man son-in-law and her only daughter. All are panting.

"What going on, West?" she asks.

My father, Westwood, has a red face, but I'm not sure it's from the running or my grandmother's frosty tone. "We were just playing," he says. "Little Eddie got scared. He thought we were fighting."

He puts his arm around my mother whose face has hardened with resignation. She shrugs her shoulders and reaches for me. I hug Grandma's flabby neck even harder. My grandmother swells her considerable girth. "As long as you live in my house, they'll be no fighting." She carries me to the house and over her shoulder I see them glance at each other.

Spring 1949

I sit on the lowest stair-step inside our farmhouse and wait for the woman to come with the needle that makes my mom stop screaming. I'm almost six, and Momma's been dying of stomach cancer for a long time. A nurse friend comes to give morphine injections as she lies in a portable bed in the downstairs parlor. But the woman also works in the hospital and is sometimes late. Those times, my mom moans and moans until they turn into screams.

My dad is a brakeman/conductor for the Chesapeake and Ohio Railroad, so we get free passes. Daddy, Momma and Sheila and Colleen, two of my three older sisters and I rode the train all the way up to

Washington, D.C. to see the Ringling Bros. and Barnum & Bailey circus. She'd gotten sick on the way back, and I'd heard Daddy say that her eating moldy lettuce had caused it. I didn't know lettuce could make you die.

I don't remember that anyone told me Momma died, though I suppose her mother who owned the house where we lived probably did. They'd set up her shiny brass casket in the same parlor where she died. One of my aunts leads me up and hoists me in her arms to see.

"Your momma went home to heaven," she says as if that explained it all. I want to tell her that she had a perfectly good home here, but am too taken by Mommy. She smells like cleaning fluid. Her flour-white skin looks ready to flake off and heavy red rouge colored cheekbones stick out above her sunken cheeks. She looks like a Christmas doll.

"She's passed to a better place now. She won't have to suffer anymore." I don't understand. I hated the screams. But sometimes she'd still take me up on her lap and look at me like I'd done something good before tears glassed up her honey-warm, brown eyes. Then she'd quickly smooth my hair from my forehead and look away so I wouldn't see her cry. Momma might not suffer anymore. I am not so sure about me.

"I just thank God," the aunt continues. I don't feel like thanking anyone. Except maybe the woman who came and stopped Momma's screaming.

That night at the wake, a lot of friends and visiting relatives get drunk. I hear people I don't know say all kinds of new things about Momma. Every time Aunt Madge from West Virginia looks my way, she bursts into tears and slams a handkerchief over her plump mouth. What am I doing that makes her so sad? She finally comes over, pats my head, erupts in shrieking cries and clutches me to her soft bosom. I cry a while and then look up. "Can I go out and play now?"

A few days later, I stand on the back seat and look out our sedan's back window at the long line of cars snaking their way up the woody road to the hilltop cemetery. It looks out over the Jackson River and the river valley. It looks like the bottom of a humongous green cup with the iron-gray mountains making the sides. Birds chirp, a man in black says words

21

and two men crank a creaking hoist that lowers her casket into a concrete grave. One day a while later, when Grandma takes me on her lap and rocks me, she says, "The last words your momma said was to take care of little Eddie."

I'm in Woolworth's one day with my oldest sister, Patsy, looking at toys in metal bins. I want a pistol that looks real. She won't buy it, and when I start whining, she walks away. My first grade teacher comes over and offers to buy it for me. Just then a man she knows walks up. She pats me on the head and explains, "This is little Eddie. His mother just died of cancer, you know."

I throw down the pistol and run from the store. I don't stop until I'm far enough away that nobody will see me cry. I sit on a deserted part of the sidewalk and fight to hold back the tears. I will never be poor little Eddie, the undersized boy pitied because his momma died.

(B) BATTLING ATTRACTIONS AND ADDICTIONS

A BAD BEGINNING

2: Bossier City Louisiana, Spring 1985

My stomach is getting upset, and I don't want to throw up, so I slide off the couch in front of our roaring fireplace and lie flat on my stomach atop the thick shag carpeting. I feel good enough to reach for the bottle of Crown Royal and take another slug. That and the full bottle of 36 Xanax should do it. Sleep will come, and my life will be over.

Debbie, my wife of 14 years, is about to leave town with a jockey friend we'd both known for years. Our two young children, Dawn and Derek, live with her. I just can't stand the thought of her traveling with another jockey, especially one I know. I have too many memories of us doing the same, too many tracks, her even being my agent and booking my mounts. We'd spent months in our motor home going from track to track like gypsies and parked it on an island in the Florida Keys and used our small boat to fish the flats. I watched our two children being born.

But the wars we fought are over. I'd become a workaholic. One evening she told me she had lied about her age for years and was only 16 when we met. She had left her home to be with me when she was no more than a kid, had never dated or had a job other than working as my agent.

Then last year, she'd found a job bartending in a local hotel, had an affair with her boss, something that let loose adolescent memories of an evil with which I had never dealt. Though not yet official, our marriage is over. Already, the unholy urges that swell within me promise a future I can't accept. My kids will hate me. I had enough brass to race Thoroughbreds for nearly 20 years. Yet I can't face a future without Debbie and one in which I will turn into something I hate. Better is the blackness about to overtake me.

*****

A green filament media inside a glass cylinder goes up and down as an electrical hum reaches my senses. I lie in an emergency room bed with a transparent tube down my throat and, no doubt, in my stomach. As the cylinder pumps and the machine hums, green bile flows from the tube and into a container I cannot see.

My first thought is that I am a failure. I had locked the front door. How had I been found? Then I see Donna standing just inside the closed curtain. She'd been a friend to both Debbie and me. I later learn Debbie had given her a key to our house and on that night, of all nights, she had grown concerned about me and made a decision to visit.

18 Months Later

My nine-year-old son, Derek, drags a suitcase up the cement pathway leading to my white brick home. A lump rises in my throat as I run to help. He's coming to live with me and my new wife, Debra, her three daughters and Derek's older sister, Dawn. I take the suitcase and bend to hug him. Never in my life have I loved anyone more than him at that moment.

A few months earlier, I'd stood atop a mountain observation tower near Hot Springs, Arkansas, and exchanged wedding vows with Debra. Turf writer Randy Moss, now a noted TV racing analyst, was our single witness. He stood near Debra's three children and watched the Oaklawn Park track chaplain seal us in holy matrimony. Bearing the same first name as my former wife, she is the same height and weight and has the same black hair. My divorce from Debbie was 10 days old.

Debbie has been gone a year, traveling with a former jockey friend. After I spent a week in a psyche ward following my suicide attempt, I started anti-depressant medication and weekly sessions with Christian psychiatrist Dr. Roper. I got well enough to have Dawn and Derek live with me, but when their mother returned, they went back with her. Desperately seeking to have a normal, heterosexual life, I had married Debra.

I'm intentionally busy, working as the turf editor for *The Dallas Morning News* out of Louisiana Downs just across the Texas border in Bossier City, Louisiana. Winner of horse racing's Eclipse Award for outstanding newspaper feature writing the previous year, I have a weekly feature on the track's TV show, host handicapping seminars in a local hotel five days a week, write a weekly column and travel across the nation to cover major races. Though the sport is loved by Texans who flock to the track, the sport is in the process of again being legalized there after a half-century absence.

Derek and I walk into the house, expecting to be greeted by his sister Dawn. Instead, Debra's three young daughters gather around Derek and chatter.

"Where's Dawn?" I ask Debra, who is busy in the kitchen.

"She's confined to her room," Debra explains, flashing wide dark eyes that make me hope for an early night. "She sassed me right in front of everybody. She's worse than your ex."

"Aren't you even going to say hello to Derek?"

"I just never expected him today." She walks to Derek and kneels to get eye level. "Of course I'm glad you're here. You always had a good time with the girls when you visited. You can stay in the room with that sister of yours. But first we'll all have dinner."

All move to the table in the dining area. "Isn't Dawn going to eat with us?"

"No. Hell no. She sassed me. Let her stay in her room. She thinks she runs the show. It's time she learned a lesson."

Dawn appears in the hall, running toward me, her face a panic. "Dad, she threw a knife at me. She cut my hand, look."

I bent to meet her eyes. "And what did you do to her?"

"She smart-mouthed me," Debra yells. "I told her to wash last night's dishes and she said she wouldn't."

"Dad, she cut me. Look at my hand."

Sure enough there was a small cut on the back of her hand. I turn to Debra. "You threw a knife at her?"

"She screamed at me like she's screaming now. She's evil. Evil like her mother." Debra plants both hands on her hips and glares at me. "Is she your wife or am I? If she's your wife then go sleep with her tonight."

Debra marches out of the room and after an awkward silence, I have the rest of us sit down and eat. Dawn goes to the couch, holding her cut hand and crying in massive sobs. I sit beside her and send one of the girls to get a Band-Aid.

"I want to go back and live with Mom."

"Just give her a chance," I say. "Things will get better. This is new to all of us."

"She's crazy, Dad. She's crazy."

"Don't be talking about her that way. If you respect her, she'll respect you."

"I hate it here, Dad. She picks on me. Tells me all the time I look like my mother."

"Oh sure, she's got a temper," I say, glancing at the couch, knowing that despite a week's absence and her flashing eyes, I'll spend the night there. We eat, mostly in silence. Derek seems particularly subdued. I feel helpless. After dinner, we clean up the table and wash the dishes. The other kids spend a time visiting while Dawn sits alone. And after a while, I send them all to bed. Glad to be alone, I pour a Crown and water and sit on the couch.

I'd just gotten back from Louisville, where I had covered the Kentucky Derby for *The Dallas Morning News*. It was won by the Jack Van Berg-trained Alysheba. Nearing the finish line, the gangly Alysheba had stumbled on a rival's heels and nearly fell, yet recovered to win. The race's favorite, Demons Begone, ridden by friend Pat Day, bled profusely from his nose during the race, causing Day to pull him to a stop. The lead of my story, sure to be teased on page one and run on the front page of the sports section, had been "Blood and Guts made the difference in the Derby." The editor killed it, telling me that many among their some one million Sunday subscribers read the paper while eating breakfast. I don't know if the lead sentence would cause any of them to be sick, but its disappearance made me ready to throw up.

My 19-year career as a jockey had ended six years earlier. At 5'4", I'd climbed down from a half-ton of honed-to-the-bone racing machine and was where I started, a foot shorter than the crowd. My sports writing career is blooming. My photo appears alongside my racing column that runs three days each week in *The Dallas Morning News*, the nation's seventh-largest newspaper. During a race meeting at Louisiana Downs, I'd picked 10 winners on an 11-race card. I am a regular on the track's weekly television show, selling handicapping tapes and am charging a large local hotel a hefty fee for holding race-day classes for their guests, complete with tips on that day's card. I'd just written a TV documentary, "Ride like the Wind," that had been nominated for a second Eclipse Award. Two years earlier, I'd stood on a stage at the Hyatt Regency Century Plaza in Los Angeles and with actor John Forsythe officiating, walked forward and received an Eclipse Award for Outstanding Newspaper Writing.

Writing had been a way for me to escape my own reality and create another one since I was 18 and wrote horrible short stories and even worse poetry. During my years of riding, I took college journalism and creative writing courses at several colleges. By the time I retired from riding, I'd sold articles to virtually every major newspaper east of the Mississippi. *The New York Times* Sunday magazine had flown me to Grand Falls, New

Brunswick, Canada, to write a story on Ron Turcotte, who won the Triple Crown aboard Secretariat and, after a racing accident, is a paraplegic.

I pour another drink, walk to our wooden deck behind the home and fire up the hot tub. Below it are nearly an acre of pine and oak trees, a trampoline for the kids in their midst. In my shorts, I ease into hot bubbling water, sip my drink and muse about my former wife, Debbie. We'd met when I was 27 and she 16. She'd grown up with me, and there was little wonder she wanted to work in a bar when we didn't need the money. For the first time in her life, she wanted to know what it was like to be on her own. I had smothered her emotionally, and when she looked elsewhere, she found a new life that didn't include me. Though she was the first to commit infidelity, it was as much my fault as hers.

Yet the thought of her in bed with another man changed something inside me. To make it easier, I've somehow bent the scene to include me. I can no longer hide from myself what happened with my stepbrother and me for two years, starting when I was 11.

Despite the hot water bubbling over me, I feel a chill. A fear of something I can't name. I remember when I was 14 and took the first puff off a cigarette. Inhaling made me feel new, a coming of age that marked my entry into manhood. Though I had stopped smoking at 25, these yearnings were like that: new, exciting and frightening. I'd always loved adventure, taking a chance, living on the edge. But the second I took that first puff off a cigarette, I'd thought of lung cancer. Tonight, I think of AIDS.

FINGER LAKES FEMME FATALE/RACETRACK RODEO

3: Finger Lakes racetrack, Farmington New York, Summer 1970

A teen with dark hair reaching halfway down her back turns her head until her eyes survey mine. She's above me, leaning over the railing of the track's indoor saddling paddock. I stand below in full jockey regalia and pretend to listen to a trainer give instructions on how I am to ride his horse. She flashes a look that says, "I know something you don't," and I wonder what it is. The trainer hoists me aboard my mount, and a groom leads us toward a short tunnel and into the bright afternoon sunlight. With stiffened back, knees pressed against withers, head held high, my intentionally detached straight-ahead stare ends as suddenly as the career of a fat jockey. My head swivels to gather in one of the most beautiful women I've seen. Her lips curl into a sly smile. I'm ready to jump off and run to meet her.

29

I manage to stay aboard and ride the race. The real race starts with me hurrying back to the jockeys' room, where I tell the clerk of scales, the presiding official, that I am sick and want to be removed from the rest of the day's scheduled mounts. Twenty-seven at the time and nine years into my jockey career, I'm a committed bachelor and well-practiced bad boy.

Still damp from my shower, I rush downstairs to the rail where she stands. I walk up, see a racing program in her hand and realize she knows exactly who I am. We shake hands, and I can't keep from grinning. We chat a minute or two before I ask her to dinner that evening. She says she has to go home with her friend Rita but provides her phone number.

That Saturday evening, I drive to Rochester and meet her dad and mom, Jim and Margaret, who live in a fairly humble apartment and are impressed that I'm a successful jockey. Both are Italian, and I soon learn that Marge makes some of the best sauce and meatballs this side of Rome. Debbie tells me she is 18 though I note she has not finished high school. We start dating and I'm smitten.

That summer a jockey strike is taking place. I'm one of the local reps for the Jockeys' Guild, the agency that represents jockeys to track management and horsemen. We strongly believe we're underpaid. Today, there's some 60 jockeys made paraplegic by racing accidents. Statistically, riding races is one of the most dangerous of all sports. Racing is something we do because we love money slightly more than we hate pain. Crossing that finish line in front of cheering fans is slightly more compelling than the fear of dying or spending the rest of your life in a wheelchair. We all know that the day fear tips to the other side is the day we need to get out.

Riders, unlike other pro athletes, don't sign contracts. At the time, the Guild—to whom each rider pays $7 for each mount—provides an injured jockey with $200 a week. Still, the organization carries a catastrophic policy underwritten by Lloyd's of London that covers the medical cost of injuries. Yet at that time, the rider of the horse who finishes second in the Kentucky Derby is paid $100. Jockeys aren't guaranteed 10 percent of the winning purse as they are now, much less 10 percent of the purse for second and third. If the purse is $4,000, the winning horse owner receives $2,400 and the jockey $240. That is if the owner and trainer happen to be generous and decide to include it. Even when they do, $25 goes to your agent, another $20 to your jockeys' room valet and $7 to the Guild. You get home with about $173 before taxes. If the trainer gets mad because he doesn't like the ride you later gave one of his horses, or you decide to ride another trainer's horse instead of his, you lose the 10 percent and earn a $35 mount fee even if you win. You take home about $20. All for risking your life.

So the better riders decide to strike, agreeing to ride only for trainers who guarantee 10 percent of the winning purse. Scabs come in from smaller half-mile bush tracks, glad to ride for $35 a race. My friend Billy McKeever comes from a local racing family and like me is holding out. We're complaining to each other in the jockeys' room, and when I notice the starting gate position of one of the scabs I get an idea.

"My my," I tell Billy. "Look at this; the scab is in seven I'm in eight and you have the six. How about I come in a little at the start and you come out a little and we scare this weasel back to the half-milers?"

His smile seems as wide as the 12-stall starting gate. Just as planned, we break from the starting gate. My horse drifts in slightly. Billy's mount sidles out a few inches. The other jockey rises in the saddle and hauls back against the reins. His horse's head goes into the air and unable to see, the horse's front hooves' tick the back heels of Billy's horse. Faster than a trap door at a hanging, the horse and rider fall.

Thinking we might have killed or at least injured the guy, my heart's in my throat as I ride the race. I breathe a long sigh of relief when I jog back to unsaddle and see him hustling toward the jockeys' room, saddle in his hand. He and his mount are unharmed. The rider packs his tack and is gone before the last race is run.

Within days, the scabs are gone, and the trainers reluctantly sign a contract, guaranteeing us 10 percent of the amount their winning horses earn. The 10 percent becomes mandatory and remains today. However, track stewards summon Billy and me to view the race's rerun tapes the next day. Unimpressed by our weak argument that it's accidental, they suspend us both from riding for 10 racing days. This means 10 racing days or two weeks with no pay. A headline in the local Rochester paper reads, "Rodeo at Finger Lakes."

Debbie's dad is actually impressed my picture makes the local paper, and Debbie and I continue our romance. One evening we ride the roller coaster at the lakeside amusement park for two hours, laughing every second. There are long rides in my small power boat on Canandaigua Lake, acid trips and love making. She practically moves into my rented lakeside cabin. We are in love.

That fall before the meeting ends and I head south to Florida with Debbie in the passenger seat, I ride a race that I'll never forget. Inside the jockeys' room, several score riders share space, jokes and after some races, punches. We party together, know each other's families and risk our lives in the same profession. But put on a helmet and goggles, climb aboard a racehorse, and walk into that starting gate and you're on your own.

On September 17, I'm warming up my mount in the crisp fall air. I look up to see a herd of geese fly in almost a perfect V. They are heading south. The leaves are in full bloom. The wind has a chill. I know it's time to soon follow them. After I warm up my mount, I'm thinking I know a little about my equine rivals, but much more about the race's jockeys. Among them is Jose Olivares, the king of riders at Finger Lakes, who consistently leads the standings. Called "Daddy Rabbit" because of many children, the Cuban speaks poor English and is one of the biggest jockeys I've met. He has to sweat off several pounds in the "hot box" each day but constantly remains jovial.

Someone once accurately compared riding a race with flying an airliner. Part of the art is to travel as far as one can, using as little fuel as possible. The crucial difference is that in a race, jockeys also have to learn to read developing patterns as well as gauge their horse's reserve fuel. On top of that, a rider has to make dozens of split-second decisions in the some 72 seconds required to run a six-furlong race. It's like navigating rush-hour traffic while you're trying to get your wife to the hospital before she has your baby in the back of the car. You have less than a second to make most decisions. You either do it or not. The time it takes to consider the move makes it too late.

This is a two-turn route race, and I'm on a horse that comes from behind and makes a late charge in the stretch. We break from the gate, and by the time we get midway around the last turn about three-eighths of a mile from the wire I'm in the middle of the pack with horses all around me. I still have fuel in the tank, but not enough to swing wide, lose ground and still win. I'm looking for a seam between the half-dozen horses in front of me. A hole opens between two horses. I guide my mount toward the space, make a loud clucking sound and slap his shoulder with the whip. He accelerates. A horse directly on my inside is also moving toward the same space.

Jockeys don't win by letting others go first. I start hand-riding my horse, pushing his neck forward. The space before us is still two horses wide. The other jockey I know is Olivares also asks his mount to accelerate. My horse is about a neck in front of his, giving me the advantage. The hole starts to close, but I'm far enough in it to maintain my position. Jose isn't so lucky. He rises to check his horse. It's too late. I feel my horse's rear dangerously sink. In one or two strides he's back on balance. My insides turn weak. I can't turn my head far enough to look directly behind me. But I know what happened. The other horse's front legs have clipped my mount's back heels and fallen.

I don't remember anything else about the race. I don't remember Daddy Rabbit hollering for room or making any sound at all. It wouldn't have mattered. I do remember that when I unsaddle I see the ambulance that follows each race sitting on the track's last turn. I also remember watching the wreck on the jockeys' room television. I made a habit of never watching when I crash, but I watch this one, and when I see it my stomach goes sour.

I dress and go to the hospital. A group of doctors surround Jose's wife. Another rider walks up to me. "Jose's gonna live," he says. "But they say he severed his spinal cord. He's never going to take another step."

The next day, I and several riders review the rerun tapes with track stewards. All agree. Jose and I are both race-riding, doing what we're paid and expected to do. I'd committed to going through the hole. Because another rider slightly behind me tries to also get into the same space is not my fault. The riders flanking the space have not dramatically altered course. All agree it was simply an accident. One of those things that sometimes happens when a dozen Thoroughbreds race around a track inches apart.

Yet Jose will spend the rest of his life as a paraplegic. I'll always wonder.

(D) LIFE TODAY

A GHOST DISSOLVE

4: Tampa Bay Downs, Oldsmar Florida, February 2007

"Hey, don't I remember you? Didn't you use to race down here?"

I turn from the straight tonic water I'm drinking to face a withered man in khaki shorts and Hawaiian shirt, a fat cigar between his thin lips puffing foul smelling smoke. I'm standing at the Tampa Bay Downs grandstand bar, wondering how this man got to be 80 without lung cancer and how he can remember 35 years into the past. "You're Eddie Donnally, aren't you? Rode for Bill Combee and Bob Van Worp all the time? I cashed a $200 trifecta one day on that Combee horse Prince Joca something-or-other."

"Prince Jacopo. I still have a win photo of him."

Particular races and horses usually blur in my memory. I'd often stand in front of trainers as they talked in detail about a race I'd ridden on one of their horses a few weeks earlier. I'd widen my eyes with recognition and nod my head, remembering nothing. But not so with some horses. Not with Prince Jacopo. He wasn't a great horse and by most standards not a good one. But at the beginning of the season here for several years, Bill Combee would crank him up and as sure as construction on the road to work, he'd win two or three races. After a month of no racing usually spent

35

with other riders, exercise boys, and an occasional valet sleeping on our tiny home's living room floor, Prince Jacopo was a paycheck. He was good for the rent, two sacks of groceries at Publix, sneakers for our toddlers, and maybe, if Debbie and I could find a sitter, a night out on the town. A lot of things get foggy in 35 years. After a while, I don't even remember why I remember the things I do. But some of those animals who paid my way through the checkout line stick with me. Prince Jacopo is one.

"He was one honest racehorse," I say.

The guy inhales and blows smoke all over me. His eyes turn sly. "More than some of you jockeys, anyway. What you do these days?"

"I'm a minister, a chaplain actually. Help the Race Track Chaplaincy of America raise money. That's why I'm down here, visiting our track chaplain."

"So you got religion, did you?"

I grin. "More like it got me." I'm ready to share my testimony when Gladys Olivares walks up. The man turns and walks off saying he's "live in the Pick-Six." The field is loading into the starting gate and we pause to watch. I think for both of us, chatting during a race is a sort of sacrilege. When it ends, I ask, "How's Jose doing?"

"Some days he's okay. But the bladder infections keep coming. You know something? That man never complains." She smiles, and I can see she's held up well, still working at the track as a mutual clerk and taking care of a husband made paraplegic four decades earlier. The some three score paraplegic jockeys face a life fraught with secondary illnesses and a life span 20 years below normal. She knows as well as I that Jose's horse had clipped my horse's heels in the race that put him in a wheelchair for life.

I'd made many trips here for the RTCA and had spoken with her regularly because she's a member of the chaplain's council. But I have never faced Jose. A week earlier I had called her and asked if I could talk to him, something I had not done since that fall day at Finger Lakes. I usually worked while flying, but on this trip I could only stare out the window and think about the race that severed his spine. I know the event is a ghost I

36

have avoided far too long. She has to go back to work, she says, but gives me directions to their house and a key to the front door. I realize Jose is not well enough to get into a wheelchair and open it.

In the lives of the repentant redeemed there are things we know need to be fixed, even while knowing they can never be fixed. I can never make the accident not happen. I don't even know if I could make myself stop thinking that it was somehow my fault. Could I have slowed my horse sooner? Maybe decide to go around and not through the hole? I don't know. I do know bettors, horse owners and trainers expect jockeys to go all out and cautious jockeys find themselves parking cars in the track's valet lot. I realize I have a case of survivor's guilt, but that doesn't stop it from being there. Though I am finally allowing myself to learn how I feel about the incident, I never before had the guts or maybe even never cared enough to learn how Jose feels about it. Today, I will.

I ease my way into the small but extraordinarily neat house, call out and walk into Jose's bedroom. He's in bed but dressed and lying atop the covers. His face is drawn, and his brown skin has a puffed-up sheen. When he greets me, his voice is raspy and weak. I sit on the bed's edge, and we talk about the people we remember at Finger Lakes and even mention some names of riders who are now dead, several by their own hands. We talk about his battle with the Jockeys' Guild and his constant bladder infections. He has far less to say than his wife. He looks tired, and I know it's time. "I remember the day you fell," I say. "I'm sorry."

Lying there with his back propped up against the bed's backboard and his lifeless legs placed before him, he shrugs his shoulders and says in a Cuban accent, "It just happened. Sometimes in races things just happen we don't want to happen. You know that."

"I do." Thoughts of a race that happened in 1974 at Boston's Suffolk Downs and changed my life flash through my mind. Regret stuns my heart. "None of us gets to go back."

He nods his head, agreeing. My eyes are glassed over and probably red-rimmed, and there's nothing I can do about it. Here is a man who'd spent half of his life in a wheelchair because he fell on my horse's heels.

Yet he doesn't hold a grudge. Would I feel the same way? How many nights had he lain in bed wishing he could make love to his wife? How many times had he wished he could bounce new babies on his lap, babies who were never born? How many more moments of savored victory during a stretch run did he never get to live . . . or relive?

"I never knew how you felt about that day," I say, realizing my voice is husky, on the edge of breaking. I clear my throat. "I'm glad I finally got around to asking."

"Me too, Eddie."

"Has God helped you cope with all this?"

He shakes his lean face up and down. "A lot."

"And Jesus?"

He nods, his black eyes blossoming with sincerity.

He agrees to prayer and halfway through asking God to give him strength and health, I hear my voice cracking. After the prayer, we sit for a time in silence. He seems content, and I feel a peace descend. One of my ghosts of races past has turned to vapor.

(A) CHILDHOOD TO ARREST

VISIT BY AN ANGEL/THE DIRTY DEED

5: Low Moor Virginia, Fall 1957

It's a school night, and the upstairs bedroom I share with my stepbrother is dark. I'm asleep but wake and sit up in my bed. Something is wrong. I don't know what. Churning over and over in my stomach is this mass of dread. Putting my feet on the floor, I look around at the drawn window curtains, the chest of drawers we share and clothes spilling out of a stand-up hamper.

A soft tapping at the door fires up my senses. My father comes in and stands over me. He's not wearing a shirt, and his face is glum. "Your grandma Effie just had a stroke. She died on the way to the hospital."

Effie is my dead mother's mother. I'm 13 and less than a year earlier I'd moved out of her house on the other side of the village to live with my dad, his new wife and her son. My grandmother had not liked my stepmother and had begged me to stay with her and my older sisters.

Though she lived less than a mile away, I'd rarely visited. The last time months earlier. After Mom died six years earlier, she'd become my mother. I was the youngest of four, the baby and the only boy. She made me cereal before I went to sleep, took me in her arms and rocked me for a few minutes each morning before I went to school, and while there was an empty bedroom, I slept with her. She always sided with me in my battles with my older sisters, even when I shot one in the arm with my BB gun. On cold nights, she'd heat the iron on the stove top, wrap it in flannel and place it at our feet. When I had earaches, she'd pour sweet oil into my ear and make over me as if I were near death.

Now Grandma is dead.

Another body will be laid out in the spacious house's parlor, another noisy wake with drinking and arguing about who knew her best and what she wanted who to have. Another long stream of cars climbing to the hilltop cemetery. She is gone and with her any hope of deserting a situation so shameful I can't talk about it to anyone, and try hard to keep from even thinking about. We'd just finished when my dad comes in. Will God punish me for the awful thing we do all the time?

I want my father to sit beside me and hug me, at least give my shoulders a little encouraging buff up. The most I get is a concerned face. At that moment, I make up my mind. What is happening to me in secret would only make me grow up faster. I won't stay home much longer.

Funny, that's all my father said or did. He walks out. I sit on the bed, watching him leave.

I lie back expecting to cry quietly so I won't wake my stepbrother. A feeling comes over me: peace, calm, well-being. It flows through my body, as sweet as the butter and honey my grandmother used to make for me. It was like the times she'd rock me or in bed on cold nights made sure the warm iron was near my feet. I am being comforted. I put my pillow over my face. It is her spirit on the way out, come to say goodbye. Or maybe an angel she or my Mom sent.

Grandma was not a religious person. I'd often heard her express doubt about preachers' money-grabbing intentions. My oldest sister, Patsy, regularly took me to the village's limestone Presbyterian Church. The few times Pastor Wood came to visit, Grandma looked uncomfortable. She never went to church or much of anywhere else except for short visits. She didn't drive, and I don't think in her entire life she traveled outside the county where she was born. I don't remember ever seeing my father in a church, much less hearing him pray. I am not much better. In church I usually nap when the aging minister explains the theological nuances of predestination. Yet the night Grandma died, I knew she or an angel was telling me my future was predestined. That I'd be all right. Eventually.

The dirty deeds with my stepbrother had started even before I moved out of my Grandma's house. Female cousins were staying with us, and for most of the night we're all in one upstairs bedroom at the back of my grandma's eight-room house. We're laughing and giggling. Touching began, and while it didn't actually lead to intercourse, I touched the girls and my stepbrother had me touch him. I was not yet 12.

Today, I know I'd never done the things I did with him without his original initiation and coaching. When my father marries his mother, and the four of us move in together, it continues. I know it is wrong from the start. I hate it most that I grow to like it.

Yet a part of me wants it to stop. I think I should tell someone but can't get up the courage. I don't dare. And at 13 and 14, my testosterone is bubbling. I soon learn how during these acts to achieve pleasure. It even begins to seem normal. There's no affection or emotional attachment. We quarrel constantly, and my dislike turns to contempt. There is just this physical act that we perform on each other. It goes on two to three times a week for at least two years. I'd heard the words "queer" and "faggot" used by the men who hung out in front of the village's lone grocery store to describe people they considered less than human. That isn't me. That isn't who I am.

One evening we're just getting started when my stepmother pushes her head through our bedroom door. I'm not sure what she sees or even thinks she sees but she quickly closes the door. Nothing is ever mentioned.

Right or wrong, good or bad, real or imagined I feel she knows but does nothing to stop it. I begin to hate her the same way I do her son.

At 14, I'm a sophomore at Central High School in Low Moor and weigh every ounce of 90 pounds. Always athletic, I try out for the junior varsity football team, but the only cleats the school has are so immense I have to stuff cotton in the toes. When my teammates catch me, they jeer and call me "cotton toes." But I'm still good enough to sub in a couple of JV games as safety. I'm not good at pass defense, but I love tackling. Diving to hit the knees and see the runner fall flat feels satisfying. Even then, my rage is starting to surface.

(B) BATTLING ATTRACTIONS AND ADDICTIONS

SHRINKING FROM MY SHRINK

6: Bossier City Louisiana, Fall 1988

"I'm thinking maybe we should be winding this thing up," I tell Dr. Ralph Roper, my Christian psychiatrist. I exhale loudly and throw my arms over the wide wooden rails of an overstuffed chair placed opposite him in an office filled with books and diplomas. "It's been well over a year now, and I think I'm as well as I'm going to get."

"As you're going to get? Sounds like you're discouraged."

Then comes silence; my cue to talk. I flash a smile I realize he'll believe is masking what I honestly feel. "Uncovering feelings. That's why you guys get the big bucks. But come on, I'm easier to read than a Dick and Jane book." I look away trying to gather my thoughts. It hasn't been a good week. I had taken the kids roller-skating, even skating with them and showing off by skating backwards and dancing as they pretended not to know me. But I had somehow left Debra's middle daughter, Mandy, at the rink and driven off with her other two and my two, only to discover when

I arrived home she was missing. Debra called the rink, and I rushed back to retrieve her. Debra had been livid, reminding me that I had not left my two children, but one of her three daughters. She had thrown a plate at me and 30 minutes later we had made love. Later she said one former boyfriend liked to dress in women's clothes and make out, and how she thought that was titillating.

"Maybe I'm turning gay," I had blurted out to her. She had only smiled in an inviting way. Her announcement had stirred something already churning in me. I told her about a party at our house shortly before my first wife, Debbie had moved out well over a year earlier. Someone had invited a swishy gay, young and handsome yet feminine. At the time I knew Debbie was having an affair with her boss at a local hotel where she worked as a bartender. But we were still trying to work through it, and most at the party were her friends from the hotel. I and the swishy guy talked, and we went into our bedroom and sat on the bed. Debbie walked in. Though we're not touching, she sensed something and later told me, "I can't compete with a man."

I want to tell Dr. Roper about what is bubbling inside me and at least get his take on it being connected with what my stepbrother and I did. He is a trained counselor and I've dumped a lot on him without him judging me. But telling him would mean going into the whole abuse thing and I had been to weekly sessions for over a year and had not brought it up. I was getting ready to move to Dallas and work for Criterion. There isn't time.

"None of us gets along," I finally say. "Dawn says she wants to go back and live with her mother. Debra is hanging in, and we genuinely want it to work. But I'm leaving the *Morning News* and buying into a TV production company in Dallas. I like writing TV features and being in front of the camera. I'm going to be moving to Dallas soon. I already won an Eclipse Award for writing. I got nothing left to prove in that area."

"You said a lot just then. It sounds like you're angry with Debra because you want to leave."

"I think I'm angry with them both. I'm mad at myself. I thought I could make this work. I know we talked a lot about this, but I'm still angry at Debbie. I wasn't a perfect husband by a long shot, but I didn't go out and sleep with someone else."

"And you're angry?"

I want to tell him I'm mad at my stepbrother for messing up my head. Trying to turn me into something I detest. "Look, I've been taking all these pills for over a year. You got me on lithium because you say I'm a manic-depressive. I read their information. The stuff can make you blind. And I'm still mad, and I'm still depressed. It's not as severe as it was. I used to go in the press box at Louisiana Downs and lean my head against the glass wall and stand there staring for hours. I didn't even realize it until a friend told me. Am I ever going to get over that woman? I thought getting married would help. I know I married when I wasn't over Debbie, and maybe I shouldn't have. But here I am, and I want to make it work."

"Eddie, if I had to make a guess, and since we will soon be parting company I will, I'd say there are some things in your family of origin that you haven't talked about."

"Nothing much really," I say sarcastically. "It was just that my stepbrother and I did all these sexual things for two years, and now I think I'm turning gay."

He sits back and rubs his chin in thought. "You want to talk about it?"

I shake my head. "I can't.

"That explains a lot. I wish we'd gotten to this sooner. That's a lot to carry around. Those feelings you're describing are fairly common among abuse victims. It's not unusual that they manifest years or even decades after it happened. It would be healthy to talk about that over a period of time. Is that what you actually wanted to say when you talked about your anger?"

"I guess so."

There's silence for a time. I can't look at his face. I drop my head in both hands.

45

"Your inability to talk about it only reinforces my belief that it would be wise if you continued counseling in Dallas. I can recommend someone."

"Look, Doctor," I say, looking up, still angry. "Just to say it right now scares me to death." I hold out my hands, trembling beyond my control. "I'm just not ready."

"I think it's vital that you understand all that suppressed anger. Unless you examine the source of your anger or call up your stepbrother and scream at him, that anger will internalize. You've already held it inside for what, 25 years? It's going to manifest, like it or not, and those feelings of same-sex attraction aren't going to disappear. Given your background and faith, they won't be easy to reconcile. You've already made an effort at suicide. Eddie, stay in counseling."

I'm silent for a time. I wish I'd never told him. I'm still shaking. "I'll consider it. I will."

"I'll call with a referral." He stands.

I nod my head and get to my feet. Part of me is scared, and part of me wants to see this unfold.

"I wish you well, Eddie. Call me if you want to see me again."

We shake hands, and I know I'm going to miss the sessions. We had explored the book of Hosea, in which his wife, Gomer, had played the harlot only to return and ask forgiveness. Hosea had welcomed her back, though as Dr. Roper pointed out, the two never again consummated their relationship. He had once told me about an angel pulling him out from behind a steering wheel embedded in his chest by a head-on crash, saving his and his wife's life. I look up at his broad face, perpetually parked in neutral.

I clear my throat, gather my composure and look at the door. "Maybe God will send me an angel just like he sent you."

(C) LIFE AS A JOCKEY

THE FALCON FLEES

7: Philadelphia Pennsylvania, Fall 1973

"So you still believe you actually became a falcon?" my first wife, Debbie, asks me as we ride through the streets of Philadelphia. We're on our way to see a serious dealer of THC (delta-9-tetrahydrocannabinol), an extremely powerful chemical formula based on the active ingredient in marijuana.

"You know I did," I tell her. "You were there. I know what it's like to be a Peregrine Falcon, drop to the earth at over 100 miles an hour, unfold to a near stop and pluck up a ground squirrel I spotted from 2,000 feet."

"God, I wish you'd never gone to the top of that mesa while you were high. Something's changed in you."

We've been together a few years, racing at a lot of tracks and that spring we'd driven to San Francisco, where I'd ridden a few races at Bay Meadows in San Mateo and bought a motor home. I'd raced that summer at the now defunct Centennial Park racetrack near Denver, and we'd just returned to the East after spending several weeks touring Colorado while snorting massive amounts of THC, a powerful hallucinogen.

I was into books by Carlos Castaneda and his peyote-using Yaqui Indian, Don Juan. The Indian supposedly had the power to break through dimensions, race through the black desert at night without stumbling and transport himself to other places. This, combined with my study of supernatural healer Edgar Cayce, Eastern religious guru Yoganada and the practice of Buddhism's hatha yoga, made me believe I could put my body through a keyhole.

A friend had taken us to the end of a deserted canyon south of Denver to view a group of Peregrine Falcons, arguably the bird world's best fliers. Behind the canyon was a mesa our friend explained contained powerful spirits. I left the party and alone climbed the mesa where I snorted even more THC and sat in a full lotus pose for hours, watching falcons hunt in the terrain below. I willed the bird's spirit to enter my body. I felt it happen. The spirit escorted me to the spirit of the falcon. He and I became one.

I realize for the first time that his hunting was more than instinctual. It requires an intellect, and I feel the falcon make decisions based on sensory input. It has a memory and thinks about his young awaiting food. The falcon doesn't feel sympathy for its prey but recognizes it as a fellow being. Killing, even for food, is something it does not take lightly. Its spirit is much like the spirit that allows me to inhabit him, and that spirit seems much like my own.

The spirit remains in me.

"Turn left here," she calls out.

It's too late for the lumbering motor home towing a small car behind. I buzz past the intersection. "You got to tell me sooner. Now we're lost."

"You've got to stop thinking about that falcon thing all the time. You're entirely spaced out."

"There's a new light in me that you don't understand. Yeah, something changed in me. But for the better. Don't you remember what happened when that cop stopped us?"

She sighs and slowly shakes her head. In Colorado, a highway patrolman had pulled us over for a minor license tag violation. Knowing we had several kinds of drugs in the motor home that pulled our car, I ran out the motor home's back door to meet the police officer. Surprised, he flung out a hand in self-defense. I backed into the metal strip that secures the car to the motor home. But instead of falling I did a standing back flip over the hitch and came up saying I'm a traveling jockey. He drove me to the magistrate's office in his squad car where I paid for expired tags, drove me back and let us go. I know my new spirit made it all possible and tell Debbie just that several times.

"We should be in Florida already," she says. "Florida Downs starts in less than three weeks. You'll never get mounts if you show up late."

"I want to go back to Colorado to live. Near the mesa."

"Are you nuts?"

She frowns at me, and I try to concentrate on driving. Her eyes hold a bewilderment I have not seen. We'd lived together three years, and she'd been my partner and ally during a litany of battles. She touches my shoulder. "We're lost anyway. Why don't we just start driving there now?"

"As soon as I get the THC. You like it as much as I do."

She scoots over to the edge of her seat away from me and looks out the window.

It's dark when we find the dealer's apartment. We pay for six ounces, an enormous amount considering that two or three snorts would nearly imitate the high of LSD. But for the first time in my life, I don't have to constantly regurgitate to make weight. I'm down to a remarkable 105 pounds. Everyone tells me I look terrible, but I have a new energy and dexterity. Because of the hatha yoga, I can slow my pulse rate down to two to three beats a minute. I'm convinced my reflex time is nearly instantaneous.

We all snort some to test it. After we talk about the metaphysical, I feel a need to meditate and again experience the love and power in my spirit guide. Coming down from the mesa on a curving mountain road, I'd curled up into a ball in the motor home's center aisle while a friend drove. My body curled up like a loose basketball, I rolled around, bouncing off the interior contours, gliding under the table and glancing off the interior

49

seats. I felt no pain. I truly believe I can perform the same acts as the Indian swamis: spend a winter night in an icy cave, survive being buried alive or slip out of a straightjacket.

I ignore their conversation, go into the full lotus and begin the breath of fire, breathing in, holding it and letting it out, all in equal time. Slower and slower comes a heartbeat I can distinctly count. I don't need to breathe. Light itself can enter my body and sustain it. I feel myself float gently above my body toward the ceiling. My breathing stops. I can see my body below me. I'm moving to the astral plane, projecting myself to another dimension, an avatar without the need of a body.

Screaming! I hear screaming, far off and disconnected. Then I feel pounding, a thumping hollow sound. I'm on my back. Debbie is above me, hollering and beating on my chest. "You stopped breathing, you fool. You've overdosed. You were dying."

I sit up, pushing her off. She slumps beside me, breathing in squeaky gasps. She's right. I nearly died. I jump to my feet, hoist Debbie up and start for the door. She gathers the bag of THC, and we run down the steps and into the motor home.

We drive through the night, south through Maryland and into Virginia on Interstate 95. At one point, Debbie drives and I rest in the back. After a couple of hours, I'm ready to drive again. But instead of stopping, we decide to switch seats while driving. Other times I'd put one hand on the wheel as she slides from beneath it. From behind, I throw one leg over the back of the driver's seat and sit at the wheel as we continue.

This time, the wheel slips in my hand, and as she slides away, we start swaying. I get into the seat. With our car behind us, hitting the breaks would cause the rig to totally jackknife. I realize it's windy. I fight the wheel as we go back and forth over the four lanes with the top-heavy, single-axle motor home. If we tip over, our propane tank might explode. Neither of us wear seat belts. Each time I try to get it straight, I oversteer, bringing another bout of across-the-freeway, recklessly swaying.

I gradually get it under control. I drive slowly and get off at the next rest stop. I hug Debbie and get out. It's dawn and the cold air lights my face. I put both hands on the brown and white sides of the motor home, bow my head and sigh deeply. I'm still shaking. I hear the spirit is telling me all is well. After all, the falcon whispers, I can fly.

(D) LIFE TODAY

DEMONS DEPART HOLLYWOOD

8: Hollywood California, April 1998

It's nearly 4:00 a.m., and the outreach team from Hope for Homeless Youth at the Los Angeles Dream Center is about to wrap up and go back to our rooms at the former 1,440-room The Queen of Angels Hospital. We've been trolling the infamous corner of Santa Monica and Highland in Hollywood for lost souls, and we have to be in church at 9:30 a.m.

We're a mere block from Hollywood and Highland, sight of the Walk of Fame and the Kodak Theatre, a place where dreams come true. Yet we're at a corner just as storied and famous for broken dreams.

We've served coffee and donuts to pimps and johns and given single roses to straight, gay and transsexual prostitutes. We've offered to pray for their safety, and many allow us. We've given out dozens of wallet-sized cards with our contact information in hope that after a beating or being raped by a pimp or john the pros will call so we can come out and pick them up. Theirs is one of the world's most dangerous professions. For the transsexuals, there is added risk. Taking beatings is part of the occupation. They live three or four in a single motel room, inject black-market

52

hormones, work without the protection of a pimp and hop into cars with groups of males who think they are anatomically women. Statistics say at least 40 percent are HIV positive.

A porn arcade and taco stand lies in the strip mall behind us. Between them several youths gather at a cement wall. They've come to maybe turn a trick, learn who's holding, buy, sell or get high. Some are there simply to acknowledge membership in a brotherhood of the homeless; divided into groups they call family or tribes. They make a circuit to other "happening places" that include nearby Santa Monica and Venice Beach, Tempe, Arizona, New York City and even Key West, Florida. In Hollywood, they come and go as fast as bad movies.

I've lived in a single room at the Dream Center for nearly a year and have come to the conclusion that if God wants, I'll gladly spend the rest of my life in street ministry. It's my kind of life. Once, we met a gay kid bleeding from a hundred cuts after a gang had decided it would be fun to throw him through a plate-glass window. Emergency 911 refused to send an ambulance, so we picked enough glass from his bleeding thighs that he could sit in our van, and I took him to a nearby ER in swanky Cedars-Sinai. With little likelihood of his being admitted, I waited until he was treated then dropped him off at his apartment.

It's one thing to go out at midnight and witness the Gospel of Jesus Christ, and it's another to tell the people of the night that if they want to push the reset button on their lives, they can come back and spend a year with us, all expenses paid. A partner and I were once in our beat-up van, bringing back one kid who was tweaking on meth. He pulled a pistol and tried to get out of the front seat of the moving van, saying he intended to shoot a man he saw at a gas station. The gun turned out to shoot BBs, but both of us stayed up all night, listening to the tweaker rave on until he wound down enough to sleep.

A few months earlier at this same intersection, I saw a girl no more than 15 sitting on the wall, jerking with sobs as tears ran from her soft face. Janie, a female team member, and I approached.

"Is there anything we can do for you honey?" she asked.

"Just leave me alone," the girl shouted as she shifted her back against the cement wall, obviously uncomfortable. She wore several layers of multi-colored clothing, red-and-white-striped tights and combat boots.

"We just want to help," I said softly. "We'd sure like to hear what you have to say."

"I'm not worth it, and I'm ready to prove it."

Janie leaned in and put one hand on her shoulder. "I know somebody out there loves you and would be very hurt if you did anything to yourself."

"I know a lot about pain and suicide," I said. "But I got healed, and I believe God can heal you. Could I put my hand on your other shoulder and say a short prayer?"

She glanced around at the other youth on the wall. None seemed to notice, and she nodded. I gently placed a hand on her shoulder and prayed. A sentence into the prayer, God gave me a word of knowledge. I ended the prayer and said, "The Lord told me you're pregnant."

Her eyes widened. "I just had a fight with my boyfriend. He wants me to have an abortion."

"And what do you want to do?" Janie asked.

"I got no place to go and don't even know how to take care of a baby."

Janie reached out and used fingers to smooth her thin brown hair. "We can fix all that. And you don't have to make up your mind tonight."

She came back with us in a raggedy van, decided to stay, and we helped her obtain support from a crisis pregnancy center. She had her baby.

*****

The streets at night hold an attraction, and I'm in my element here. As we end the night, my ministry partner, Bill and I start the walk back to our parked van, a place we know the rest of our crew will be waiting. Bill abruptly stops.

"Wait a minute," he says as he walks to a clump of bushes lining the sidewalk. He peers into the area behind the bushes, obviously seeing something I do not. A man is squatting behind a row of thick shrubbery, peering out with eyes so wide he has to either be on speed or horrified.

Bill squats in front of him. "You all right back there?"

"Go away, they're looking for me." The voice is Hispanic and reminds me of a growling dog.

I lean close. "You want to come back with us? You'll be safe at the Dream Center."

He shakes his head. "Go away."

"Look," I say. "Walk with us. Whoever it is after you aren't going to bother you with us around."

He stands up, shaking his head. "You don't know this gang. I want to get out, but if they jump me out, they'll kill me in the process."

He's in his twenties, wearing the street gang uniform of oversized baggy pants and a new white T-shirt that reaches his knees. I figure he's from Boyle Heights in East L.A., but now he's in the neutral territory of Los Angeles. "How do they know you're here?" I ask.

"We came together, and I got in a beef with them." He walks from behind the hedges and glances around. "Look, I got to get out of here."

His eyes narrow and burn with anger, the kind I've only seen on schizophrenics and the demonized. His chin twists constantly and his skin seems stretched taut over a young face that sports a long, thin goatee. He's either mentally ill or he's been making nice with Satan.

"Walk back to the van and we'll give you a ride out of here," I offer.

"I need to disappear," he says. "Get invisible."

Bill and I exchange glances. "Son," my partner from Texas says in a drawl, "I think you got more on your back than your homies."

I lean in, looking him dead in his eyes. "I think Satan wants to kill you more than they do. I think you been dealing him in."

"How you know all that?"

"Sometimes God tells me things about people so he can save their lives," I say. "He's telling me right now that there is a part of you that wants to get set free."

"Not here. We got to go somewhere else."

55

We walk toward the place where the van is parked and where we will meet our crew. He tells me his name is Roberto but says little else. Bill and I silently pray in our spirit language. I know he'll stop and protest.

He stops and spins, heading the other way. I sprint to his front and stand square in his path. I've been cursed, spit on and swung at. But the Bible is true: resist the devil and he will flee. Demons make a sizable show, but I've yet to see one stand in front of a Spirit-filled Christian.

"Roberto," I say, putting my hands on both his shoulders, "You want to get set free? I know you do. I think you know something about God's mercy no matter what you've done."

Something registers in his dark eyes; a spark of humanity I know is real. My partner is beside me. Roberto stares at us for several seconds. I know a battle is going on for his life. He sinks back, but I put one hand on his shoulder and keep it there. "Let me pray for your safety."

It may seem odd, but pimps, prostitutes, drug addicts and even most of the demonized will let you pray for safety. Some probably think the prayer is no more than a good luck charm and fear denying it will bring down rotten luck or even bad karma. I don't care. If I can put my hands on a person and pray, something happens in the spirit world. Something that's always good.

My friend steps back. I can see his mouth moving silently. I know he's praying in his prayer language. It's part of our procedure: one talks, the other prays. I even say a silent prayer to be led by the spirit because I know my partner is praying for our spiritual and physical protection. Demons always interfere when one of their kind is in danger of being evicted.

I pray, first for protection for him and then for all of us. Exactly how the other team members know where we are, I never understand. Yet, suddenly they're beside us.

"Roberto here is being plagued by an unwanted visitor," I tell them, not about to raise my hands from his shoulders. I turn to him. "These are all strong Christians. They want to lay hands on you and pray too."

"I don't want nobody else touching me," he bellows. "You're the one God told me about." I'm not sure what he's talking about. I bow my head as a chorus of prayers spring up around me. I can feel the atmosphere change. Some speak in tongues. I hear a female voice sing in long harmonic notes, a language I don't think originated on earth. The crew is made up of strong Christian volunteers who dedicated at least a year to ministry and came to the Dream Center to live out their beliefs. All have done street ministry and praying out a demon in front of a porn parlor at 4:00 a.m. is something they live for.

My intent is to call out the demon while not allowing him to speak and to cast it out in the name of Jesus Christ. I know that I know that I know about Christ's authority. I know it from the Bible. I know it from the changes of others. I also know the miracle that happened to me. This is hardly new. A young man had come to Hope for Homeless Youth, dragging the coffin he slept in. His incisors have been surgically sharpened, and he says he regularly drinks human blood. The ministry's founder and director, Pastor Clayton Golliher leads and we spend nearly all night praying for him. The young man is set free and begins a new life. But that man came to the point of reaching out for help. I'm not that sure about Roberto.

"I saw Satan," he says.

We all look at him expectantly. "My friend and I used an Ouija board to contact him. We wanted his power. We were in a basement one night doing a rite we read about in a book and praying for him to come to us." He looks around, fear twisting his face. His entire being is back in the place where he'd met the devil. "An empty bottle of vodka broke right in front of us for no reason. I felt this power come over me. Manuel felt it too. He's the one I just got in a fight with. He said he's coming back with his homies. He plans on killing me."

"Stand in a circle with us as we all pray. I think you need our connection."

He shakes his head, not understanding. Yet he joins hands with the others, and I stand inside the circle. I ask God how I should pray. Using a tiny capsule of oil that's in my pocket, I anoint his head with oil. He screams and begins a series of expletives.

57

"Roberto," I interrupt. "Do you renounce Satan and ask God to forgive you right now?"

His head is hanging limply. Saliva drips from his open mouth. "Ahhhh, Ahhh," comes a tortured voice.

"Ask Jesus to forgive you," I say firmly. "If you're forgiven the demon has no right to you. You have to ask Christ to forgive you."

I don't know why I believe he has to do this. I just believe that is what the Holy Spirit is saying to me at the time. At least seven of the some 35 miracles Jesus performed involved casting out demons. Jesus simply told them to go, and they went. But once when his disciples failed, he told them they needed to first fast and pray. Before we leave for Hollywood, we always stand in a circle and pray that Jesus will first bind the "strongman." (Matthew 12:29)

He's breathing hard as if he'd been running and can't seem to stop the thick, wet wheezing that makes him sound like human bellows. I glance around. We all pray harder, loud enough to be heard blocks away. None of us cares. Just as an evil spirit has overtaken Roberto, the Spirit of God has overtaken us.

"Demon," I say, putting one hand on his forehead. "I declare in the name of Jesus Christ that any device, contract or plan by any imp, demon, power or principality over this man be declared null and void this instant."

I press, feeling the oil on his head heat under my palm. He's taller than me and I look up into closed eyes. Yet I can still see his pupils dart about. The hate and anger inside his head are burning my hand. "For you, Lord, have not given us a spirit of fear but of power and of love and of a sound mind," I quote the verse in Timothy. "For you, Christ, have given us all authority in heaven and on earth and declared that: behold I give you power to tread on the serpent and the scorpion and over all the powers of the enemy. We take that authority now and declare that any demon be cast out right this instant and be removed to the dry places of the earth."

I look up. Everyone is praying and agreeing with the words given by Jesus. Roberto's sweat has wet my hand, but I keep it in place. "Can you say the name of Jesus?" I ask, amazed that my voice sounds so calm. "It's important you say Jesus' name."

Roberto sinks to his knees. Retching loudly, he throws up a wide puddle on the sidewalk. We're making headway. Someone runs to the van and gets a towel he uses to wipe Roberto's hands and mouth. He struggles to his feet, and this time I join hands with the others, praying loudly as cars drive past. "Say Jesus," one of us calls out periodically. After what seems like ages, he sinks to his knees again. But instead of throwing up, he cries out, "Jesus."

"If you acknowledge him as Savior, say his name again," I say.

"Jesus," he moans, and then cries out as if in defiance, "Jesus. Jesus."

We help him up. One of the ladies wipes his mouth with a handkerchief. He's breathing in gasps, but his eyes have cleared. The others start clapping and shouting hallelujah. I start laughing. But we quickly say another prayer of protection over him and hurry him to our van. I seem to know a lot about demons. I learned the hard way.

(A) CHILDHOOD TO ARREST

RAGING WITH MY FATHER

9: Covington Virginia May 1960

"The woman is driving you crazy. Can't you see that?" I can't keep my voice from rising when I talk to my father. I sit at the kitchen table in the back of the drab, stucco house in Covington, wondering about dinner. At 16, I'm convinced I'm more mature than my father. My older sisters are all living away, and it's me and my dad. We had moved the eight miles from the village of Low Moor two years earlier, and several months earlier my stepbrother and stepmother moved out, taking my young half sister with her. My father is convinced she's having an affair with her boss. He'd been a good father, but these days he's consumed with talking on the phone to enlist friends to spy on my stepmother. She's apparently not trying to keep it a secret because friends regularly report sightings of the two.

"Why do you care, Dad?" I ask. "She doesn't give a flip about you."

"She used to." He reaches over piles of dirty dishes, grabs a bottle of gin from the wall cabinet and pours a healthy slug into a smeared glass. "This guy is her boss. She's only with him because he tells her what to do."

"She wanted YOU to tell her what to do, but you never did." I hate being hard on him, but this has been going on for a while. He downs the gin, and I shake my head in disgust. He doesn't go to work much, and she's all he talks about. "Dad, she always asked where you wanted to eat, what movie you wanted to see, but you always left that up to her. She wanted you to lead, but you wouldn't."

With eyes glazed over and chin tucked into his chest, he moves toward me. Is this the time I always thought would come? He'd hit me only once. Cuffed me on the cheek with the back of his hand when I was in the fourth grade because I couldn't understand a math problem. But that was it. He'd been mostly a good father, taking me on trains all over the country. Maybe the traveling was part of the reason I wanted to leave now. I stand up, my chair sliding back with a grating sound. I'm all of 5'4" and 95 pounds. Dad is 5'11" and 180 pounds. But I'm mad and disgusted with his whining. I'm glad my stepbrother is gone and trying to forget what went on. "Hit me, Dad, and I'm out of here, forever."

He stops and looks at me a long time, like maybe he sees my mother in me or is thinking about her dying. "Give up on her, Dad," I say. "She's left you, and there's nothing you can do about it. You couldn't stop Mom from dying and you can't keep somebody from leaving if that's what they want."

Inside his gaunt face, his eyes glisten. I turn away. I don't want to see my father cry. I'd seen enough crying already. He pours another slug and slings it back. Standing over the sink with both hands planted on the counter, he shakes his head as if the gin hurt when it hit his belly. It's dark, but I walk out of the house, not bothering to tell him where I'm going.

I walk down to Paul's Lunch-Counter restaurant that sells the best hot dogs in the world, buy one, sit on a swivel stool and eat it. I'm going to miss the place. But saying goodbye to the rest of this town won't be hard. Still, I'm enjoying Covington High. I've made a host of friends from the highbrows to the hoods. Yet it too will soon end.

Despite my small size or perhaps because of it, I work at being popular. At initiation day as a freshman, I wore one of my father's suits which practically fell off me and sang, "I was a Big Man Yesterday, But Boy You Ought to See me Now." I dress up in sequined tuxes, wear blackface and am an end man in our high school minstrel, telling lousy jokes and even falling off the stage. One night I covered an arm with ketchup, climbed into a car trunk and dangled it in clear sight of the highway as we parked at the entrance to a cemetery. Another night, I walked down the sidewalk in front of this older lady who always sat on her porch and stared out at the street. Suddenly my friends in a prearranged gag pulled up, jumped out and faked beating me up and throwing me into the back seat. Before we went two blocks, we got pulled over by the cops. Late one night, drunk on Country Club Beer, I took off all of my clothes to accept a dare and swam over and back across the Jackson River. When I got back, my buddies had taken my clothes and I had to run beside the car before they gave them back. I became a wrestler in the 95-pound weight class, never had to sweat to make the weight and lost only one of my eight matches my senior year. I had my first date at the prom with Mary Ellen, and I was one of the best dancers in the school gym.

My chili dog and Pepsi dinner over, I pay my bill and walk out. The bracing May air wakes me up, and I decide to walk awhile. I'm 16, and because there are only 11 grades in our school system, I'm due to graduate next month. I'm determined to leave. Covington has this enormous paper mill where everybody who is not going to college gets a job, works 40 years, takes a pension, gets a gold watch at a banquet and retires. Only the town is so polluted, they usually die before 65 of lung disease.

A few years earlier, a barber noticed my small size and said I'd make a good jockey. The only horse I'd ridden plowed our garden in Low Moor. Yet the idea stuck. I'd gotten a *Turf and Sport Digest* magazine when I was visiting my sister Colleen in Petersburg, Virginia. I'd read a story about Bill Hartack, a Pennsylvania country boy who was the nation's leading rider and in 1957 won the Kentucky Derby aboard Iron Liege. It sealed the deal. My grades were fine, but I had no interest or money to attend college, anyway. I'd written a letter talking about my desire to become a jockey and asking for a job. My sister Sheila made copies and I'd mailed them to a bunch of horse farms in Lexington, Kentucky, a place I learned through our town's library was the center of the Thoroughbred breeding industry. None responded.

(B) Battling Attractions and Addictions

A BIPOLAR LIFE

10: Richardson Texas, Spring 1991

Things are going as planned. My life is disintegrating into warped pieces. I'm vice president of production for Criterion Productions, a video and TV show production company located in the trendy north Dallas suburb of Richardson. I run a staff of 24, make more money than I ever did as a jockey or journalist and the company has grown from six to 32 employees.

While writing for the Dallas Morning News three years earlier, I interviewed R.D. Hubbard in his Fort Worth penthouse office for a story. On the way out, I dropped on his desk a proposal for him to buy 40 percent of Criterion Productions, in exchange for our producing live race and weekly television shows at his Ruidoso Downs. I would get half his stock and $50 an hour for doing a personal services tour of that track and a North Dakota off-track betting parlor venture he partially owned. I toured North Dakota, New Mexico and Texas doing public handicapping contests and we produced several live races for TV. Our yearly revenues had grown from $600,000 to over $3 million and the company had bought back Hubbard's stock, giving him a healthy profit.

I have two assistants, Thomas and Ernie, both vying for the top spot under me. My partner, Bob, supervises a staff of high-line telemarketers, selling six-minute videos to corporations of every ilk and wrapping four of them into half-hour shows. We buy air time on a host of emerging networks that air our shows in time slots attractive to insomniacs. But the company that pays us gets a promotional video and its consistently egotistical CEO can say he was on national television. I or one of my two writers draft out a script, send one videographer out to shoot, and we edit in three edit bays, often going around the clock to produce six weekly shows. I also produce and host "On the Right Track," a horse racing show, for which we sell commercials to real sponsors. It airs on the Houston-based Home Sports Network, later purchased by ESPN, and in my years at Criterion I will produce 167 of the shows. At Criterion, every day is a deadline.

My oldest daughter, Dawn is back in Louisiana with her mother. Though my son, Derek and Debra's three daughters live with us, Debra and I sometimes get a sitter and go to swing clubs. Worse, I do a quickie encounter with a man who never sees my face, something I prefer. I don't find a shrink in Dallas because as strange as it seems, I'm too shamed to talk about my life with anyone. I can't face peeling the onion of my soul.

This day, I'm standing at the head of our conference room table running a production meeting. We can't keep up, and we're trying to find a faster way to edit the features we're airing.

"Look," I say, suddenly getting up, pacing in circles and waving my arms as my two competing assistants sit and watch. "If we don't get the shows in on time, the networks run an old show and we have trouble collecting from clients who stay awake all night to see their face on TV."

Both look at me like I'm the god of the airwaves. Ernie chimes in. "Well, we could edit the video, pick out the best sound bites, and then write the script to match the video. It's easier than trying to find video to match the writing." Ernie is 25, Jewish and understands both video and profits.

Thomas, who has a family and is Christian, shakes his head. "The writing is going to be weaker, and the features won't be as good."

Quality vs. Speed. An age-old business argument. These are pre-digital video times when editing is done in "assembly," which means that every shot has to be laid down in sequence. If the editor wants to change one shot, or one sound bite, he has to make it the same length or start from the beginning.

Ernie leans in. "We do it his way, we either have to hire more people or live with reruns. It's easier and cheaper to write to the video."

Thomas puts his elbows on the table and uses his palms to rub his face. He's older than Ernie and was working for my partner when I came on board. He's a terrific editor; not fast but thorough and highly creative. He's having a problem with me promoting Ernie to be his equal. He stares at me. "Doesn't anybody care about what comes out of here anymore? We're all so obsessed with speed. What's happened to our product?"

"Tom, I hate to burst your bubble," I say. "But other than airing once and being played at corporate picnics, nobody here's getting any Emmy nominations."

I'm flying now. Making decisions that will put paychecks in our workers' pockets. My heart is racing, and a feeling of power and well-being fills my brain faster than a line of cocaine. So what if Thomas is a good guy and I wound him? He stands and shoves his chair under the table. "I don't want to be a part of this anymore."

He walks out and starts down the hall toward my partner's office. Bob has told me Thomas had threatened to quit. Yet the department belongs to me. I do what I want.

I smile at Ernie, walk to my office and close the door. My hands are shaking. My head is buzzing. Inside my desk, I find my flask of Jack Daniel's and take a long toke. It bites my tongue and makes my face shudder. But the buzz slows me down. I'd been a year sober before Debra and I vacationed in Huatulco, Mexico, and now I'm having two beers with lunch and an afternoon nip or two of Crown Royal before I get serious after work.

Meeting over, I sit on my padded swivel chair in my corner office and stare at the busy street. I know Thomas has quit. I remember the curly hair framing the faces of his two little girls. Tears run down my cheeks. I've found another reason to hate myself.

Debra also works for Criterion, and when we drive home that evening I'm silent. I want to talk but can't. It is like my depression set up camp in silence. My head hurts, and I flash back to when I was 19 and had headaches so severe I wound up in Boston's Massachusetts General Hospital. Debra and I share a bucket of fried chicken and trimmings with Derek and the three girls. I wish Dawn would be with us. Derek gets along with his three stepsisters, though the oldest talks mean to me and tells her mom I'm crazy. The relationship between Debra and me has mostly to do with sex, and she is willing to stretch the envelope as far as I like. Our only requirement is that whatever we do we do it in the same room. In many ways, we're a match, especially our tempers. Only I believe I'm a little smarter.

It's a school night, and the kids go to bed early. We stay up in our large bedroom, doing lines of cocaine and shots of whiskey. Her anger over an office incident a few days earlier bubbles to the surface. "You went in Minnie's office and told her I was crazy, didn't you?" she says.

Debra dislikes Bob's sister, a former schoolteacher who knows little about video production but is becoming increasingly prominent in the company. Debra doesn't work directly under her, but Debra sometimes gets mad at staff members who do. Debra and I often argue behind the closed doors of my office. Today for the first time she and Minnie had argued in front of the staff. Debra was correct: alone in Minnie's office I admitted that she has a temper problem.

"You've got to stop arguing in front of people at work," I say to her. "They can hear us in the office. Maybe you should stay home. God knows I'm making enough money."

"Maybe you got your eyes on that new girl they hired. I see how she keeps looking at you."

I laugh in a mocking tone. For some reason, I need to make fun of her. Indeed, I need to put down women in general. Maybe it is because I think my stepmother had known about her son and me. I don't know.

Women, from my mother to my grandmother to my first wife, always left me. I hate being abandoned. But if I make it happen, at least I'm in control. This way it hurts less. "I can't believe after all the things we've done together, you're jealous of some woman I work with. You afraid you might want to be with her, too?"

I'd never seen her with a woman, but we had talked about it. She lunges at me, her fingernails raking across my cheeks. Somehow the pain affirms my anger. I grab both her hands. She leans in and bites my arm. I let go and shove her away. I make for the back door. I stand against a light pole outside and call 911.

She runs through the door, just as I knew she would. When she tries to hit me, I hold her hands and laugh. She stops and screams at me. A squad car pulls to the curb. She erupts at the cops, screaming profanities. They arrest her. The kids come out in their pajamas and watch as the police take her away. I usher them back inside. Debra's three girls cry when they see my scratched face and realize their mom is going to spend the night in jail.

I get everyone back in bed with promises to get Debra out as soon as she sobers up. Back in my room, I put everything away and sit on the rumpled bed. Part of me celebrates my cunning and control. I know my marriage to Debra will soon be over. I know there will be more same-sex encounters. I put my head in my hands and watch as tears drip to the hardwood floor.

*****

I'm driving in downtown Dallas. It's night as I pass the towering bank building with its famous green piping running the length of its sides. I come out of my deep daze as if I'm waking up. I realize I'd set out to go somewhere, a definite place. Only now I can't remember where. The same thing has happened several times recently. Like my mind is a tape recording, playing scenes where I'm angry or engaged in doing things I hate play over and over. They override all other thoughts. I can't stop them. Sometimes I lose a block of time in my immediate past. I can't remember what I've done, causing a black fear to flood my insides. A few times before I'd come back to a sense of time and place wondering why I am where I am. Now, I'm in downtown Dallas at 1:00 a.m. I don't know why. I don't know where I'd been, where I'm going or even if I'm carrying cocaine. Panic sweeps over me.

*****

A few days later, my mind again rises to the surface of awareness, and at first I can't tell if it's a scene I'm dreaming or if it's real. I'm wearing pajamas and sitting on a straight-back metal chair in front of woman in a turtleneck and lab coat. She studies me like I'm a specimen in a jar.

I remember now. I'd cried in front of everyone at work. Debra had gotten me into Bob's office. He'd made some phone calls and had driven me to a private psychiatric hospital. Nurses and orderlies had met me at the door of the one-story white brick building. I couldn't seem to make coherent sentences, something that frustrated me deeply. I was taken to a room and given several shots. I pass out, and I think the next morning I'm here, probably in front of a shrink. It's my second trip to a ward with locks on the doors.

The thirty-something woman with straight black hair that looks ironed sits behind a black metal desk, clutching a clipboard with both hands. "How are you feeling this morning, Mr. Donnally?"

"Like my head spent last week in a London fog and my body got left behind in a brothel."

She doesn't smile. "You'll be detoxing. But we won't leave you in pain."

"Too bad, I was beginning to get the hang of insanity." She writes on the clipboard page, probably something about my arrogance. "My guess is you're bipolar, have fairly acute depression and had a psychotic episode, a break if you will. But I wouldn't term you insane."

"You make it sound like I caught a cold."

"People with mental health issues, they get sick and they get well just like other ill people. At least you didn't try to harm yourself this time."

"How you know about that?"

"Debra told me. She said you've been in counseling and were previously hospitalized over in Louisiana."

"She's got no right telling you that."

"That makes you angry?"

I shake my head, realizing that moving it around makes it hurt worse. "What's the difference at this point? We're history, anyway."

"We'll get to that. Are you willing to sign a release so I can get information from the doctor you were seeing in Louisiana?"

"I don't think so. He recommended I get counseling here. But some things I'm just not ready to talk about."

"I'm not here to lecture you or even say it's something we can talk about today. But I would like you to consider that holding all that in may have contributed to your current mental state."

I take a deep breath. Debbie, my first wife, had suspected my same-sex attraction and I'd lived it out in front of Debra, though she didn't know its source. I'd never talked about the times with my stepbrother with anyone, except mentioning it to Dr. Roper in Louisiana. But I'm falling apart, and I want to change.

"My stepbrother and I played around sexually when I was growing up, like from 11 to 13 or 14. It wasn't that big a deal. It's just when I got divorced from my first wife, it got all twisted up in my head, and now I'm doing some things that scare me to death. I always thought I was straight. I was a jockey for a long time, nothing pansy about that. Every day I took a shower with a bunch of naked men. Never a thought about any of them. Now I'm going to wind up with AIDS if I don't stop messing around with other guys."

"Promiscuity is one thing, but a lot of perfectly sane people have relationships with persons of the same sex. You want a relationship with a man?"

"The thought makes me want to vomit. I got Debra involved in swinging. Now I've started encounters. Ten minutes, and most of the time I don't even see their faces. It makes me feel awful."

"Guilty?"

70

"God yes. I became a Christian a long time ago. I'm not going to church or anything, but I still believe. I know what I'm doing is wrong."

"And is what your stepbrother did to you wrong?"

"Did to me? I could have stopped it, but I didn't. I could have told someone, but I didn't. I must have liked it, that's why I'm doing what I'm doing now, right?"

"Of course, the physical response felt good. Our bodies are built that way. It's . . . "

I'm squirming in my seat and interrupt. "Why'd it hit me like that? It wasn't in my mind for years and all of a sudden it falls on me like a brick wall."

"That's not unusual. Actually, it often happens that way after abuse."

"Hell, I wasn't abused. He was almost my age, maybe younger, though I keep thinking of him as older. I went along with it. God, after a while I even enjoyed it."

"Would it have happened if he didn't start it?"

"No. He started it, and the whole time I felt like he was teaching me."

"You're a victim of sibling sexual trauma, whether you realize it or not. It came during a crucial time in your development. Sometimes society tends to minimize sexual acts between siblings and experimentation is common and not necessarily harmful. But even a younger sibling who initiates and continues these acts can cause lasting psychological damage and leave a deep imprint on one's sexuality. It's something that's likely to continue to drastically affect you without long-term counseling and medication."

"I can die of AIDS."

"You can. However up to now you're fine. We tested."

"It's a matter of time unless I stop. And I can't."

"You can't stop?"

"Right now I can't stop anything. The cocaine, then the drinking and grass to come down. I'm always so buzzed I feel like I can do anything. Two seconds later I come down and fall apart. I'm a runaway racehorse.

Part of me knows I need a jockey to slow me down, but part of me wants to run faster. Racehorses feel safe when they're being controlled, but sometimes they get blitzed out by their own power and their love of speed and don't want to stop."

"And where does this horse end up?"

"I know a lot about runaway horses. The track is a giant circle, so sometimes when they run off they just get tired and stop. But sometimes, they scare themselves so much with their own power that they run over the rail and fall. They usually break legs and have to be put down."

"And where is this horse you say you're riding?"

"It looks like over the rail. I'm in a dangerous spot. If I don't get a disease, I'm likely to get busted for drugs. You know, once when I was a jockey, a horse I was on broke from the gate and when I started to steer him, I couldn't. The metal part of the bit that goes in his mouth had broken of all things. I had no control at all. I was surrounded by a bunch of horses, all of us racing. It was scary."

"What happened?"

"I tapped him on the shoulder with my whip to steer him down to the rail when I was clear of other horses. I kept him there that way by occasionally waving my whip beside his head. I yelled at the other jockeys to let them know I had no control. We got around okay, and after the race the outrider saw what was happening and pulled me up. I got back in one piece."

"What about now? Can you make it around the track safely?"

"My jockey would have to be an angel."

We talk about my relationship with Debra and the words "codependent" and "enabler" come up. She says we're like two roots that still fit together because we're both twisted and suggests we both get counseling. Soon the session is over, and I'm escorted back to my room.

For the next week, I'm stuck behind locked doors. Attendants constantly watch us. The sound of the metal doors opening and closing slam through my head day and night. Each day I talk briefly with the doctor, who suggests a resident program and counseling. I'm just not ready.

I take enough medication to make a dead horse race. None of it keeps my need for isolation from covering me like a down blanket in a snowstorm. I refuse to allow Debra or Bob to visit, and I don't talk much during group therapy. I do have a couple of conversations with my roommate, an older man who is practically catatonic. "I'm going home tomorrow," I tell him one day as we sit together in our room.

"Can you find your car?"

"I didn't bring one. Why?"

"I lose my car all the time."

"So what?" I ask, trying to cheer him up. "I lose mine, too."

"Yes, but you eventually find yours."

(C) LIFE AS A JOCKEY

SHAKEN DOWN/DERBY DISASTER

11: Philippe Park on Tampa Bay, March 17, 1974

Out over the placid, blue-green water of Tampa Bay, the dawning sun is a smear of pink behind translucent silver clouds. Some 15 of us stand atop an Indian mound in Safety Harbor's Philippe Park. Debbie and I, along with fellow jockey Ronnie Fairholm and Vicki are exchanging duel wedding vows before the chaplain at Florida Downs (Now Tampa Bay Downs). I stand facing Debbie and recite words a combination of my own and Kahil Gibran's *The Prophet*. "Let there be space in our togetherness. And let the winds of the heavens dance between us. May we stand together yet not too near together: For the pillars of the temple stand apart, and the oak tree and the cypress grow not in each other's shadow."

We're standing on a grassy knoll ringed by stately date palms and live oaks, decorated with hanging Spanish moss. Historians don't know what the mound was used for, but we thought it would make a grand place for a wedding. Debbie wears a long yellow and white dress that drapes her lithe body like an opera glove. As the chaplain pronounces us man and wife, a part of me is scared the commitment will mess it up.

That afternoon, we hold our reception in a grassy field next to The Barn, a popular tavern just down the street from the track's entrance. Next to the bar is an open field and we've set up a tent to house the six kegs of beer Ronnie and I have ordered. Our fellow trackers are manning a giant iron pot filled with crabs and shrimp. The place is swarming with people, walking, talking, drinking, eating and sprawling on blankets spread out in the sun. However much I like it, beer is not something I can drink. I'm regurgitating at least eight times daily to make weight, and unlike some liquids, my system instantly absorbs beer. My stomach is trained so that the instant I bend over from a standing position, my stomach contracts in a spasm, allowing it to empty with no more ado than brushing my teeth. But beer tastes terrible coming up, even if it's only been down a few minutes.

"Yuck," I say to Ronnie as I return from the bathroom and lay down on a blanket next to my friend. Scores of people are milling about, stopping to offer congratulations while a band is playing hoedown Bluegrass. Our wives are gone, going from blanket to blanket to visit. "God, I hate to heave beer," I say.

"That's why I sip it. Never could get the heaving part down."

I shake my head. "I used to get so hungry I'd go into supermarkets and walk down the aisles just to look at food. If I couldn't heave I'd never be able to ride."

"Guess it's like Scotch. Have to acquire a taste for it."

"Taste indeed. A bad one." I'm so aware of my weight I know within a pound day or night exactly what I weigh.

"Where you going when the meet ends next month?" I ask.

"Back to Cleveland. Looks like Thistledown is my permanent home. How about you?"

"Keeneland, Churchill, probably back to Rockingham Park."

"Not me," he says. "I used to think hanging out at Churchill Downs might get me a Derby mount. Now I know that's not true."

"You know, it's so crazy. Any time someone learns you're a jockey, the first question they ask is, 'Did you ride in the Derby?' Like it's the only race in the world."

"It's the granddaddy of them all. You and me, we're not that old. We still got a shot."

It's partially true. I'm 33, and he's a couple of years older. We still have much of our career in front of us. "I've noticed one thing," I say. "If you don't establish yourself as a stakes rider in your early twenties, the owners of top horses aren't going to be calling your agent when a Derby mount comes open."

"It used to be different. Trainers stuck with riders, thick or thin. If a horse got good, they weren't on the phone to an agent for a top stakes race rider like they are today. Just look at Red Pollard and Seabiscuit. He was a nobody until he landed on the horse. And the trainer stuck with him."

"I met Red Pollard once when he was a valet at Narragansett. I came in to ride one day, and he was my valet. I spent a lot of time with him, nearly all of it talking about Seabiscuit. He told me Seabiscuit was a machine horse until he learned to win and started to like racing."

Ronnie grins. "Makes sense. They ran him so many times when he was two, he probably got sour and learned to cheat."

Machines, joints, batteries are tiny two-pronged hand-held electrical devices designed to deliver a harmless, but attention-getting shock to a Thoroughbred in the midst of a race. I'd seen green riders whip a horse's belly instead of the rump; something I knew was far more painful and likely to make a horse sulk in a race and quit trying. To me that was far crueler than a machine. I use them on occasion, mostly either to satisfy a trainer's demands or to cash a bet. In reality, they are horribly overrated and hardly worthy of the risk, which can include up to a lifetime ban if caught. At least 80 percent of horses try their best in races, and a whip is a stronger incentive than a machine for most of the rest. But in the case of that rare underachieving horse that cheats despite the whip, a mild electrical shock from a "joint" will get its attention.

I'm a strong left-handed rider, and I can lay stripes on a horse with my whip. But some horses learn to ignore the whip and loaf. This made those few horses incredibly powerful betting tools. Leave off the machine and ride hard, use the whip even, and the horse still runs poorly. Light him up at the top of the stretch with a little electricity and he finds new life.

"I don't know if it's true, but that's what he told me. I don't think he had a reason to lie. But I don't think you're right about stakes race riders. I think even today you get on a horse that gets good and some trainers will stick with you. They go to the Derby, and you go with them. That's what happened to Mike Manganello."

The rider led the Florida Downs standings for many years and while riding here four years earlier, he'd picked up the mount on the gangly three-year-old Dust Commander in the City of Miami Beach Handicap at Tropical Park in Miami. The colt won, then went on to win the Blue Grass Stakes at Keeneland, and then the Derby itself. "I was at his party after the race," I say. "Some shindig."

"I heard."

"Maybe I'll have that party myself this year." I say it with an exaggerated grin meant to be funny. "That colt, Consigliori, I'm riding for Jimmy Foster. He tells me the owner is dead set on running him in the Derby. I don't know how good he is, but one thing's for sure, you can't win if you're not in the starting gate."

"You go, guy. We still have a chance at the Derby. Just have to get good. Learn to horseback with the best of them. Just become excellent. It can still happen."

"What do you think is different between us and say maybe Angel Cordero?" I ask. "Guts, the ability to read pace, maybe finish like a banshee. A great agent? Luck? What?"

"It'd be too easy to say it's because of the good horses he gets to ride. He didn't get to ride them because he's a crazy Puerto Rican who would slit your throat to win a claiming race. No, he's good. Good in a lot of ways."

I look at Ronnie and raise my red cup of beer. He touches his to mine. I say, "To us getting that good."

"To us winning the Derby." We toast again and lay back to greet friends.

A few weeks later, Debbie and I sign the mortgage and buy a house at 5 ½ Georgia Avenue in Crystal Beach, a tiny waterfront community not far from the track. The house is small, but it has a yard and a dock on a canal that runs into the Gulf of Mexico. I use our 14-foot boat for all-night shark fishing and to take us to Honeymoon Island, where Debbie and I camp out.

One afternoon during a dark day at the track, I'm sitting in our yard, facing the canal and wearing only a pair of shorts and a thick layer of homemade tanning oil. My legs are folded into a painful full lotus pose with upturned palms resting on my knees as thumbs and index fingers form two circles. I do the breath of fire, chant Om as I exhale, and seek to rid my mind of all thought, including the pain in my legs. I feel someone softly tap my shoulder and stop to look up at an older woman, who stares down at me with sorrow. "God is going to use you in a mighty way one day, son."

I unfold my legs and turn to tell her she's crazy, but she's already walking away. I go back to meditating, but I can't erase her words from my mind. Later I tell Debbie, and she says the woman is Mary Ellen and all in the community know she is a Pentecostal zealot, whose own family shuns her because they think she's crazy. Still, her words haunt me.

A few days later in the jockeys' room, I'm standing beside my locker, which is actually a wooden shelf in a wall-length set of large open boxes, and helping my valet by fitting a colored cap over my riding helmet. Two men in suits and ties walk in the door and head toward me.

I stiffen and my insides shrivel. They're agents from the Thoroughbred Racing Protective Bureau (TRPB), an arm of Thoroughbred Racing Associations. The organization was founded to protect the sport of kings by none other than former FBI head J. Edgar Hoover. We call them "track dicks." I'm about to be shaken down and searched for a machine.

Somehow they know I'll be using one in the race I am scheduled to ride 30 minutes later. How, I couldn't imagine. When I was "hot" I never told anyone. Not even an "egg" who would be placing a large bet for me in exchange for a guarantee the horse would win. The track dicks had to be guessing.

The lead agent is young, probably recruited, as many are, from the ranks of the FBI. He scowls at me. "Let's go upstairs. We're going to do a search."

"I'm entitled to a witness. You can't search me unless another jockey is there. "

Billy McKeever stands nearby and like me is one of the track's three or four representatives to the Jockeys' Guild, an organization that represents riders to racing's agencies, including the TRPB. I look over at him and realize he already knows what's going down. The three of us walk up the steps to the recreation area, dining area and sleeping room. The other agent stays back and ruffles through my locker. My mouth goes dry, and I start to sweat.

Upstairs, the agent peeks into the tiny sleeping room, walks in and gently shakes the lone napping jockey. "We need some privacy. You can come back in a few minutes."

He turns on the light, and I can see by the glint in the agent's eyes that he's having a good time. The second agent returns and gives a shoulder shrug to let his partner know his search was fruitless. The plump older one, whose tie is sinking into his flabby throat, closes the door, leaving the four of us alone. Billy looks at me as if he is waiting for a cue, and I get the feeling he thinks it's in my clothes.

I can't help but consider if machines are worth the trouble. They are about three inches long, with one side a copper coil and the other a place for the battery, usually one used in a hearing aid. Covered with flesh-colored tape, they fit neatly inside the hand. When handling one, the user is as likely to get shocked as the horse. I had practiced shocking myself on an arm until I wouldn't flinch.

If I'm busted, I will almost certainly be banned from racing for years, possibly life. I had started going to college in hopes of becoming a racing writer, but that dream would disappear. My life as I know it would be over. I'd be lucky to get a job shining shoes at the airport. A high price to pay for carrying a device that improves the performance of remarkably few horses. Sometimes riders are coerced into carrying a machine by trainers, who as a group believe in their effectiveness more than riders. But in this case it is greed. I had a friend make a $200 bet on my mount. If the horse wins—and even with a machine there are no guarantees—I will probably net less than a thousand dollars.

The agents and Billy watch intently as I disrobe. First I remove my silks and drop the bright top. The skinny agent picks it up and shakes it. I start to tell him, "I'm a jockey, not a magician," but keep quiet. Then comes my thin T-shirt, kangaroo skin boots and white nylon pants. The agent shakes them all. When I get to my jock strap, I stop. "Take it off," one commands.

This time I can't hold it. "Where you think I keep it, up my butt?"

The young one stiffens then growls, "You said it. Turn around and spread them."

I give him a hard look but comply. I just want it over with. I want out of that room. They both look at me as if I crawled out of a hole with a ratchet tail. The younger nods to the older and they both leave. Billy uses expressive fingers to wipe imaginary sweat from his head.

"I can't believe they looked up your behind."

"What I get for mouthing off."

He leaves and I get dressed. There's no way I can stop my friend from making the $200 bet. If my mount wins, he'll do it on his own. Before I leave, I glance at the bed in the far corner, the one with a mattress so stained and brown no one uses it. Tucked neatly between the wire springs and the bottom of the bunk mattress is my machine.

I had learned from the best. Never keep it in my locker. Never put it in my hand until I walk into the saddling paddock. Don't give anyone the chance to see a pony rider pass it to you in the post parade. After a race, instead of dropping it to the track and drawing heat, stand in the irons and in the normal downward motion of pulling down my goggles continue with the hand that holds the machine and drop it inside the front of my T-shirt. If I get stung, so what?

Staying calm is essential. I'd returned to the jockeys' room after a race at Keeneland Race Course in Kentucky and watched an angry rider rip off his helmet and throw it into his locker. He'd forgotten he'd stashed his machine in his helmet after the race. The device, wrapped in black tape, slid across the floor, skidding to a stop a few inches from the heels of the clerk of scales. With half the room watching, he ran over and scooped it up before the official noticed. One rider was searched in the shed behind the starting gate. The agents found nothing. But one decided to look at the horse in the starting gate. The machine was tucked inside the knot riders tie to shorten long reins.

Why do riders risk their careers to carry a machine? Trainers and jockeys base their careers on tilting ever so slightly the level playing field regulators work to maintain. We're all looking for an edge. For riders, it's going as far out on a legal line in a race as possible. It's allowing your mount to drift outside a foot or two as you approach the stretch in order to start the horse outside you toward the outside, then having your horse switch back to his left lead a little late and move back toward the rail in order to gain perhaps a half-length. It's hanging back and then accelerating just enough to keep your foe penned in behind another horse in what's called a "blind switch." The difference between clever and dirty race riding is a gray area existing largely in varying degrees in the eyes of track stewards. Jockeys go as far as they can without overtly putting another rider in danger. When they receive what they give, crying about it is considered bad form.

Likewise, trainers look for that edge in everything from a new vitamin or herb to concoctions of cooked-up food and injections by an elite crew of racehorse vets who adhere to the motto "Better Living Through Chemistry." I don't want to come down on vets. On the whole, they are among the most benevolent animal lovers alive. But in the world of commerce we all want to succeed. We're all looking for that edge. Given the fallen nature of humans, any place there is money, there's certain to be chicanery.

I'd been asked to carry machines on horses I knew in my heart weren't cheating and would not improve. There were some 120 riders who escaped the cold and raced at Florida Downs during the winter. Each race-day card contained some 70 horses and a losing jockey made $35. Did that mean I didn't respect the animals I rode? I admit my sense of right and wrong was skewed at the time. Yet it's impossible to ride races for decades and not develop an abiding admiration for the animals that pay your way through the check-out line. Was using a machine on a horse cruel? Perhaps, but not as cruel as leaving welts or whipping one under the belly. Was it cheating and was I wrong? Absolutely.

Of the 10,000 plus races I rode, I carried a machine in at least 50. Sometimes the fear of getting caught kept me awake all of the previous night. During the race, I'd try to save the jolt until the appropriate time, usually a half to a quarter mile before the finish line. I would try not to hit the horse more than once or twice. A machine is about surprise and not pain. Each successive jolt is less effective. And it was that surprising rare touch and not the persistent pressing the machine against the horse's neck that was most effective.

My shakedown for a machine proved fruitless. Yet, I'm still shaken. But not enough to end my occasional foray into being a "machine rider."

Near the end of the winter season, I win an allowance race on Consigliori for trainer Jimmy Foster. After the race, he tells me the horse will run in the Kentucky Derby. Winning an allowance race at a second-tier track like Florida Downs might make him rank among the top 200 three-years-olds at the time. But in those days, all an owner has to do is pay the fee and his horse runs. I don't care that in reality he has little chance of winning. I'm going to ride in the Derby. I will be horseback when the entrants walk onto the track and the band plays, "My Old Kentucky Home." During the week before the Derby, I will talk to the press about what it feels like to ride in the world's most famous race. Best of all, the next time I get on a plane, with my whip tied to the top of my tack bag, I can tell the person I sat beside, "Yeah I rode the Derby."

Foster is a friend, and we rent a large sailboat. He and his girlfriend along with Debbie and I spend an enjoyable day sailing in the Gulf, smoking pot, drinking beer and talking about the horse and the most famous race on earth. The day after the meeting ends, Debbie and I have our utility trailer loaded, ready to move north and give up our house until late the next fall. Foster calls and wants to meet me at his barn. He then hangs up.

"What's up?" I ask on arriving at the nearly empty barn area. "The big horse all right?"

Foster, young and thin with curly hair, is looking down at the ground, moving around dirt with the toe on one of his boots. "I got bad news for you."

"What is it?"

"I decided to ride Darrell Brown in the Derby."

My heart skips a beat. Darrell's won fewer races here than I have. I'm ready to punch him.

"Why, what'd I do? I just won on the horse."

He finally lifts his head and looks at me. "You got to understand. This is a chance of a lifetime for me. I got to take my best hold."

"And that means taking me off? I thought we were friends. We just spent a great day together cruising around on a sailboat."

"That's the trouble. I don't want to use a rider who smokes dope."

"You smoked with me, for heaven's sake."

"But I won't be on the horse's back when the gates open. I want a rider that's straight. This might be the only chance I get to win the Derby."

I stand there, rage bubbling into my face. I want to tell him it might also be my only chance. Instead, I suggest an anatomically impossible act and walk away.

When I get home, the woman who came into my yard when I was in a lotus pose is standing in my kitchen. Debbie holds up a knitted afghan folded over one arm, it's pink, white, yellow and brown stripes making it look a bit garish. "Look what she brought us, Hon."

"I knitted it myself," the woman says. "I want you two to have it."

83

I nod, not wanting to be impolite. Yet I'm in no state to deal with the neighborhood tongue-talking Pentecostal, one so zealous her family hardly speaks to her.

"You know, Buddha is not God," she says. "But Jesus Christ is. I'd like you to know him as Lord and Savior."

I shake my head. "God exists in many forms. What makes him right and every other religion wrong? But this just isn't a good time to discuss it."

"We never know how much time we have. If you died today, do you know where you'd spend eternity?"

"I'm sorry, Mary Ellen, but I think a little part of me died today, and I need to talk to Debbie about it. Look, we'll talk again, okay? And thanks for the comforter."

I walk into our bedroom and stand looking out my window at the fence we'd just built and the dock beyond where my boat is riding tiny swells. How will I handle it? Standing in the Churchill Downs jockeys' room and watching Darrell Brown put on Consigliori's silks and walk down to the saddling paddock and ride onto the track, with fans lining the outside and inside fence and a TV audience of millions. The woman had asked where I would spend eternity. Right now I can't get past the first Saturday in May.

A month later, Consigliori is one of a record 23 entrants in the 100th Kentucky Derby. As a then-record crowd of over 140,000 view the race in person, I watch on the monitor in the Churchill Downs jockeys' room recreation area that houses a ping pong table and café. My ears roar and my chest feels like it belongs on a sparrow. Brown and Consigliori are eighth when they reach the first turn. I'm starting to think maybe one of racing's most major miracles is about to take place. But they soon fade to the rear, and at the finish the horse is in front of only three others, one of which is lame. Cannonade, the favorite and winner, is in front nearly every step, expertly ridden by Angel Cordero Jr. Still, it's Darrell and not me who gets to tell his grandchildren about the time he rode in the Kentucky Derby.

(D) LIFE TODAY

METROLINK MINISTER

12: Chatsworth High School near Los Angeles, September 13, 2008

It's 4:00 a.m. and I'm in a high school hallway kneeling on one knee before a thin middle-aged man who shifts his Toy Poodle in his lap and absently rocks back and forth as tears stream down his face. He sits on a brown metal folding chair among a crowd of other equally distraught victims, haphazardly seated inside a hallway at the Chatsworth, California High School. The man's cell phone rings and he presses it to an ear. "Is that you calling? I know you're alive. You have to be. Say something to me. Say something, please. I love you darling, you know I do."

That afternoon I was driving home from work at Race Track Chaplaincy of America headquarters at Hollywood Park Racetrack in Inglewood, a Los Angeles suburb. Radio news was consumed by a train crash in the northwestern burg of Chatsworth. At 4:23 p.m. the commuter train filled with workers returning home collided with a freight train. Later we learn 225 people left Union Station near downtown Los Angeles or boarded the train along the way with the final destination point Moorpark, some 35 miles away. While sending a text message, the Metrolink engineer had blown through a red signal, and after emerging from a tunnel ran headlong into a freight train. The collision was so violent the freight train's gargantuan diesel engine plowed through several passenger cars.

I know I am about to get a call out from the Los Angeles Mayor's Crisis Response Team (CRT). My wife, Sandi, and I had taken 47 hours of training at a Los Angeles Police Department training academy. After fingerprints and a background check, we'd become members of the volunteer organization. Activated by the LAPD and LAFD to aid victims and liaison with officials, I'd been on several dozen call outs for homicides, suicides, drive-by shootings and even natural deaths, some with Sandi along. I'd been with families whose members were killed in gang shootings, taken hostage and watched those they loved die in apartment fires.

My cell rings and in less than an hour, I'm in Chatsworth assigned to help set up our location at their high school. The Red Cross sets up a shelter in the school gymnasium. Swarms of people flood the school. Many bring sandwiches, bottled water and enough pizza to feed a city. Other CRT members arrive, and when we meet our leader, Jeff briefs us as does the female police captain acting as incident commander. She says the site will become a reunification center where families of those on the train will meet with the crash's uninjured and then leave with them. Those with loved ones in hospitals will be given a police escort there. Fatalities will be identified by the coroner's office at the crash site, and their loved ones, gathered here, will be notified. It sounds simple. It isn't.

The school is a campus the size of a small college. Hundreds gather in the outdoor plaza, mill about and help set up and staff a food line. Our team can't tell the victims' families and friends from onlookers. Civic groups, charities and churches show up. With no formal training and little experience, they become groups our team members have to manage.

Police officers inform our group that we're to sort through the crowd, identify victims' relatives and friends and escort them to a section inside the school that will become a communications center. People stand and mill about in groups and alone, talking and fuming. Others stumble over each other to get to the food. All want to know about the people on the train. There's a group of young people standing in a circle, holding hands, heads bowed. Each one is taking a turn at praying. I stop and bow my head and silently join in their prayers.

"Oh Chaplain, can you come over here?" I see an Asian woman wearing a name tag I know is from a Buddhist charity, one with excellent training. Leaning into her shoulder and crying in loud sobs is a young woman clutching a wad of tissue.

"She's Christian, and she said she wants prayer."

My heart melts. A Buddhist has seen me praying, assumes I'm a Christian and asks me to pray for a Christian she is helping. I walk to the folding chairs where they sit and sink to my knees to be eye level. "Would you like prayer?" I ask softly.

The woman lifts her head and faces me. "Please."

"You obviously have someone you love on the train."

"My husband." She says his name and hunches back into the other woman's shoulder and cries again. I bow my head and pray, and the Buddhist instantly translates the prayer into the language the woman speaks. I use her husband's name and ask God to bring him home alive and to bring peace and comfort to her and her family, ending with the thought that God will provide the peace that passes all understanding.

The relief worker puts an arm under the Christian woman's arm, helps her get up and delicately escorts her inside. I see a well-dressed man ask people if they know anyone on the train as he hands out law firm business cards. Thankfully the exit and entrance to the building where families and friends wait can be controlled.

In another quick briefing, we're asked to obtain ongoing listings of victims and hospitals and inform those waiting. Yet the crash had been so violent, many victims' clothing containing their IDs has been ripped from their bodies. Some are badly injured, mangled or unconscious. Quickly identifying them is impossible. In a few hours, all the victims' families are in the long hallway, sitting on chairs, standing, pacing or leaning against the wall. The talk is loud and often angry. Information is sketchy.

Both L.A. County Sheriff Lee Baca and L.A. Mayor Antonio Villaraigosa show up and talk with the victims' families. The mayor holds a press conference in the school's gym before rows of media cameras. Many of those waiting attend, though the press is not allowed in their hallway.

It's nearly 11 hours after the accident, and we've been told all the injured have been removed from the scene. The firemen are searching only for bodies, something the police ask us not to relay to the victims' families. I spot the thin man sitting alone, his chair a distance from others. He looks frail with the dog in his lap and his cell phone clutched to his chest. He stares into space, resolve hardening his eyes. I move to him and with no chairs available bow on one knee. "Is there anything I can get for you, coffee or water perhaps?"

He shakes his head, not looking at me.

The cell rings.

Shoving it to one ear, he answers. His eyes flood with expectation. "Talk to me, baby. I know you're there. I know you're alive. They're coming for you. Hold on. They'll find you. Just hold on." He looks to the ceiling, tears running down the sides of his nose. "Just don't die, baby. I couldn't stand that, okay? Just don't die."

He holds the phone to an ear, listening and then asking for his baby to speak to him, time and time again. He finally shakes his head in tight shudders, closes the phone then shoves it back against his chest. "Gracie keeps calling me. I know she's alive. I know she's alive."

My hope rises with his. "Has anyone checked the hospitals for you? Maybe she's there."

"She's not in any we know of. I think she's still on the train. Maybe buried under something. Can't get out. Calling but too weak to talk."

"How awful."

He shakes his head but says nothing.

I remain silent for a long time. He looks away, still shaking his head.

"Have you told the police?"

He looks back at me. "A couple of times. The commander had the signal triangulated. The phone is on the train. I believe she still has it."

I wait for more, but he's silent. I'm not going to diminish his hope. "Can I pet your dog?"

His shoulders shrug. I want to help, but not intrude. I gently stroke the tiny dog. "How did you hear about the accident?"

"Heard on the news. She was due home. She'd called me from the station. She was working out of town and just got in today. It's the train she always took. I know she's on it."

"And to hear her phone call you and not hear her, I can't imagine what that's like."

He nods his head and glances down at the phone. I remain silent. He's not ready to talk. That's fine. I say nothing, just pet the dog. If denial is going to get him through the night, then so be it. Still I feel woefully inadequate. I say a silent, open-eyed prayer, asking for wisdom for myself, comfort for him and safety for his fiancée. I rise and walk away. But his hope is contagious.

The list of those hospitalized is complete. The number of those still waiting thins. When the remaining ask for information, we say we have none, allow them to draw whatever conclusions they find helpful and give them ample space to express their emotions. Some cry, others pace, a few sit in silence. The Red Cross has set up cots for those who wish to spend the night. Yet, all seem to prefer the hallway, waiting for news they increasingly believe has to be bad.

Jeff calls us into a huddle. The L.A. coroners are on their way. Just after 4:00 a.m. he escorts me outside. He notes that I'm a licensed chaplain and asks me to be part of one of the support teams present when coroners deliver death notifications. In this instance, I know if my spiritual background conforms to that of the victims, I am free to be Christian. For the others, I will listen, console, advocate to other helping organizations and silently pray. He takes me to the school's band room, whose walls are lined with tubas, drums and portable keyboards. I sit in a brown metal folding chair at a long folding table. At the table are county and city mental health workers and a chaplain or two of other faiths. Other CRT members, all with extreme kindness, usher the victims' family members into the room.

They are asked to sit. The coroner, a middle-aged woman with concern on her broad face, tells each that someone he or she loved is now dead. Some seem to understand before they even sit and burst into tears when they see the coroner's badge.

All look tired and haggard. Some have tight defensive faces as they sit. Some I'd been with shoot me a glance filled with anger. I realize they believe I knew the fate of those they loved but did not tell them. A few put on looks of optimism I know are defense mechanisms. These take the news the hardest, with some asking the coroner if she is sure. In those cases, she showed them pictures taken at the morgue, something I knew she didn't want to do. I'd been part of other notifications. I knew what to expect. Experts have described intense grief as waves of varying strength washing over the bereaved. Here there is pain and little else.

I know words can never halt an avalanche of misery. In the privacy of intense grief, especially if another loved one is present to provide comfort, words are not always welcomed. Yet I've learned two things: simply being there means a vast deal to the victim, and silent prayer is not only fitting but has the power to bring peace and comfort.

On it goes. Entire families, some with teenage children, husbands, wives, brothers and sisters, and close friends file in. Some are shocked. Others numb. I offer condolences, encourage them to talk. Before they leave, I and the other team members give referrals to grief counselors, help them think through practical matters, asking if they are under a doctor's care and taking medication, have others to be with, and for those alone if they're capable of driving home. Police officers are there to drive or escort them.

Our group's coroner gives a notification for a member of a Spanish-speaking family. I find an interpreter and say the Lord's Prayer and recite comforting Bible verses, but I know they're Catholic and a Spanish-speaking priest is needed. As the family mourns loudly, I confer with my team. One, a rabbi, miraculously produces a list of Catholic churches in the area. I call and though it's 5:00 a.m. on a Saturday morning, I get a priest on the phone. We dispatch a police car to bring him here. A Jewish Rabbi helping a Protestant find a Catholic priest has the makings of a barroom joke. Yet for me, it's a remarkable memory.

I move back to the coroner's group. Some who are notified want to know if their loved ones died quickly or suffered as firemen removed rubble to pull them out of the carnage. The coroner tells all she thought they died quickly. Before one notification, I learn the family is Buddhist and realize I know a Buddhist professional mental health worker on another notification team. I call, only to learn he's already left. He agrees to return.

It's nearly daylight when they escort in the thin man, the one who believed his fiancée was alive and calling him on his cell phone. I know she's dead. The sadness I had accumulated in the past few hours hits me. I turn away, wipe the moisture from my eyes and regain my composure. It's the price I pay for allowing myself to hope.

After the notification, he's not crying and looks numb, stunned beyond belief. His dog sits in his lap and stares around at us. Tears fall from his stoic face, but he remains stiff, almost formal. He remains defiant, but his tears are unstoppable. We gather around him, and I want to give him a hug, but the coroner hugs him, and he hugs back. I summon the words, so meaningful yet so meaningless. "I'm so sorry. I know you loved her deeply."

He tells us about her, what it was like the last time they were together and says he was glad he'd said he loved her when she called from the station. He keeps talking, and I mirror his words, giving him room to expand on his feelings. I give him a bottle of water, and after a while ask if he is on medication, would like us to help contact others in his support system—family, friends, and a spiritual leader perhaps. We offer a ride home, but he declines, saying a friend is coming to pick him up. He leaves, a bit wobbly and his body sags beneath the weight of a stark realization that a future with a fiancée he loves has died with her.

As the day dawns, I walk outside and hear traffic and birds chirping in the new day as if nothing of significance had happened. It's 7:30 a.m., at least 13 hours after I arrived. I hunt up my CRT supervisor.

"I'm done, Jeff. I've hit the wall."

"You've done an incredible job. Go home get some sleep. We'll all debrief soon. I'll call."

I nod and go search for my car. Feeling the same numbness I encountered in the band room, I wander around a bit in the massive lot, finally finding it. I drive down the interstate toward our Culver City apartment. I count, remembering seven separate notifications. I do my best to remember what God's word says about hope but little comes. At home I decide not to wake Sandi, sit on the couch and lay my head back against the afghan Mary Ellen had knitted for me some 30 years earlier. I remembered the words she spoke to me as I sat in my yard in a lotus pose, chanting to Buddha: "Son, the Lord is going to use you in a mighty way one day."

I smile. Yet I still see the twisted anguish on the man's face that had held on to hope throughout a dark night only to have it dashed when the sun came up. His fiancée had probably sat in that train seat, tired from traveling and thinking about nothing more significant than getting home to him. One striking fact about all who didn't make it home that night becomes painfully clear. Their day was routine, the trip just another small hurdle to being home with those they loved. I realize that in the end, those moments we hardly count are the ones most significant. It's doubtful any suspected anything was wrong until the second they died. Sometimes it takes death to make us aware of what is most valuable in our lives.

Life is precious. That I too had not died several times was a miracle. I finally cry, allowing myself for the first time to feel the pain that had fallen on me like acid rain I can't escape. My face is wet, but I allow the tears to linger. Tears too are precious. Proof I can still feel. Proof I'm still alive. Proof God changed me.

(A) CHILDHOOD TO ARREST: LEARNING TO RIDE

LEAVING MY HOME, NOT MY PAIN

13: Low Moor Virginia, August 1960

I'm in a backward-facing seat on a C&O passenger train as it pulls out of the Covington station. The engineer in the bright blue locomotive revs its diesel engine and the small-town backyards and slat-board fences start to disappear. I see my dad stop and wave and then walk off the station platform. Somehow I believe my leaving home at 16, seven weeks after graduating, will help his mental state. I know it will mine. I don't have to worry about him getting back with my stepmother and my stepbrother coming back into my life. The train crosses the Jackson River, heading west and starting up the grade into the mountains and West Virginia. On the other side is Kentucky, Lexington to be exact. In a letter I still have, Herman Goodpaster, the manager at Patchen Wilkes Farm, wrote me back, offering me a job. I would earn $40 per week riding unbroken Thoroughbred yearlings.

Dad bought me a one-way train ticket and put two twenties in my hand. We'd hugged briefly on the platform. He'd been a good father for the most part, but all that's gone now. In a few weeks I'll be 17 and officially grown up. I'm ready to do anything to become a jockey.

*****

It's 4:30 a.m. in Lexington on a humid August morning. Summer air blows over my tight crew cut as I sit Indian-style in the back of a pickup and stare at the outline of rolling hills moving past in near darkness. It's my first day on the job and I wonder if my hero, Bill Hartack, started this way. The train from Covington had pulled into the downtown Lexington station the previous day. I lug my lone suitcase the few blocks up the hill to a red brick boarding house on the 300 block of Third Street. I'm going to make $40 a week breaking yearlings. I pay $17 a week for the boarding house semi-private room and all of Ms. Johnson's food I can eat. I'm only 97 pounds but have already heard stories of good jockeys quickly outgrowing the saddle, and with my dad nearly 6' and 180 pounds, I pledge to contain myself.

The pickup stops at the end of the tree-lined lane at Patchen Wilkes Farm just outside of town. We all pile out including the rotund driver and our foreman, Lit. He shifts the wad of Red Man in his jaw, spits a pancake-size dollop of juice onto the road and yells, "Herman, we got your new bug boy out here."

A man with a ruddy outdoor face beneath a tweed porkpie hat marches up the incline from a barn, grinning as if he's about to meet his new mail-order bride. "Well, lookie here," he says, walking around me and appraising me like a yearling he might buy. He cocks his head, his wry smile friendly and challenging. "Think you got what it takes to be a jockey, do you?"

At that instant, I have little idea of what it takes to be a jockey, other than being a lot smaller than everyone else. After learning that Lexington is home to nearly all the leading Thoroughbred farms, I'd written a letter to the city's Chamber of Commerce, who sent me a map with all the horse farms. I wrote a letter to each, and Herman Goodpaster replied with a job offer. "Well I heard you have to have good rhythm to ride racehorses," I say. "So I play the drums."

"Do you now? You're going to get throwed, you know. Sure you're not afraid?"

The crew of workers had gathered around in the soft dawn light and gave me the attention usually deserved for a team mascot in a beaver suit.

"Hell, he don't know enough to be afraid," says one of the exercise boys. "He ain't dry behind the ears yet."

I'm not sure what that means. But, I realize Mr. Goodpaster is playing to the crowd.

"I take it you haven't ridden much," he says.

"I rode plow horses, but I think I was real little and sitting in front of somebody."

Snickers float up from the crowd like passed gas.

"That's good," the boss says. "I don't have to unlearn anything some amateur taught you. I'll teach you right." He turns to the others. "We got 30 head of babies to break before the snow hits, and we start tomorrow. We're going to have to get along and work hard. Most weeks, we'll be riding in the morning and the afternoons."

He looks back at me. "You know our policy. You get thrown you buy a case of Pepsi to go with lunch."

I follow the dozen exercise riders and grooms to the barn. Inside, they chat about the personalities of the unbroken babies. Mr. Goodpaster motions for me to follow him as he walks down the training barn's packed-dirt center aisle between opposite rows of 15 stalls. At the stall closest to the tack room, where the riders are starting to inspect and clean saddles and bridles, he flips a light switch; slides open a wood-barred stall door and walks inside. I'd never been in a stall with a horse, but I follow as he slides the door shut behind us. Standing in the back and gazing at us with curiosity is a horse, looking full grown and a little fat.

"This a yearling I get to ride?" I gingerly move to the horse to show him I'm not afraid.

"This is a mare, son. She's in foal. I just keep her here so I can watch her."

I nod and keep a look of fake understanding on my face. "So she's already raced?"

"That she has. And she was a fast one too. Her name's Filly O' Mine and I own her."

I can't help but note the horse's odd color. Inside the lit stall, her coat has round dapples with a reddish hue. It's somewhere between auburn and gray, the color of iron ore when it comes from the ground.

"She's what's called a strawberry roan," he explains. "She'll eventually turn gray, but at least that's what she is now. "

His face lights up. "You want to ride her?"

"Yes sir, that'd be fine." I stand there nodding and agreeing.

"Then let's get going."

A lump the size of a softball runs up my throat, and I cough. I never meant now, this instant. "Sure thing," I say.

He walks to the stall door and asks the group in the tack room to bring us a helmet, saddle, bridle and girth. The entire group walks to the stall's front and unloads the tack into the boss's arms. But instead of leaving they stand there looking at me as if I'm a vaudeville act.

Mr. Goodpaster tacks up the filly, explaining in detail every piece of tack and its purpose. An exercise saddle is maybe six inches across at the widest part of the seat. It's like nothing I've seen. Filly O' Mine stands there eyeing us curiously. Is this going to make her mad? Outside, the crowd watches in silence. Grins sprout up like crab grass.

I knew I'd be breaking untamed yearling racehorses when I got on the train back in Virginia. I'd envisioned myself as some kind of bronco rider, leaning back and putting out one hand for balance as the yearlings bucked their way around a corral. Somehow climbing aboard a pregnant mare in a stall in front of funning exercise riders was not part of the picture. This looked so easy that anything I did wrong or any fear I might show is sure to set off the group watching. And the helmet they brought is black, with no colored covering, and is several sizes too large. I snap the chin strap to discover it dangles well below my chin like a noose. With green canvas tennis shoes and a helmet bouncing around on my head, I know I don't look anything like Bill Hartack posing on a Derby winner in *Turf and Sports Digest*.

The boss shoots me a knowing grin. "Always remember with racehorses, the left side is the right side and the right side is the wrong side." The crowd outside laughs. I feel like a show they've seen before. As he explains each part of the tack, he puts it on the horse while he has me hold one rein. After he tightens the girth on the saddle, he takes the rein I'm holding and turns toward the horse's rear.

"Now, you'll need a leg up."

I'd seen this before, in movies at least.

"Put your hands on top of the withers and spring a little to help me hoist you up." He looks around at the crew and smiles. "Just try to land in the middle and don't fall off the other side. And gather up the reins. You never get on a horse or sit on one without having the reins in your hands. They're your lifeline. Lose them and you can lose your life."

My life; my Lord, he said my life. I gather the reins in my left hand and raise my ankle and foot. I barely spring and only get halfway up. He lets go, and my front slides painfully down over the stirrup edge. Laughs. Lots of laughs.

I raise my leg again. He grasps my ankle, and I jump hard. Too hard. Instead of going up and coming back down in the saddle, I teeter on the horse's far side, clutching at the mane with my left hand to right myself. My body is so far forward my face hits the horse's neck. She flips up her head, pushing my helmet over my eyes. The boss has to steady her.

Giggles this time. One laughs in donkey snorts. Another cries out, "We going to be drinking a lot of Pepsi this fall."

"You're doing fine," the boss says seriously. "A natural-born rider."

With his hand on one rein, he leads us around the stall. I get my feet in the stirrups and have a rein in each hand. I raise my head, arch my back and feel like Caesar crossing the Rubicon, returning triumphant to Rome. He lets go, and the mare stops. I hunch my hips forward a few times and shake the reins. She doesn't move.

97

"Don't forget," he says as he opens the stall door and starts out. "You're the rider and she's the horse."

I'm stumped. Do I dare kick a pregnant mare that belongs to my boss? He probably has her winners' circle photos in his living room right alongside those of his wife. What if I kick her and she lunges into the wall, breaks me up and aborts her baby? I knew there is some clucking sound riders make to get horses moving. I hunch my hips back and forth in the saddle, purse my lips and make a kissing sound.

More laughter. I hear slapping and realize some are poking ribs and pounding thighs.

But she's walking again. We make a few more laps and when she slows I kick her gently with the heels of my sneakers. She walks faster. I'm actually riding, controlling the show.

Cheers erupt. A shrill whistle. One yells, "Look at you. You got a seat like Eddie Arcaro."

(B) BATTLING ATTRACTIONS AND ADDICTIONS

A BANNER DAY/ LEAVING AGAIN AND GOING NOWHERE

14: Richardson Texas, December 21, 1992

I'm packing my new-car-smelling, fire engine red Datsun 280Z coupe, ready to leave Richardson, Texas, and travel to the sunny shores of Southern California. Earlier that morning I dropped Derek off at his mother's apartment in Bossier City. We said an awkward goodbye and I told him that being with his mother is best for now. I drove west, stopping in Richardson to pick up my clothes and say goodbye to my second wife, Debra. Why was I taking the trouble? In my suitcase are the divorce papers, dissolving our marriage of six years, its length a tribute to the power of physical attraction. A few weeks earlier, we'd sat in a lawyer's office and agreed to terms. She didn't even hire her own attorney. We'd worked it out.

"It just wasn't meant to be," I say as we stand in the street just outside our apartment.

"It wasn't fun while it lasted."

99

She stares at me with sharp black eyes, the Marine in her coming out. She is one tough lady and not about to cry.

"You know, I think we're both relieved," I say. "Irreconcilable differences are a fact."

"Wrong time, wrong reasons."

"I was wrong to get involved in the first place. I wasn't over Debbie. I should never have gotten married. I did you a terrible disservice. I hope you and the girls will forgive me."

"I think they will."

"Maybe I should have spent more time with them and less time with you in bed."

"We had some kicks, but I think in the end the bedroom kicked us both."

I nod, remembering the swinging. She'd never discouraged it, and her kicks seemed to be as enjoyable as mine. It made our relationship more solid on one hand because we, in a warped way, needed each other to get our highs. But on the other, it was so unnatural; the bond of marriage became meaningless. Any chance at love had been overcome by lust.

"Probably shouldn't have gotten into all that," I say. "I could have stopped it and you'd been fine with that. But I didn't, so I can't blame you. I think we just went crazy together."

"I'll miss you."

"You too," I say, bending to kiss her cheek.

She raises her chin and looks at me with eyes that make me wonder if she'd like one for the road. "You actually think leaving is going to make a difference with you? Eddie, what you're dealing with isn't going to go away because you change states."

I look at the car, remembering how I freaked out the car salesman by speed shifting and laying rubber in his parking lot.

"Eddie, I think you've been running from what you really are all your life. Why don't you let it be and learn to live with yourself? Gotta be easier than this."

"Yeah, sure," I said. "I'll get over this thing just like I'll get over you, Debra."

"We'll see." She smiles and I fight the urge to take her in my arms. Make it a real send off. I get in the car, rev the engine and squeal out, feeling the rush of power.

As the sun sets over Dallas, I head west on Interstate 10. It's a road I know ends on the Santa Monica beach. I'm eager to see the ocean. As a boy I'd gone to Virginia Beach, Myrtle Beach and even Miami Beach with my father and sisters. I love the beach. Its fresh smell, its constant movement, the way the salt water splashes over my body when I charge into a wave. It always makes me feel so clean. I ache to feel clean.

As a single jockey, I loved the feeling of driving all night and arriving at dawn at a new track where I knew almost no one. A fresh start. A new day. Races to ride and girls to meet. I want that back, those days when I didn't have to deal with what I'd become. Yet as much as I want it to, this doesn't feel like that. The thought crosses my mind that I'm still the 6-year-old boy, running from the five-and-dime and my schoolteacher's tag of "poor little Eddie." My short run down the street and my youthful bravado only masked the pain. Maybe Debra is right. The 1,600 mile drive to the West Coast won't stop my unholy urges. But in a new place I might be stronger.

As the sun sets in front of me and the Dallas skyline flits across my rearview mirror, I say something out loud I often said as a rider, traveling from town to town like a 1930s Bible salesman. "I've never been anyplace I wasn't glad to leave."

Laguna Beach California, One Year Later

The year is three hours old, and I've drunk myself silly. I'm walking back to my apartment overlooking the beach. I see a swanky hotel bar and decide to stop. Inside I see a woman with long black hair and dark eyes that glow with an intelligent confidence. I sit in the chair next to her and her girlfriend. "Don't you consider New Year's celebrations hollow?" I ask.

"Depends on whom you're spending them with," she says.

"Well, I spent mine alone in a bar filled with people."

"Sounds like you like your own company."

"Not more than anything. Perhaps, no one liked mine."

She looks at her friend, exasperated. "That's what I need in my life. Another loser."

"I'm not a loser; I'm just bored with the superficial."

"I'll drink to that."

"I never drink with people I don't know."

"I bet," she says, flashing a wry smile. "I'm Pam O'Neill

"Eddie Donnally."

We hang out in the hotel bar and talk for over an hour. Her girlfriend excuses herself and leaves. We talk some more. Pam is well read, divorced from a successful businessman, has a catering business and apparently is not looking to fall into bed with someone she just met. That's okay with me. I have more than enough partners of both sexes. I need a friend. She proves to be one of the best I've ever had. And never did we allow sex to mess with that.

At the time, nonphysical relationships are rare. The proceeds from selling my Criterion Productions stock back in Dallas allow me to rent a small apartment on the beach in Laguna Beach, about 30 miles south of Los Angeles. I honestly didn't know at the time I moved there that it had a large gay population. I started writing the as-yet-unpublished "Golden Altar," a story about a drug-addicted jockey barred from racing who discovers a woman he loves and a horse that can take him back to glory. Yet to take that ride on the talented but illegally registered colt in the Kentucky Derby, he must sacrifice what few morals he has left and his relationship with the woman he loves. He must also risk his life as well as the life of a horse that is like none other he's encountered.

I buy a sailboat; write each day and each night drink a half-dozen gin and tonics in a local bar I come to consider the center of the universe. Opportunities for brief same-sex contacts abound. I once try to develop a relationship with a man I meet. We go sailing and have dinner together. But

I can never go as far as hold his hand in public. A romantic relationship with a male is beyond my scope. Nameless and sometimes faceless contacts are not.

I also date women, and through one dating service have lunch with at least 25. A few develop into casual relationships. I want desperately to be straight. I meet a woman from Israel, and we date for nearly a year. Those few with whom I am intimate don't know about my other side, though it is obvious I am a player. I realize now I was unfairly jeopardizing their health, but at the time I was caught up in this giant hookup game where our mutual behaviors outside fun times are not discussed.

Oddly, Debra moves to nearby Covina to live with her daughter and we begin seeing each other again. We quickly resume swinging. My same-sex contacts are not the most dangerous type, yet I constantly worry about AIDS. During one period, I'm so afraid I won't get tested. A positive will put me over the edge.

On some level, I'm using other men and women not so much for gratification, but as a way to make me forget my divorce from Debbie, my growing estrangement from my children and, oddly enough, what started me down this path. Somehow, same-sex encounters are not necessarily a product of what happened to me as a youth but an outcome I want to incorporate into the present in order to make that earlier time less aberrant. I ache to view it, not as punishment for the past but as a means for new pleasure. This keeps me from dealing with the memories and the impact. If the outcome is in my present, and the present is acceptable, the past seems less dangerous. I keep trying to tell myself that some people are just bisexual and that doesn't make them horrible. I've never honestly talked about what is going on with anyone. Counseling will force me to confront my past, something I don't have the courage to undertake.

After each same-sex encounter, a part of me that won't go away causes my stomach to churn in fear and self hate. I can never accept myself as gay. Yet another part of me wants to believe I am living as I want, writing the "Great American Novel," sailing my boat to Catalina Island and indulging in behaviors fed by an appetite that challenges my very being. I tell myself my actions are consistent with talented writers, whose genius is enhanced by tortures and appetites that invade their lives and their art, appearing on the page as depth of soul. Yet a part of me realizes the alcohol and drugs are just a way to keep my mind numb enough to maintain this facade of useful self-flagellation.

On occasion I go to a local church, trying to feel something I'd lost. I even ask God to forgive me. Even when I pray for help, a part of me doesn't want help. I'm free and in some sense enjoying my life. Yet I can't shake this feeling that my appetite is consuming me and this dark hunger is going to get worse. Turns out I'm right.

(C) LIFE AS A JOCKEY

A LIFE CHANGING RACE

15: Suffolk Downs, East Boston Massachusetts, October 16, 1974

A chilling wind blows sleeting rain in from Broad Sound as I stand just inside a shabby Suffolk Downs barn and consider why I haven't left for Florida. I half-listen to trainer Jeanne Patterson talk about Society Boy, a horse she trains and I'm listed to ride that afternoon. I never suspect that before the day ends I will take part in an event that will alter my life in ways I can never imagine.

I'd finished fourth aboard the horse in his last start at Rockingham Park as the favorite and doubt he has much chance today. My windbreaker and jeans are wet and muddy from working out horses that morning on the sloppy track. As Jeanne talks and the wind howls, my mind wanders to Florida. In a few weeks, I'll be living in Crystal Beach, driving my boat down a canal and into the Gulf, fishing poles tilting up like dual antennas.

Jeanne clears her throat. "It's raining and I don't think he'll like the track," she says. "I wanted to scratch him from the race because of the mud, but the racing secretary promised he'll write a race that fits him better if I stayed in today. But if he can't handle the mud today, give him a sanitary, and we'll wait for a fast track."

I nod my head and hold off a grin. The four-year-old apparently dislikes all kinds of track surfaces. He had no excuse in his last race when he was beaten nearly 10 lengths by similar company. In 38 previous races, he had won only once and in three years of racing had earned only several thousand dollars. His owner has spent far more in training bills and jockey fees.

While not the most kosher pickle in the deli, giving a horse a "sanitary," or easy race, on a surface it dislikes is as much humane as illegal and sometimes done. Any bettor who could read the *Daily Racing Form* would realize the horse had little chance on any surface. Only a grandmother betting on jockey's colors or a New Ager doing numerology would bet on this horse.

In most cases, trainers are far closer to the horses they train than the jockeys who ride them. I'll spend 10 minutes in the post parade and then race the same animal they've spent weeks and even months preparing. In the end, all their work depends on a series of decisions made in little more than a minute by a 110-pound guy who wears a size six hat and trainers sometimes call "pinheads."

And then there is the betting public. This group of abstract faces fuels the pari-mutuel machines that turn the cogs and grease the wheels inside the giant horse racing industry. I guess on some level I know that without them it all grinds to a wheezing halt. Yet at the time they seem far removed from my life. Those same nameless persons have taunted me with insults when I'm hot, dirty and pock-marked by flying dirt and just risked my life trying to get a half-ton racehorse into a shrinking space moving as fast as my mount. They also seem to have an affinity for cheering and jeering when a racehorse gets loose and charges pell-mell down the track in front of the grandstand. That the panicked horse can kill itself or someone else seems as far removed from their sentiments as my sentiment is removed from theirs. To me, they are not only irreverent but irrelevant.

It's all about politics, I stand there thinking. Run your horse in a race he can't win in order to fill a race and save the racing secretary from canceling it and trying to get enough entrants to fill another so he'll card a race that perfectly fits this or another of the trainers' horses. So I hear Jeanne loud and clear. Go get a race into her horse to help him get fit enough to perform better the next time he is in a race with company as weak as himself. I would get the chance to ride him again in his next start. Quid pro quo—it's what makes the world and racehorses go around.

Riding a horse worth less than a 10-year-old used car in chilling sleet for a winning fee that won't pay for two nights in a decent motel makes Florida dreaming addictive. Weeks earlier, I'd finished the summer meeting at Rockingham Park in Salem, New Hampshire, 60 miles north, as the fourth-leading rider. I have a pocketful of money and am just killing time before Debbie and I head south. The cold wind haunting the track just outside Boston is beginning to kick up sleet. Snow will not be far behind.

It's nearly 10:00 a.m. The track has closed for training, and I walk away, ready for a nap in the jockeys' room. A rider I hardly know falls in beside me. "You got a minute?" he asks.

I stop, and he looks around to see if anyone is nearby. We're standing on a concrete apron between two barns. Grooms are in their horse's stalls by now, doing them up in bandages and medications to help their all-important legs. I know the rider but not well.

"This horse you're on in the third race … you know much about him?"

My ears prick. I sense what's coming. "The trainer said he won't like the track. Not much stock to begin with. Why?"

"You want to make some money today? Some real money?"

"How?"

The rider, older and with a wrinkled face as if his best days are behind him, pulls a wad of $100 bills from his jeans. "I got eight hundred if you can make sure he finishes worse than third."

This time I take a look around and do some quick math. The purse is a whopping $2,500, meaning the winning horse gets $1,500, and my 10 percent is $150 before I pay my valet and the IRS. I am far from a saint, but I had turned down bribes before, one a few weeks earlier at Rockingham. I've never taken part in race fixing. The decision to abstain has little to do with those abstract faces in the crowd. I'd worked with trainers in a race or two to help them put their horse's worst foot forward, so to speak. Then when the horse was ready and in a field we were confident the animal could beat, we'd made significant bets. I worked out horses at 5:00 a.m. before the track officially opened and the clockers arrived. I worked out young horses that hadn't yet raced at speeds below their potential in order to heighten the potential payoff when they made their first starts. But to deliberately cheat a trainer I'm working for is a line I have not yet crossed.

The trainer said she wanted to scratch the horse from the race because of track conditions and told me to give him an easy race. Besides, on his best day, the horse could run as fast as a man with gout. And why hadn't they given her the money? She didn't own the horse, and her commission for winning would be the same as mine. There were subtle things she could have done to make sure the horse didn't perform well. Or perhaps they had paid her. Maybe the $800 they wanted to give me was merely the fixers' purchasing insurance.

I take a final glance around and open my hand. He plants the bills in my palm and scurries away. Easy money, I think, remembering an old racetrack expression that speaks to the chicanery present in horse racing yet applies to every other form of commerce that involves people and money. It doesn't turn out to be easy. The decision is the worst in my entire life.

*****

In the post parade, Society Boy warms up like he'd rather be in his dry stall. He is so calm his trainer doesn't hire a pony and rider to accompany us to the starting gate. It's still chilly and drizzling. The track is wet but still officially listed as fast. Beneath my silks is a plastic rain jacket. My riding breeches are plastic and on my helmet are four sets of goggles for the one-mile race. At this point, I've been riding races for 13 years and the fact that I lived through it and can still compete on a middle-level grade gives some degree of testimony to my ability. I have some idea of how to help and how to hinder a horse's performance. Rain pelts my helmet and I line Society Boy up with the rest of the field and walk toward the starting gate that sits in front of the grandstand. Among the couple of thousand people in the aging grandstand could there be any who paid me to lose?

I'd heard the stories about New England racing and its influence by reputed mob boss Raymond Patriarca of Providence, Rhode Island. A rider who rides each summer at the lowly New England fairs bragged that so many races were fixed he had to reserve one well in advance. He said he once had two groups of gangsters fix the same race and collected double. I heard a story of a mob member who came to a trainer's barn after the man had claimed one of their horses who's running at a lower level than the horse could handle and was being "held" and set up for a bet. When the trainer refused to sell the horse back, he was kidnapped and put in the back of a car as they held a gun to his head. The trainer changed his mind. Despite my mount's lack of ability and his apparent dislike for the mud, I wished I could change mine.

In reality, fixing a race by picking out one horse to win is far from a sure thing. The horse weighs over 1,000 pounds, the jockey little more than 100. If his mount is superior, the rider would have to stand in the irons and muscle the horse down so strongly the track stewards watching each race would be sure to see it. Even then, if the horse was that much the best, he'd still win. During morning gallops, horses often run off at a full race pace with dead fit 145 pound exercise riders struggling to slow them down.

Also, four cameras mounted in towers film the race from separate angles. Patrol judges watch with binoculars from several strategically placed stands along the outside rail. Three stewards high up in the grandstand watch the race with binoculars and on monitors and take instant reports from the patrol judges. If it's obvious a jockey deliberately keeps a horse from winning, suspensions can range up to a lifetime.

The nearly black Society Boy has the one post on the rail in the eight-horse field, something I think is good. I can bury him early behind the field and the massive amount of mud being hurled in his face will remove any inkling of courage he might have. In a race on a wet track, the kickback stings your face as if a man three feet away were hurling mud into it.

109

The four goggles I wear can also be used to an advantage. Behind horses during a race, the flying mud makes the top pair opaque within a quarter mile and must be gently removed. On horseback, in the middle of a pack of horses going nearly 40 mph and racing inches apart, removing them from the top layer down is no mean feat. A clumsy move and they all come tumbling to your chest. Putting them back up is impossible. If I have to, I can pull all of them down, rise on the horse and pull him to the outside, something the stewards would likely forgive given the wet track.

An assistant starter walks up and puts a thin leather lead through the bridle's chinstrap. He leads us into the first stall and leaves. I consider gigging the horse with my heels to get him excited, something that might give him a lousy start, but he stands there as if he's asleep. I decide to leave him alone.

The seven horses outside me load quickly, and the starter squeezes a pair of prongs that break the electric circuit that keeps the front doors closed. They spring open and off we go into the rain and mud. As we enter the first turn, less than an eighth mile (one furlong) from the gate, we're fourth. Mud hits us like we're inside a car wash. Oddly, Society Boy doesn't seem to mind. He has his head down and is firmly into the bit. Horses have an extra covering over their eyes that allows them to keep them open even when a wall of water is ripping into their faces. I'm not worried. Not yet.

As the field straightens into the backstretch, a space opens in front of us, and he literally drags me through it. He's fourth. The three in front of me are staggered and wide apart. No mud is hitting us. I decide to give the reins slack, thus depriving the horse of the support my firm hold is providing. I cautiously move my hands up his neck, not to signal for more speed but to let him flounder a bit on the muddy track. This I believe will discourage him.

To my dismay the early leader slows, and I and another horse pass him. I'm still fourth but in the clear and only about four lengths off the lead. I pull him behind horses again, but instead of slowing, he's gaining. I'm nervous now. I realize that in a fixed race other horses are being held, and I know the entire field is running slowly, even for bargain-basement $2,000 claimers.

As we approach the final turn, I have an idea. Horses race with one of their front legs leading. On the backstretch and in the homestretch, that normally is their right leg. To properly negotiate a turn, they must switch to the left lead. I decide to keep Society Boy on the wrong lead, something I think will force him to race wide and lose valuable ground.

To induce a horse to change leads entering the turn, the rider shifts his weight to the left or inside while gently pulling the right rein to the outside. I do the opposite, shifting my weight outside while putting pressure on the left rein. Society Boy ignores my leading and shifts perfectly to his left lead. I decide to keep him wide. He's on the outside, but still moves into third. The two leaders are racing head to head with me alone in third. I'm getting the perfect trip, damn it. In a near panic, I tighten the reins.

Society Boy sees it as a sign to accelerate and despite my strong hold moves into second at the top of the stretch with less than a quarter mile remaining. The only horse in front of me is starting to tire. I can jump off or muzzle him back so hard the stewards can't help but notice and likely finish second. The only other option is to win. Jumping off a perfectly good racehorse is like jumping out of a perfectly good plane—without a parachute. Behind me are a half-dozen racehorses. If I keep a stranglehold, I'll draw the attention of the stewards, who might rule me off for years. Even worse, they'd investigate the race and interview its riders. It would not only put a lot of heat on me but on the people who were fixing the race.

There's a point in nearly every race at which a jockey is sure he's going to win. Because it hasn't happened yet, that moment is more thrilling than even going under the wire in front. I never heard the roaring crowd because my every fiber is overwhelmed by a sense-numbing moment when the horse and I melt into a single purpose. The line where I end and the horse begins is blurred. For a few brief seconds it ceases to exist.

It's the reason riders come back from near-crippling injuries to again climb aboard a Thoroughbred. It's why they return from retirement and hang on long after their best days, tamping down the naturally recurring fear that crops up in the frontal lobe like divots on a golf course. That singular, silver sliver of a split second is something I still dream about.

To make this horse finish worse than third in front of three track stewards and a battery of cameras would not shoot my career in the foot but the temple. No more silver sliver moments. My fellow jockeys in the race will have to answer questions that might also end their careers. I don't know what the race fixers would do. I am sure what the track stewards and the racing commission would do.

I decide to win.

With less than a furlong to go, I cock my whip, give Society Boy a reminding tap and start hand riding. He wins by a length and a half.

We walk into the winner's circle, and Jeanne is there, happy and carefree. I don't think she knew what was going down. The race's final time for a mile is 1:44 2/5, at least three seconds or 15 lengths slower than normal for even $2,000 claimers. This is the only race Society Boy will win in 24 starts that year. Nearly three weeks later I ride him over the wet track at a distance only 70 yards farther and in a cheaper $1,500 claiming race. He is never closer than sixth and in a field of eight finishes seventh. This time I try hard. His 101 race career ends at age 10 with total earnings of $19,308.

But on this day Society Boy is the winner. As I walk back to the jockeys' room covered from head to toe with mud, I look again into the nearly empty grandstand, half expecting a crazed Italian to run down the steps and start shooting.

I know there will be retribution. I just don't know what it will look like.

(D) LIFE TODAY

AN ABUSED CHAPLAIN/ A NEW DIRECTION; MAYBE

16: Time and Place Anonymous

"I was sexually abused when I was a kid, and it's coming back on me." The chaplain before me is near tears. Anger spews from my gut, leaving me suspended somewhere between screaming and crying. I clinch my fists, marveling that I can still be affected this deeply by sexual abuse.

I catch myself, take a deep breath and look at the track chaplain sitting behind his desk opposite me. This is new ground. I'm director of development for the Race Track Chaplaincy of America, which sanctions and oversees some 70 chaplains. I raise funds and communicate our message to the racing world and beyond. After five years of night classes on fundraising and communication at UCLA and eight years as a writer for a major newspaper, I'm fairly well equipped for the job. It also involves visiting our chaplains across the nation to teach them and their councils (boards) and volunteers how to do what I've learned. I know most of the chaplains well and encouraging them is part of what I do. Yet, hearing one talk about the late-coming effects of sexual abuse has thrown me like a barroom bull.

"Sexual abuse is one of the most damaging things that can happen," I say.

"I thought I'd put it behind me, but I'm starting to think about it again, all the time it seems. I'm in counseling, but I think it's starting to affect my work here at the track. I'm having trouble concentrating, and there are times when I just want to go sit down by myself and cry."

Part of me wants to cry out my own story. But this is about him, and I decide to hear him out. "Sounds like depression."

His head lowers, and he stares his desk's edge. "I'm taking medication. Just not sure it's helping. I just can't be close to my wife right now. I don't want to divorce, but all this going on with me isn't fair to her, and I know it."

I note that he's feeling guilty, a normal but inappropriate response. "Not fair?" I ask.

"I finally got up the courage to tell her about it, and she says she understands and all. I just feel awful about all this."

"Guilty."

He looks up for a brief second. "I know God has forgiven me, but it's all still going on in my head right now. I don't know if he can keep on forgiving me for what I'm likely to do."

My anger at his abuser is getting the best of me now, and while I am just beginning to learn about counseling, I know it can harm my effectiveness. "You still believe it was your fault, the abuse I mean?"

"You sound like my counselor. One side of me knows it wasn't, but one part of me says I didn't try to stop it. There is a lot I could have done."

"Did you cause your abuse?"

"I didn't start it, that's for sure."

"It sounds like you feel responsible for it."

114

The chaplain gives me some details about how it came about. It's repulsive, and my anger keeps coming back. But I at least recognize it and try to be calm.

"That's horrible."

"I'm not sure I want to stay married. Crazy urges, if you know what I mean."

"I do. I lived them out for seven years, and by the grace of God I'm still here. But at least you're getting help. That can change a lot of things."

"I thought it was behind me. Look Eddie, I've heard you talk about what happened to you, and I knew you wouldn't judge me."

"And you think others will?"

"If I told the members of my council what I told you, they'd find a new chaplain." Tears glisten at the red rims of his eyes.

"You've told your wife and your counselor. And you told me. That's probably enough, at least for now. You know self-destruction comes with this stuff. I was in counseling for two years and never mentioned it until I knew the shrink wasn't going to counsel me anymore. It takes guts to talk about it."

"It makes me feel so dirty, and sometimes I get so mad at myself."

"Crazy thing about sexual abuse. The abused wants to take the blame. That way we get to beat ourselves up. Makes us feel better. We don't have to feel guilty because we're already suffering."

I realize my tone has an edge, one out of place. I make my voice softer. "Chaplain, you've been a man of God for a long time and you still are. God built into us a desire to make things right. You were brutally abused, and your anger is justified. But it sounds like you can't or won't be angry at your abuser or maybe he isn't even available. So your anger has to go somewhere and it goes inside. You can only suppress it so long and it has to come out. You can't hurt your abuser, so you hurt yourself."

"I think I've forgiven the person that abused me. I know about God's grace, so it's crazy that I have a hard time forgiving myself."

"Abuse is a deep wound."

"Would you pray for me?"

115

I pray, asking God to bring the right people beside him to help, that God would strengthen his relationship with his wife and give him the courage to get through this tough time. I remind him in prayer that God says that which we sow we also reap, and hold the chaplain up as one who has sown generously, helping others get through their problems for many years.

We talk some more, sticking to mundane things. We end and when I get into my rented car, I feel a subtle shift in my spirit. I know that my work with RTCA has made a difference in the lives of thousands of backstretch workers. I've raised a lot of funds and the money has helped a lot of chaplains and track workers. We've added chaplains, and I've found funding for the White Horse Community Events in which we provided hygiene kits, clothing, free haircuts, a children's carnival and a superb barbecue meal. Kentucky Derby-winning jockey Pat Day shares how Christ had brought him out of drug use and helped him become one of the world's most successful jockeys. In one series alone, over 1,000 had accepted Christ as Savior, many praying that Jesus would change their lives a few feet away from pari-mutuel machines.

Yet the compassion stirred in me by this chaplain's story is something new. I've learned that the power of confidential, genuine listening, combined with a few short but correct responses and point-of-need prayer, are powerful agents in helping others heal or at least in getting through a long night. At this point, the International Church of the Foursquare Gospel—a Pentecostal denomination with doctrine similar to the larger Assembly of God—has ordained me and commissioned me as a chaplain. I have an enormous respect for track chaplains, who are genuine missionaries to some 150,000 who live on the backstretches of our nation's horse tracks, a group who would never be reached otherwise. I felt in my spirit that I'd helped. Yet my work in administration is at the rear of the battlefield of human struggle. As I drive back to my motel, I can't help but consider that God is moving me to the front lines.

(A) CHILDHOOD TO ARREST: STILL LEARNING

PAIN ON A HORSE/HURT IN MY HEART

17: Patchen Wilkes Farm, Lexington Kentucky, August 1960

On the morning after I sat on my first horse and gave the crew a show, Mr. Goodpaster leads me to a stall with a towering white horse and gives me pointers as I put on the saddle and bridle. He explains that the horse is his "pony," Buck. Beside him is a white Boxer he says is named Sugar. When I say she's the first white Boxer I've seen, he explains that the American Kennel Club refuses to register the color, and he drove 80 miles to Cincinnati to rescue her from death. A white Boxer. A white pony. Herman has a thing for white animals.

Doubt creases my face. "On the track, any horse that isn't racing is a pony," he explains. "Buck's been turned out all summer so he'll be a little fresh." His eyes light up, and one eyebrow lifts with revelation. "But I believe you can handle him. Just don't let him run off."

Buck did run off. I tried for a while to restrain him but I feel like a toddler lifting an anvil. In the end I bend over like a jockey and let him rip. Amazingly, Herman isn't mad. The next morning Buck stays in the stall and so do I. That doesn't mean I don't ride. These are the days before the round high-sided "breaking pens," became an integral part of training a young horse to accept a rider. At Patchen Wilkes, we put tack on an unbroken yearling minus the dangling stirrups. As the groom leads the horse in tiny circles around the stall, the rider pats the horse all over, then "bellies up," or puts an increasing amount of weight on the horse's back. If a horse throws a fit or bucks, the rider safely slides off as the groom leads the horse in tight left-handed circles.

I'm assigned six yearlings. I manage to belly up on all six to some degree and find that some accept me quicker than others. One rears and nearly falls, but by that time I'm on the ground. I live to ride home in the back of the pickup and eat one of Mrs. Johnson's pot roasts.

A month later, I'm riding a small unnamed filly, galloping her around the track. She's on the outside of two others, going head to head as all three who seem to gain courage from each other. There are two things every jockey remembers. One is the name of the horse and the details of the first winning race or "breaking your maiden." Another is the first time you walk onto a track with a racehorse under you, jog off and break into a gallop. With stirrup leathers shortened to provide the leverage needed for control, only knees and lower thighs grip the horse for purchase. I train my hands to become kind while firmly holding the crossed reins against the withers. My butt is to always be lower than my head.

The first time I feel a Thoroughbred's instant acceleration and realize the power between my legs, the experience is forever etched into my soul. At Patchen Wilkes, I become aware that I am no more than a passenger, possessing only the control granted by an unpredictable half-ton animal exclusively bred for some 250 years to race and win.

Access to Bluegrass horse farms is easy at this time, and just beyond the outside rail on the first turn of our five-furlong track is a stand where tourists watch young horses train. I relish being watched as I sit atop this young filly and gallop toward the stand housing several tourists. I know how to arch my back, insert only boots' tips in the thin metal stirrups and drop my heels to "cock my toe." The fall breeze blows across my face. I'm alive in a new and different way.

One of the tourists raises a video camera. I fight tensing. Thoroughbreds essentially learn only to accept what they encounter time after time. A racehorse can see a lone fence post every day for a month and never shy, then one day think it's a horse eating monster and make a "drop-you-on-a-dime" U-turn. It's vital that I recognize the objects that might panic my mount but not telegraph fear through the reins. Tighten up and their fear is assured. I concentrate on being loose and all seems well.

The filly plants her two front hooves into the track. I'm thrown forward, but bend my knees and sit back. Then she drops a shoulder and turns left. I plow into the track, landing on my right shoulder. She runs over me, stepping on the top of my foot.

Pain scalds its way up my leg. I let out a yelp. Sitting up on the track, I hold one of my new Kroop boots with both hands. I know my foot is broken. Herman, standing in the saddle, races past on Buck on his way to pick up the panicked filly. I learn a valuable first lesson. Some trainers think of jockeys as busses: one comes along every 15 minutes. Not so with a talented racehorse. Finally, Lit drives down the outside of the track in the pickup. In minutes, I'm inside a local emergency room, watching in horror as a nurse uses a thick pair of scissors to cut off one of my new high-heel boots that had cost me a week's salary. Fiberglass casts are years into the future, and a doctor fits me with a plaster of Paris model thick enough to withstand a sledge hammer. It has a heel that allows me to walk; something I realize later is as much a curse as a blessing. The next morning all the crew sign it. That day I walk seven yearlings for at least 30 minutes each to cool them after morning gallops. The night before I'd called home and proudly told my dad I'd broken my foot. As I lay in my bed that night, I saw a vision of my high school classmates walking across safe, green college campuses. I ached for a chili hot dog from Paul's.

After six weeks, my cast is removed. A day later, Herman studies my eyes as a groom gives me a leg up on the filly that threw me. I manage to grin through it all, but I'm glad no tourists show up that day. The filly is eventually named Be Stepping in my honor. She proves extremely fast on her feet indeed, winning several races.

I'm glad to be back riding. Being on top of a racehorse always seems to cure a lot of things. At Patchen Wilkes, I begin to understand and foster cooperation between horse and rider, guiding but not forcing the animal by subtle moves of my hands and body weight. I learn to think like a horse and start to get a feel for when to let the horse be the horse and when to intervene.

The first time I jog a young racehorse down the farm's track and rise in the irons as my mount surges into a fast gallop, my father's anger, my mother and grandmother's deaths and all that happened with my stepbrother in our bedroom begin to sink into the past. I want to ride races as much as I want to breathe. I have a new life, a new purpose. The power and control I feel aboard a racehorse allows me to bury in the lost memory file a former life I couldn't control.

And, oh yes, the Pepsi. By the time the spring meet opened at nearby Keeneland Race Course the following April, we had started or broke some 64 yearlings, half before January and half after. While every one of the six riders bought a case or more of Pepsi, I set a farm record that probably still stands. I bought 32.

(B) BATTLING ATTRACTIONS AND ADDICTIONS

A NEW CITY/A NEW ADDICTION

18: Sam Houston Race Park, Houston Texas, April 24, 1994

"I'd like you to serve on my council here," says Randy Weaver, the track chaplain who stands beside me in the glass-enclosed press box as I gaze down at a field of horses entering the track.

As we watch from high atop the gleaming new green and white grandstand, guilt spreads through my body like an injection of cocaine. "I'd love to. I'm honored you asked."

Randy and his older brother, Russ, were professional rodeo ropers before becoming track chaplains. When the late jockey Sammy Maple and I started the chaplaincy program at Arkansas's Oaklawn Park racetrack in 1978, we assembled a group who hired Russ as our first chaplain. A couple of years later, I'd worked with Russ and others to help start the Racetrack Chaplaincy of Texas. It was natural his younger brother would want me to serve on what amounted to a board of elders for his ministry. Yet I'd just been divorced for the second time, was smoking marijuana and fighting a losing battle with same-sex attraction. I'd driven here from Laguna Beach seeking a fresh start and a paycheck.

"Love to help any way I can," I say. "I'm starting a new TV show. I'll do a feature on the chaplaincy here."

"Great. How about we pray for that show right now?" He removes his white straw cowboy hat and places a hand on my shoulder. I look around at the crowd of reporters throwing glances our way. With bowed head and closed eyes, he prays. I see others watching, feel embarrassed and wonder how God can hear me when I'm so enmeshed in sin. Yet I bow my head and close my eyes. I'm glad when he finishes. "Thanks, I need a lot of prayer these days."

"Don't we all?" he says, excusing himself.

I watch him go, hoping he won't find me out.

It's opening night at Texas' first major racetrack to open after the state in 1986 legalized pari-mutuel racing for the second time. It's a huge triumph for the state's many racing fans and horse community. I chronicled the effort as the horse racing writer for *The Dallas Morning News* and a few weeks earlier landed a job writing and handicapping here for the *Austin American-Statesman*. I am also contacting potential sponsors and arranging to buy air time for my horse racing TV show, "Trackside Texas."

I'd spent the buyout money from Criterion during the nearly two years I lived at Laguna Beach, living a raucous if not outright depraved lifestyle. I'd found a literary agent who'd shopped my novel, *Golden Altar*, which had gotten close but was never sold. I'm taking the anti-depressants Lithium and Paxil every day. I've decided to slow down on drinking and stick to smoking a joint or two each day to relax. I'm nearing the end of the line. If I don't make my writing and TV show work, I'll not only be broke, but flirting with a third stay in a psyche ward. I've rented a nice apartment and am casually dating a girl who knows little of my past. I'm determined to be heterosexual. It's a new start in a new city, but part of me knows I'm white-knuckling the whole thing.

A few days later I accidentally drive past a video porn shop, and after driving around the block several times give in to the urge and go in. A girl stands before the raised counter, fast talking the worker who sells booth tokens. She turns to me, smiling. It's obvious she's speeding and looking to turn a trick, probably in one of the booths, and later share part of the proceeds with the worker. Still her smile is engaging. She's mildly pretty, young and obviously available. Maybe a girlfriend, a real girl to sleep with is what I need to stay straight, put me back on the road to being strictly hetero. Anything is better than the alternative.

We talk, and she comes back to my apartment. Sitting on stools at my kitchen bar, I pour two beers and chat. I'm not surprised she makes a quick assessment of my wealth, status and potential generosity. I hit the glamour spots of being a jockey and a newspaper reporter and tell her about my new job and the TV show. With a mischievous smile, she removes a tubular glass pipe from her purse. She pours several white misshapen cubes the size of a fingernail onto my kitchen counter. It's my first look at rock cocaine.

"I like to make out when I'm high," she says. "Look, this is evil stuff, and you're better off if you never do it. You can if you want, but I advise you not to."

She puts a rock in the pipe's end, tilts it to nearly vertical and uses a lighter to artfully dab at it. As she inhales the white rock melts. "Hey girl, you're talking to me," I say. "I've done every drug known to man except antifreeze. I've snorted more cocaine than you could put on this counter, tried opium, Dilaudid and probably smoked a bale of grass. I've never been addicted. Don't expect to now."

She grins and hands me the pipe. "I'll show you how."

She coaches me through inhaling the heated residue. My lungs expand, and my head explodes. A locomotive of pleasure roars into my brain. It sizzles, snaps, crackles and pops at the same time. I'm the king of the hill, the man of the hour and the prince of pleasure. I want to shout, giggle and make love. Instead I stay still and feel something like a rocket that takes off in my loins. It's a buzz like none other. Addicts always say they're chasing that first hit, the one purest, the holy grail of highs, the one that every toke after it always fails to meet the first one. And no matter how many hits you take or how large the rock, the high always seems to be less and less. I'd heard it was like a dog chasing his tail as it grows shorter and shorter. This feels too good. I know I am in trouble.

A few days later she knocks on my door at 1:00 a.m. and comes walking in with a man she introduces as T.C. Within 20 minutes, he takes from his jacket pocket a round pie of crack cocaine the size of pita bread. We smoke. He takes off all his clothes, stands on his head and spins around on my hardwood floors. He's in his thirties, handsome and clearly uninhibited. I'm intrigued.

Intelligent with a clever tongue, he owns a thriving courier firm he runs from home, taking calls and dispatching drivers with the intensity and focus of a 911 operator. His company becomes one of my show's sponsors, and often the three of us go to the track to film with the couple I've hired to help produce the show. The female helps on camera. Her husband shoots the footage and works with me to edit it into a show, something I'd learned at Criterion. I contract for a weekly 10:30 a.m. Saturday slot, a good time for fans thinking about going to the track. It airs on Home Sports Network, a company later purchased by ESPN that at the time was the nation's third-largest sports network. I write the features, produce them and co-host. The track itself has no production facilities, producer or host and it soon comes on board as a sponsor.

T.C., Cindy and I hang out and smoke a lot of crack. But the three of us never get it on together, and T.C. and I become friends. However, we openly share Cindy, only separately. Cindy, free spirit that she is, no doubt shares her favors with others.

She never has a key to my apartment, but she shows up virtually any time day or night she likes, sometimes at 4:00 a.m., bringing along female friends who she had talked into climbing into bed with me. She also brings around a cross-dressing male. In turn, I buy her crack, which we often smoke together. T.C. is married and lives in a giant double-wide permanent mobile home surrounded by tall, chain-link fences. But he, like me, is spending more and more time getting and smoking crack.

124

*****

"You have to start getting your stuff here on time," warns the sports editor at the *Austin American-Statesman* one evening. I'd submitted my picks for the next day's races on top of the deadline for making the next morning's paper. "You're jamming us up here, and my desk man is going crazy."

Part of my job with the paper is to email a list of graded entries the night before the next night's racing. I rank each field of horses in the order in which I think they will finish and give comments on the first three. I'd come to the job with a record of picking the race's winner nearly 40 percent of the time at *The Dallas Morning News*. Once in the *News*, I picked 10 winners on an 11-race card with the 11th race winner picked second, a feat achieved by few professional handicappers.

"I'll try to do better," I say.

"You sure you're all right, Eddie? Your voice sounds hoarse all the time."

"Just a little thing I got going with my throat right now."

"Your TV show looks good. I know you got to be busy."

"I can handle it. I'm okay."

"I'm counting on you. You got a lot of readers, you know."

"Look, I got to go. Need to go do an interview."

"Sure, fine. Just give my editors a break, all right?"

I hang up, realizing I sit on a kitchen stool with no clothes on, a crack pipe in my hand.

(C) LIFE AS A JOCKEY

A BOTCHED FIX/WHAT NOW?

19: Salem New Hampshire, Evening, October 16, 1974

After Society Boy won the race I'd been paid to lose, I meet Debbie outside the jockeys' room and we walk to the track's lot reserved for jockey parking. She's aware of what happened and like me is not surprised to see the jockey who paid me leaning against our hatchback.

"Nothing I could do but jump off," I say. "The race was so jiggered I was in a gallop and still won. I was afraid I'd draw a lot of heat on us all." I reach in my jeans, glance around and hand him the money I'd taken. He shrugs his shoulders nonchalantly but his eyes smolder and tighten at the corners.

He walks away and Debbie and I give each other long, exasperated looks. On the ride back, I give my logic again, and I can tell by the fear on her face it's not convincing. If she is not buying it, I realize whoever put up the money is not going to buy it either. At the time, she's still working as my agent, booking my mounts at the recently concluded Rockingham Park season. We're saving the 25 percent fee I pay an agent, but all we do is talk horses, trainers and upcoming races.

126

"Wonder who put up the money?" I ask.

"Don't the Italians run this town? They run everything everywhere I've been."

Debbie's maiden name is Bonazza. She's from Rochester and members of her extended family have names like Guido and Luigi. She'd said she thought some were "connected."

"They got the Irish here too, you know," I say.

"I hope one of them is named Donnally."

She looks longingly out the window and into the night. "Time to get out of Dodge," she says. "We're getting ready to go home in a couple of weeks anyway. We can drive our motor home out of here tomorrow."

The previous fall, we'd purchased a small house in Crystal Beach with a backyard that fronted on a canal. A 10-minute ride from my backyard dock in my little 16-footer is the Gulf of Mexico. We love fishing and camping out on nearby Anclote Key. At that moment, the house, the fishing and camping and especially the children we want to have seem light years away. This summer we'd parked our 24-ft motor home in a tiny RV park beside a lake. It'd been a good year and we saved up several thousand.

"No use running," I say. "They know where we live. I'll ride here a couple more weeks like we planned and see what happens. Where's my pistol?"

"In my underwear drawer where it always is. Why?"

"I don't know. Just thinking."

"Eddie, if these guys are the real thing, a pistol is only going to get you shot a lot faster."

"I gave the money back. Maybe that's enough."

"They had to lose a lot more than that."

"What was I going to do, jump off?"

"These guys don't play, Eddie."

"They mess with me there'll be a lot of heat. They don't want that."

She shakes her head and exhales loudly. "They kill judges and cops just to let everyone know where they stand. Maybe they want to make an example out of you just to let others know they don't play. You actually think this is the first time they've done this?"

I know it isn't. I'd turned down offers that summer at Rockingham. I grip the steering wheel and shake my head. I can't believe this is happening.

"I'm so dumb. We don't even need the money." I glance over at her. "But I'm not going to let them break my legs. So help me God I'll start shooting first."

Debbie leans over and lays her arm on my shoulder. She weighs every bit of 90 pounds and we've been in some crazy situations before. But for the first time I see fear in her face.

"If they come after us," she says. "We won't even see it coming."

*****

The next day I'm named on several horses. But because we're planning to leave for Florida as soon as feasible and we'd both slept poorly, we decide to forgo hustling mounts and we show up after the track closed for training at 10:00 a.m. I'd brought my pistol, a German Mauser 32 my father said was taken off a Nazi. It's loaded and under the front seat, but I've never shot it. When we get out of our car, I see the same jockey walking toward us. He had to be waiting several hours.

"The boys want to talk to you," he says. He makes it sound casual as if it's something I do every day. "They just want to have breakfast and talk."

I glance at Debbie whose face is twisted with suspicion. "I'll meet them some place that's public, a restaurant maybe," I say. I know it's risky for a jockey to meet publically with gangsters, but I don't think I'm being watched by the cops or track police. It's better than being beaten or killed in private. "What do they want to talk about?"

"They just figure you owe them one. Don't worry, it'll be in a restaurant. Nothing's going to happen to you. They just want to know you'll make it up to them down the line."

I'll get a phone call one day and one of them will say that a certain horse I ride that day will finish out of the money. Case closed. I'd be off the hook. Not have to look over my shoulder every day of my life. "Can't

128

you just tell them I'm in? I owe them one. I'll make it up. We're getting ready to go back to Florida. I'm done here anyway."

"Don't think that would be smart." His voice takes on an edge. "You meet with them in a public place and they're not going to be mad on you. You run, and they don't know where your head is on this and they'll start to worry." He pauses. "Eddie, my brother, you don't want to make these guys worry. They don't do worry well."

I sigh deeply and look at Debbie whose pinched eyes are saying no. He gives me the address of Danny's Bar in Somerville, not far from the track. I get a pen from Debbie and write it down.

He seems relieved. "I'll meet you there in a half-hour. Spend a few minutes and you go ride like nothing happened."

He walks away and I turn to Debbie. "I got to go meet with these guys," I say. It's a public place. What are they going to do, shoot me or beat me up in a restaurant? I'll take my pistol."

"That'd be stupid. It'd be like pulling a pistol on cops. They'd blow you away on the spot."

"Look, I just know I can't run. I'm not going to spend my life wondering when they're going to show up."

"I'm going with you."

"What? You're the one talking crazy now."

"Not really. They do anything to you, I'm a witness."

"Meaning what? They'd have to kill us both?"

"I'm Italian remember. I know how they think. I'll be safe."

I look at her a long time and finally shake my head. She puts her arms around me, and we hug. "Can't you just wait at the track?"

She pushes me away. "We've been together through a lot of stuff. We either stay together, or we don't. If we split on this, we might as well split on the rest."

(D) LIFE TODAY

WHITE HORSE BATTLES/ WHITE HORSE WINS

20: Lexington Kentucky, October 2006

At 89, Herman Goodpaster lives in the same Hume Road house as the day I walked onto Patchen Wilkes Farm, a few miles away and 46 years earlier. I have visited previously, and finding his house isn't hard. I recognize the three dogs that roam his 10-acre backyard. His wife, Mary, comes to the door, ushers me into the large one-story home and soon Herman shuffles in, wearing a brown robe, slippers and a grin he'd probably wear in his coffin.

The previous winter he broke a hip when he slipped on the ice as he retrieved his mail and now uses a walker. His hair is the color of the white Thoroughbreds he loved, and I had discovered only a few years earlier that he had been a Christian and active in his church, even during the days he ran Mrs. Joe Goodwin's Patchen Wilkes Farm.

As always, we talk about old times and with three dogs at his feet, I recall the story of Sugar, his white Boxer who hid in the tall grass and when the yearling I rode got close leaped two feet in the air. "Herman, you always loved white animals. Maybe that's why God gave you the first white Thoroughbred."

His face takes on a hard look, one of resolve and anger. I think I understand why. In the language of horse racing, Kentucky horsemen are called "Hardboots." The Bluegrass is the headwaters of the Thoroughbred breeding industry, Horse racing is part of the culture and its horsepersons are typically traditionalists. Once at Patchen Wilkes I mentioned that I had a more efficient way of getting the feed tubs inside stalls. Herman rejected the idea, saying, "We been doing it this way 200 years, I'm not about to change now."

That might have been why he had to fight to have White Beauty, born at Patchen Wilkes in 1963, registered as the first white Thoroughbred. The Jockey Club, which officially registers all Thoroughbreds, had not been kind.

"They thought I was lying," Herman says. "I finally told them that if they found out I was lying, they could rule me off the rest of my life and put me in jail if they wanted."

Hardboots are not only old-school, they have this thing called honor. Lying to those who run the hallowed sport of horse racing is simply not part of the culture.

"But she was finally registered," I remind him.

"Not before they said I'd be ruined if I was wrong. I had to put my name on the line."

White Beauty's dam is Herman's Filly O' Mine, the Thoroughbred he had hoisted me aboard the day after I had arrived at the farm.

Over 200 years of breeding had failed to produce a white Thoroughbred. The pure white filly was foaled in the spring of 1963, less than a year after I left the farm for Camden, South Carolina, and a job Herman had gotten for me with the prestigious C.V. Whitney Racing Stable. In the fall of 1963, less than a year after her birth, I rode in my first race.

131

I am also well acquainted with White Beauty's sire, Ky. Colonel. At Patchen Wilkes in the early spring of 1961, I was helping in the breeding shed where Ky. Colonel was the farm's prize stud. Big and muscular with a burnished chestnut coat, he had an odd white spot on his belly. I held a long leather lead shank attached to his halter in one end of the breeding shed while his groom brushed him down. A worker pulled apart a sliding partition to reveal a mare in heat a few yards away. The stallion understood exactly what was expected and suddenly reared into the air. I gave slack as I knew was correct, but my heart nearly stopped. The groom laughed at me, took the shank and led the "Colonel" to the waiting mare.

"I had to hire a lawyer and fight The Jockey Club all the way," Herman says. "My pony Buck was white, so they sent vets out to do a fertility test on him. He'd been gelded for years, but they didn't believe me. It was like they were saying I did something wrong."

White Beauty was eventually registered and went on to win races at two and three. She produced the unraced white filly Beauty 'n Motion and is the great-granddam of the white Patchen Beauty, who won two races and has several white offspring.

"Well, Herman, there was a man who lived 2,000 years ago, and they tried to ruin his name too. The Bible says he was also God and that when he returns he'll be riding a white horse, and that everybody who believes in him will be riding back with him on white horses."

His eyebrows rise with skepticism. I take my skinny chaplain's Bible from my back pocket and turn to the back, Revelation 19:11and read, "Now I saw heaven opened, and behold a white horse. And He who sat on it (Jesus) was called Faithful and True, and in righteousness He judges and makes war." And then verse 14: "And the armies in heaven clothed in fine linen, white and clean, follow Him on white horses. Herman, a lot of theologians believe that army is made up of Christians."

I look over to see tears run down his ruddy cheeks. "Herman, we're going to get to follow Christ back to earth, and we'll all be riding white horses."

A few days later at Churchill Downs, I help with the Race Track Chaplaincy of America's White Horse Award. God had given me the idea for honoring unheralded track workers each year in conjunction with the Breeders' Cup, giving the award to the one person judged by major donors who became members of the White Horse Fellowship to have performed the most heroic act in behalf of horse or human. I'd convinced our executive committee, the closest thing to an RTCA board, that it was a good idea. Then I took the idea to Sherwood Chillingworth, one of racing's old line gentleman managers and the executive vice president at the Oak Tree meeting at Santa Anita Park. He agreed to have the first White Horse Award presentation at the track the day before the start of their 2003 Breeders' Cup, Thoroughbred racing's season-ending championships that do much to determine the year's champions.

In 2006, the White Horse Award takes place when the Breeders' Cup is at Louisville's Churchill Downs. It's now backed by Christian Kenny Trout, the billionaire owner of WinStar Farm and substantial RTCA donor. We bring the five finalists and their significant others and work to treat them as royalty during the week. This is our fourth edition, and at this one we have a white Thoroughbred.

That summer, I'd visited Patchen Wilkes and met owner Warren Rosenthal, a Jewish businessman who founded Long John Silver's. In another oddity, he had fallen in love with white Thoroughbreds and had bred several. During our meeting, he gave me permission to use in our promotional materials a photo of Patchen Beauty with her white foal, The White Fox. The photo, taken by famed horse racing photographer Barbara Livingston, shows the two lying atop thick wheat straw in a stall that had rays of sunbeams flowing through the window. Mr. Rosenthal had asked me why Christians were interested in white horses, and I had politely explained that our Bible says Christ will return to earth riding one.

At the ceremony, the White Horse Award is presented to Clinton Beck, an assistant starter at Pimlico Race Course in Baltimore who pulled two children from the back of a car fully engulfed in flames seconds before it exploded. Mr. Rosenthal brought one of his white Thoroughbreds to

Churchill Downs. I have a saddle towel made that says, "Faithful" on one side and "True" on the other as in the scripture in Revelation. Between races, the colt is walked around the famous track and into the winners circle while the now-deceased track announcer Luke Kruytbosch reads a few paragraphs I've written, explaining to the thousands in attendance what the White Horse means to Christians. I stand beside Mr. Rosenthal in the track's winner's circle. As he listens, a grin spreads across his face.

The unseen network of connections within God's universe is apparent. We just don't always have the tools to comprehend. Humble, small-time breeder Herman Goodpaster, who loved Jesus and white animals, became the caretaker of the first white Thoroughbred to be registered and race. God had given the idea for the White Horse Award to a former jockey whose first Thoroughbred mount was the first white Thoroughbred's mother. And here was a Jewish man who took the time and expense to show the racing world a fourth-generation offspring of that first white Thoroughbred. This, during an event at which the track announcer tells thousands of racing fans that Jesus, a Jew like Mr. Rosenthal, will return to earth aboard a white horse. Only an odds maker with heavenly wings could calculate the odds.

CHEATING; RISKY BUT PROFITABLE

21: Bowie Race Course, Bowie Maryland, March 1963

It's barely 4:00 a.m. and I sit atop Thoroughbred Cover of Stars and watch the horse's trainer, Kenny McLaughlin, slide back the telescope outside rail that opens the entrance to the racetrack. It's two hours before the track officially opens and clockers climb into their heated stand, expensive stopwatches in hand. This is one workout they won't see.

It's early March, bitter cold, and I wear a down vest and beneath my jeans long underwear. But my hands are intentionally bare. I hate racing in gloves. I didn't wear them a month earlier when the McLaughlin-trained Monono charged to the lead in the final eighth mile during a snowstorm at the same track. I "broke my maiden," a once in a lifetime event. Back in the jockeys' room, riders poured ice water over my head, wrestled me to the floor, and in hoots of laugher ripped down my pants and used liquid shoe polish to decorate my privates. So what? I was officially a jockey.

However, darkness is more forbidding than the snowstorm and this day is even colder. I communicate through the reins and covering my hands creates static on the line. In races, I wear gloves to the starting gate and take them off. What I am about to do is even hairier than riding a race during a snowstorm.

The track is as dark as a black hole, and I'm totally dependent on the horse's senses, which I know are far more acute than mine. If a harrow were somehow left on the track or if a deer ran from the surrounding woods across the track, Cover of Stars might not see it in time. I know I won't. I also don't know how Cover of Stars will react to the total darkness, but my boss assures me all will be fine. Of course, he's standing on the ground and I'm on a horse that will be running through the night at some 40 mph. And except for one incident when I helped him bring his clothes into a motel room and tossed his hat on the bed, which resulted in a 10-minute tirade about bad luck, he held my apprentice contract and had allowed me to ride all 15 horses he trained.

Herman Goodpaster had gotten me a job with the racing stable of C.V. Whitney, who at the time owned more stakes race winners than any owner in Thoroughbred racing. After spending over a year exercising some of the best horses in training, including Bug Brush and Silver Spoon, I rode my first horse, Angel Fish, in my first race at Aqueduct in Whitney's famous Eton blue and brown silks on September 4, 1962. However, I started at the top and worked my way down. I was riding infrequently at New York tracks when "Wilkie," a Maryland jockey agent scouting for talent, got in touch with me and started booking mounts for me at far less competitive Maryland tracks. He also arranged for McLaughlin to lease my apprentice contract. I won several races at Bowie Race Track near Washington while competing with the likes of Canadian Ronnie Turcotte, who would later win the Triple Crown on Secretariat and is a friend today.

I'm all of 19, and I don't feel good about working a horse in the dark. It's illegal and obviously dangerous. The few lights on in the grandstand on the other side of the track comfort me and my right hand holds a tiny flashlight, but it's not there to see with. Once on the track, I turn left and we jog clockwise or the opposite of the way horses train and race. Backstretch work starts notoriously early but I see no one along the rail. The ambulance parked just outside another track entrance will not be manned by paramedics until the track opens. It's dark, and I know if I fall no one but my boss will be there to help. He's old and on foot. Cover of Stars, a tall bay with a long head, seems comfortable enough as we jog all the way back to the seven-eighths pole, an eighth mile before the finish line (a furlong is an eighth of a mile). The boss said not to jog all the way back to the partially lit grandstand, fearing a worker would see me. I stop the horse and turn him toward the inside rail, allowing him to "stand out" or simply relax and look at everything around him. Does Cover of Stars think this is as strange as I do?

We jog off going the right way and quickly go into a gallop. A quarter mile away is the five-eighths pole, where we have to be in a full breeze when we pass it. The distance is not sufficient for the horse to properly warm up. This increases the likelihood of him breaking a leg in a race and falling, something even at this early stage in my career I've already experienced.

The numbing wind hits my face, and for a second I feel dishonest. I'm breaking the rules. Yet the trainer has trusted me with his entire stable and encourages other trainers he knows to give me mounts. I had just won my fifth race and my horses still receive a seven-pound weight allowance until I win another 35, when it will go to five pounds until a year anniversary from winning my first race. On the racing program, the weight allowance is denoted by an asterisk, hence the title "bug boy." I make a decision to be loyal to the trainer. Something I stick to until that fateful day in Boston.

Cover of Stars is more eager than I anticipated and tugs at the reins, wanting to break into a dead run. His confidence is comforting. But the small flashlight I carry in my right hand is thicker than a whip handle and it keeps me from gripping the reins as firmly as needed. Suddenly I'm glad the five-furlong pole is close. I rear back, using as much restraint as possible. I allow him to gradually accelerate, feeling the cold wind flash across my face until it aches. My bare hands are getting stiff. I'm supposed to hit a button and flash the light at the exact time I pass the five-furlong pole and again when I pass the finish line. The time between the flashes will be the time of the five-furlong workout. If I drop the light or don't hit the button at the exact instant the whole thing is ruined.

As we near the pole, I tuck into the neat monkey crouch behind the horse's bobbing ears. As we pass the pole I press the flashlight's button, glad to see a flash of light. In those days, trainers knew how to clock a workout as well as a professional clocker. Today, trainers have to report their horses' workout distance to the clockers when the horse enters the track and most trainers don't even own stopwatches.

We race around the turn. I'm still developing that instinctual "clock in my head," something all good jockeys have, but I know we are traveling about 12 seconds per eighth mile, a fast pace. When we straighten into the stretch, I concentrate on switching the flashlight to my left hand so the boss can see it from the backstretch when I can flash it again as we hit the finish line. I am naturally left-handed, meaning I can whip harder with my left hand. I had long mastered the art of switching sticks in the middle of a stretch drive, but a flashlight is far shorter than a whip handle and I can hardly feel my hands. Switching the stick to my left hand means reaching for the stick already cocked upright with the opposite hand and lifting it out of one hand with the other. This happens while the giving hand holds both reins in a full cross.

But the flashlight is short, meaning my left hand has to go deep into my right hand and grasp its barely protruding top before pulling it out. All this while aboard a Thoroughbred running full-tilt-boogie through train-tunnel darkness in subfreezing temperatures.

I take my hand off the left rein and reach for the flashlight top. It takes longer than I expect and when I let go of the left rein that long, the horse starts to drift to the right and the middle of the track. I take the left rein again and straighten him. The wire is coming up. I reach again. This time I grab the light and pull it so hard the right rein starts to slip from my right hand. The horse veers to the left. Something far more dangerous. The inside rail is only a few feet away. Does the horse even know it's there? Hit it and we could go over it or bounce back so hard I could be unseated. Falling to the track at this speed is something I have done once or twice before. It was not pleasant, and while uninjured, I was sore for weeks. I also remember Be Stepping running over my foot and breaking it a few years earlier in Kentucky. Explaining an injury now would be as painful as having one.

But I finally have the flashlight in the grip of my left hand and lift it out of the other hand. I find the button and push as we cross the wire. It flashes.

I fumble and drop it to the track. What will the track maintenance worker who finds it think? It matters little. I know the workout is fast. It will not show up in the *Daily Racing Form*. The bettors will never know. The boss will bet big.

A week later, Cover of Stars goes off at odds of over 70-1. He finishes an honest second with no excuses. McLaughlin buys me an almost new and decidedly sporty Mercury Monterey. It's my first car.

Nine Months Later

"You can't ride today until you see the track doctor," says the clerk of scales at Aqueduct when I come into the jockeys' room carrying my tack bag.

"What's the deal?" I ask. "I got some terminal disease?"

"You'll have to ask," the racing official says and walks off. I make my way through the track's bowels of cement block hallways painted a dull yellow and find the doctor's office. A few weeks earlier when I renewed my New York jockey's license I'd taken a mandatory physical examination and given a blood sample. What on earth had the doctor found?

I'd raced nearly a year, and the one-year apprentice weight allowance that induces trainers to ride the less experienced is about to expire. In the coming months, I'll face off with riders on equal terms. But now I'm living in a high-rise apartment building near downtown Baltimore, driving a new Lincoln Riviera and escorting pretty women all over town. This year I will make more money than my father did in any 10 years he worked as a C&O Railway brakeman/conductor. I'm winning races and have had several write-ups about me in local papers and papers back home in Virginia. Famous racing writer Bill Boniface even allowed me to write a retort in *The Baltimore Sun* to an article he wrote criticizing jockeys for stopping racing on what we felt was a dangerous racing surface. I'm recognized in restaurants and bars and soon discover a lot of people want to hang out with me. They invite me to all the right parties, and I'd been introduced to marijuana, LSD and cocaine.

"Would you please pull down your trousers?" says the older doctor.

I give him a suspicious look, but lower my pants.

"Your underwear, too," he says, pulling on thin rubber gloves.

With little ado, he delicately handles my penis, bending to carefully examine it. I look away, trying to distance myself from the event.

"Your blood test came back positive," he says looking up. "You have syphilis."

My mind flashes to the girls I've been with. Which one is guilty?

"You have no sore or lesion," he said. "Have you had one in the past?"

"Never," I say, telling the truth.

"You'll have to give us the names and addresses of anyone you've had sex with. It's a matter of public health."

"I got names. Don't know the addresses of some." There is only one I am serious about, the daughter of a trainer I've dated for several months. I dread telling her but know I have to.

"The health department in Baltimore will be in touch with you. They'll contact everyone you were with. And I would advise you strongly to abstain until it's cleared up. Without massive doses of penicillin, syphilis can kill you."

"But I never had a sore. And I'd have to have relations with someone to infect them, right? So I can ride here, right?"

"No, you can't. I don't know about other states, but you don't pass the physical here you don't ride here."

I'm afraid to ask if he'll report my condition to the racing authorities in Maryland. New York is the only state I know that requires jockeys to pass a physical to get a license. If Maryland racing officials hear about my contagious disease and bar me, I'd probably be the first rider ever to be ruled off for having syphilis. And in most states, I'm not yet old enough to drink.

(B) BATTLING ATTRACTIONS AND ADDICTIONS

HOOKED

22: Houston Texas, Summer 1994

Crack is crackling in my glass pipe, and down the stretch comes my mind. The white horse is racing into nirvana.

A woman Cindy brought around is on my apartment couch, and Cindy and T.C. are in my bedroom. I share a rock with the woman and after a while Cindy and T.C. return and the four of us sit around my kitchen table smoking, none of us with clothes. T.C. has a wealth of connections for crack and like me is willing to spend a considerable deal of money for it. He even brings a hand-held acetylene torch and passes its flame under the crack pipe because he believes a short blast of intense heat melts the rock faster and increases the high. Tonight he's turning it on and off like a cigarette lighter.

"Cindy, you know those two guys you had call me and then showed up?" I ask her. "I gave them $300, and they give me cornmeal pellets. I called them back after they left and they told me to go to hell."

She says she didn't give them my number and has no idea who they are.

T.C. gets up from twirling around on his head and sits beside her. "You tell me who they are, and I'll break their legs."

T.C. is not large but doesn't have an ounce of fat on his body and clearly is not afraid of much. He goes in and out of crack houses carrying large sums of money to buy crack and has had to fight his way out of a few places. I've seen a pistol in his belt more than once.

"Why you being mean?" she asks. She gets up and goes into a giggling fit, dancing to rock music on the radio. "I want to move in with you and your wife."

"I got my daughter. She's a teen now and sees everything."

She moves to T.C. and shakes her hips. "Send her to grandmas and we'll all party."

I met his wife once, and she seemed normal enough and according to T.C. didn't use drugs. He puts a hand on my shoulder. "What's my buddy here think about that?"

She grins at me. "He doesn't care. He's a faggot."

So fast I hardly see it happen, he throws a right hook into the side of Cindy's smooth jaw. She lands on her back in front of the refrigerator. The other woman jumps up and screams. I go into panic mode. The cops can be here any minute.

He lights the blowtorch and stands over her. She comes to and stares at it. "You ever, ever at any time call my friend a name, and I'll burn the face off you."

Cindy's eyes widen then close as her face contorts. She commonly jumped into cars and got men to take her where she wanted, and pulled her switch-blade any time someone argued with her. But right now she's petrified.

I'm not sure what I should do, if anything, and am much less aware of how I feel about her announcing that she wants to live with him or his standing up for me because she called me a "faggot."

I'm hardly heartbroken over Cindy. She's explosive, given to actual fights with those who oppose her and scary to be with in public. T.C. taking care of her is okay with me. In the end, she'd do what she wants anyway. One of the apartment managers has told me to keep the noise from parties down, and I live in fear of getting busted.

Plus T.C. and I have bonded in an odd sort of way, like gnarled misshapen tree roots that had twisted to intertwine around each other solely because they are so close together they have to share sunlight and darkness. That he would hit our girlfriend because she dissed me feels good.

Yet feeling good about it scares me because I had never had those kinds of feelings about another man. I'm unable to think clearly. Crack has a way of taking over your brain. It physically constricts the blood vessels, the reason over half the emergency room visits related to drugs involve crack. Heart attacks and strokes are common among crack addicts. Crack heads constantly make decisions that will put them in jail, destroy valued relationships and even cause them to die, all for reasons that have nothing to do with logic.

It's all about the crack. My life has become consumed by three things: getting the money to get high, getting the crack to get high and getting high. I don't know who I am. I have become a creature a part of me hates, yet another part relishes.

The rest of the night is a blur. T.C. and Cindy retire to my bedroom. I ask the other girl to leave, and she starts to go ballistic, shouting that she came with Cindy and would leave with her. She wants to stay with the crack. In between hits off the pipe I make out with another stranger I don't know or remotely like.

Sometime near dawn, I wake up in the quiet, lying on the couch, my naked partner draped over a chair and softly snoring. Cindy and T.C. are in the bedroom. I need to get up and do an on-camera interview but can't remember the subject or what time I've promised to be where. The tape that is my memory is again skipping spots. I'm about to enter another dark tunnel, with little light and no end. I remember the short prayer Chaplain Randy Weaver said for me. It doesn't help.

In the midst of all of this chaos, my son, Derek, then 15, comes to visit for a few days. I stay straight, and we drive down to the beach in

Galveston, have dinner and try to talk. I catch him giving me odd looks, and when I look at my stand-ups on my TV show, I see sunken cheeks and a paleness that belongs on a corpse. When I put him on a plane for the trip back to Bossier City, I realize that he is growing up and I'm missing it. Dawn is scheduled to graduate from high school the following spring, and I will likely miss that, too.

But that doesn't stop me from driving to a rundown section of town, going around a particular block until a dealer appears in my headlights. I give him $80, and then drive a half-block to a deserted field where his stash is located. He walks to my rolled-down window and hands me a tiny plastic bag containing several white rocks of crack cocaine. I drive home, the tiny bag open and the contents ready to pour into my mouth if a black-and-white pulls me over. If I get busted, my life as I know it is over. Once parked, I jog to my apartment, find my glass pipe, load it and light it. I watch as a tiny white rock dissolves in the flames. I suck the smoke into my lungs, hold it and exhale to glory in the buzz. Once more, a racehorse of rush races off a cliff.

I ride it to a mind-bending exhilaration that lifts me to the heavens. For a split second, I think I know what it feels like to be God. I drift back to earth and catch the ride again. I smoke the bag in less than an hour.

I feel hollow inside. Any meaning my life contained had been sucked out by chasing a high that can never be enough. I want to feel something but can't. Remorse, self-hate, even the blackness of depression would be better than this. Am I still human?

One morning T.C. and a friend I never met knock on my front door. They're going to cop crack and ask if I want to go along. It's early and I shake my head, trying to clear it. They say they've found a new dealer and are going to try him out. Going on crack runs with T.C. is nothing new. He sits in the back seat, loads the pipe and we take turns. It's risky but fun.

"Let me get on a pair of jeans," I say and walk back to my bedroom. I feel a presence. Despite all I've done in the room, I keep a tiny silver cross and chain pinned to the wall behind my bed. As I turn to look at it, a feeling of dread invades me. How had I gotten to this point? Every ugly

145

thing I'd done in this room had been done beneath a cross. Why have I left it there? Was I feeling some kind of penance for all I had done here because I had defiled it?

I walk to the cross, snatch it off the wall, slide it into my robe pocket and walk back to the living room.

"Don't think I want to go this time," I say. "My crew's coming to shoot an interview at the track this morning. I'd forgotten about it."

T.C. nods, his face sinking with disappointment.

"Be careful," I say.

He gives me a long look and a reply I'll never forget. "It's too late for me to be careful."

They leave. T.C. has lost weight in the past few months. His face has a pale, grayish cast, and I see his usual vigor only when he is high. His top assistant in his courier company has quit in disgust and started a rival company. According to T.C., he's taken his best clients. His daughter and wife have moved out. He's writing bogus checks and ducking creditors. I'm no better.

I drive to the track and go through the motions of producing a TV show a few months earlier had been well received. The track was not producing its own show and hiring me was cheaper than setting up a production studio. The track is ready to sign a long-term contract. But the quality has slipped. Word is out I'm using drugs. The deal disappeared.

When I go home, Cindy is sitting on a curb in the parking lot. I stop, and she leans into the window. "T.C. and his buddy had an accident. His friend ran off the road and hit a bridge abutment. The other guy's injured, but T.C. is in a coma. He's not expected to live."

A rush like a nightmare surges through me. I remember the prayer the chaplain had prayed, the presence in my bedroom that morning and the tiny cross that stood over my bed and is now in my pocket. Despite the accident, we go inside, smoke the crack we have and make out. It's all crazy. Everything is crazy. Nothing makes sense anymore.

T.C.'s family won't allow Cindy to visit in the ICU, but I go. He's unconscious with a breathing machine stuck down his throat. I learn he's

146

bleeding inside and has a brain injury. A half-dozen tubes, some attached to machines, flow from his body. His eyes are shut and he looks peaceful. I can't seem to feel anything. It's like my soul has disappeared. I'm a person I no longer recognize. I've become one corpulent appetite whose sole focus is satisfaction.

Yet realization floods my thoughts, and I sink back from the bed with a cold shiver that shakes my chest. T.C. always rode in the back. Had I gone I would have been in the shotgun seat, the one he sat in when the driver hit the abutment.

I walk out and find myself in a hallway with his wife, daughter and other relatives. "I'm sorry," I tell his wife. "I almost went with him."

She searches my face as if it held some answer as to how her husband could become addicted to crack and as a result become comatose. Her pretty face twists with a pain I remember seeing on my mother before she died. Her mouth opens, and her lips start to form words as tears stream down her milky white face. I stand there, no more words to give, no more tears to share. I want her to feel sorry for me. I want her to realize that I had become entrapped just like her husband.

Her mouth closes. Our intended words a silent echo, louder than anything either of us can say. An older woman engulfs her with loving arms. They lay heads on each other's shoulders and sob. I look around at a roomful of staring eyes. I turn and flee.

A week later, T.C.'s doctors find no brain activity. They disconnect him from the ventilator. He quickly dies. I simply cannot attend the funeral. But alone I visit his fresh grave, a big lump of brown dirt in a level green field of tiny nondescript tombstones. Out there in this lonely place with crowing birds and a cold breeze, it's as if his life had no meaning, had stood for nothing and had been wasted. Fear comes as a chill that makes me cross my arms and shiver. I can die the same way.

I drive home and call Chaplain Randy.

The next morning I walk into his tiny backstretch office. He's sitting behind his desk and before I sit in one the chairs along the wall I announce, "I'm addicted to crack cocaine."

He stands and walks toward me. Compassion I don't expect fills his wiry face. I'd produced and aired on my show several times a six-minute feature on his ministry. He has a copy to show at churches and to other groups interested in helping his ministry. I'd been ashamed of others seeing us when he came to the press box on opening night to pray for me. Now that makes me ashamed.

He locks the door, ushers me to a plastic chair and sits beside me. I lower my head and without looking up tell him the entire story. My descent into homosexuality, debauchery, an addiction to crack and the death of a man whose feelings for I can't define. He listens, giving me space and time to say it all.

"So you want to get set free?"

"Randy, I smoked more marijuana than you can put in this room. I've snorted a couple of pounds of cocaine, and I don't think you could name a drug I haven't tried. I tried to kill myself and been in two psyche wards. I'd been on depression medication for years. But this is the first time I actually got addicted."

"Crack is some evil stuff."

"It takes your soul and rubs it into the ground. Right and wrong turn into the same thing. It puts you so into yourself that the whole world is determined by how everything makes you feel, physically I mean. Getting high is all that matters. I got lost in it. I don't know who I am anymore. I've done some rotten things, but on crack I plowed new ground."

He takes off his white straw cowboy hat and places it in a chair beside him as if he's getting ready to do something that his hat would hamper. "You haven't done anything God can't forgive. And you're still a child of God whether you know it right now or not."

"I feel dirty. My body smells of crack. It comes out of my pores when I sweat. I don't want to think about "detoxing." I'm already crazy. Doing without it will send me over the edge. I want to make it all go away. I want to feel, but I know feelings will be so horrible I'll want to die."

I look into his eyes a few inches from mine and see pain as if my wounds, anger and self-hate are being absorbed by this professional-roper-turned-racetrack-chaplain. For a second, I hate it that I'm hurting him just like I'd hurt Debbie, my children, Debra, her children and a herd of others. He kneels in front of me, puts both hands over my shoulders and prays. He first prays for wisdom for himself in helping me. Then he asks God to touch me and ends by praying that I will make my way back to Christ.

I feel only self-hate. But that's better than nothing. "I'm too far gone. I need to get out of Dodge. There's nothing here for me but death."

I sit in the office as he makes several phone calls and soon other council members file in. Randy tells them only that I need prayer for a serious problem. He anoints my head with oil and the members lay their hands on my shoulders and pray for me.

Within days I quit my job with the *Austin American-Statesman*, turn in the last of my contracted shows to Home Sports Entertainment, load my few belongings into a used Honda and head back to California. I'd called Pam O'Neill, my friend from my days at Laguna Beach, and she'd wired me $200. I also called Jack Van Berg, a Hall of Fame trainer. His charge, Alysheba had run in all three 1986 Triple Crown races, which I had covered for *The Dallas Morning News*. He promised me a job at Hollywood Park grooming horses. I want one exercising horses, but when I explain my situation, he insisted I start as a groom. That he would hire me at all is a kind and generous act.

I'd covered the first Breeders' Cup at Hollywood Park in 1984, mingling at a party attended by Liz Taylor and Frank Sinatra. A few months later and a few miles away in the Century Plaza Hotel, John Forsythe had placed in my waiting hands an Eclipse Award for outstanding newspaper writing. This time if my 10-year-old Honda holds out and I get to Hollywood Park, I'll be a groom living in a cement-walled dorm room on the backside. Worse, I think as I head west on I-10 with my sole belongings piled onto the back seat, my addiction will not disappear in my rearview mirror.

(C) LIFE AS A JOCKEY

GETTING COZY WITH KILLERS

23: Somerville Massachusetts, October 17, 1974

"I still think I should take my pistol," I tell Debbie as we exit our hatchback and walk down a street in Somerville, a decaying burg north of Boston. We walk past mom-and-pop grocery stores, dry-cleaning shops and a shoe repair shop with a picture of a giant shoe stretcher in the front window. Everything looks old, used up and as gray as the slate sky.

Debbie shoots me a frown. "They see a gun, they've got an excuse to shoot us both."

"If you think it's so dangerous, why'd you have to come?"

"I'm Italian, remember. I'll know how to talk to them."

It's 10:30 a.m. and drizzle is wetting my bare head. Debbie, her 95 pounds crammed inside jeans and a pink down jacket, wears a suspicious smirk. We move with deliberate steps to the front door of Danny's Bar and Grill. We stop and peer through its glass door. It looks like an ordinary neighborhood bar and grill. Several men sit at the bar chatting and watching television. Scattered couples sit in the booths eating what looks like breakfast.

I can't suppress a sigh. "I'd rather be in a dentist chair with an abscessed tooth."

She stretches a hand over her forehead to see inside. "Let's get this over with. I'm ready to head south."

We walk in, glancing around, trying to look casual. No one looks up except the jockey who a day earlier had paid me $800 to finish no better than fourth on Society Boy. Less than an hour after the horse won, I met him in the parking lot and returned the wad of $100 bills. That morning he had been waiting in the track's parking lot, and I agreed to meet the men who had put up the money, as long as it's in a public place. He told me about the bar and grill. I wanted to come alone and carry my pistol, but Debbie had talked me into substituting the gun with herself.

A middle-aged man whose shoulders look as wide as the sidewalk outside appears beside the jockey, smiling and looking friendly. The rider glares at Debbie, and it's obvious no one is expecting her. She orders a grapefruit juice and sits on a bar stool. The jockey asks, "How come she came?"

"I'm his agent, remember," she pipes up before I can say anything. "I handle his business. This, I assume, is business."

I stiffen and fake a confident smile. "She's Italian," I say, grinning. "Ever try to tell an Italian what to do?"

The guy who looks like he got kicked off the football team for being too big is not smiling. He doesn't look Italian.

"Around here, we tell Italians what to do," he says. He glances around at everyone in the bar. "Let your wife stay here and we'll go in the back room and talk."

The bar looks public with booths, a mini pool table and a back room with no door to close. A round green velvet card table sits in the middle. The entrance is wide and open and in sight of the bar and restaurant. I give Debbie a reassuring nod, and I follow the jockey and the heavyweight into the room. We sit on folding chairs, and I put my elbows on the table, ready to give my best speech. I look up, and five other men file into the room, two from the back and three from the front.

They look like the front line for the New England Patriots. I stand, thinking we should walk out. The bouncer type I talked to when I came in walks to the room's wide entrance and nods to the folks in the restaurant. Everyone there gets up and files out the front door. One of the five walks over, locks the door and lowers the window shades.

Two men walk to me, and one pushes me to the chair. Two guys sit on either side, one of them fat, weighing at least 300 pounds. The bouncer guy sits in front of me. Flanking him is a man in his forties with sandy hair, clean shaven and wearing slacks and a sports coat. The porkpie hat parked on his wide Irish-looking head makes him look natty and neat. He's smiling, but it's not a gotcha grin. It has professional warmth, like he's about to sell me a used car.

"Look, about yesterday," I start. "I gave the money back. There was nothing I could do. The whole race was jimmied. I was hardly in a gallop. A pony could have run the race faster. We went the mile in a minute forty-five, that's a little better than a two-minute lick, guys."

I look around. They're glancing at Debbie and back and forth at each other. I get the feeling they're adjusting their plan. They turn to glare at me, and I know they're not convinced. All are huge, except for the fairly short man in the porkpie hat who seems to be the boss. Everywhere I look are faces, middle-aged, vibrant and seething. Much of their shtick is scaring people. They do it well. I'm packed in between two guys I realize may have killed before. None remotely looks or sounds Italian. "Look," I continue. "If I jerked the horse back to fourth, it would have been obvious. The stewards would have investigated the race. There would have been major heat on all the riders. Someone might have cracked. I knew you wouldn't want that."

No one seems to be listening. With the exception of the man in the porkpie hat, they all look mad. "Look, I owe you one. I'll make it up. I'll call you the second I got a winner at good odds. I know I can do this, I've …"

152

"We lost $50,000 on the race," says the fat guy to my left. He says it dryly as if they plunk down that kind of cash every day. But I'm amazed. I know that if they put that kind of money through the betting windows at the track, the horse's odds will drop faster than a running horse that breaks a knee. I don't believe him.

"You rode the first part of the race for us, and you rode the last part of the race for the stewards," the fat guy says.

I shake my head, suddenly feeling like the place is overheated and making me sweat. I ache to be outside in the cool drizzle. "The only thing I could do was jump off. If I do something stupid like that I could not only get killed, but the stews would be all over the race. I didn't think you'd want them looking. It'd just bring a lot of heat on you guys. I didn't want to do …"

The back of a hand the size and texture of a cured ham slaps me across the face. My head feels like it exploded. The blow sends me reeling backward. The chair tips for a second. I think it's going to turn over, spilling me out into the floor.

The guy who hit me says nothing. His glare makes me think he's just getting started. Somewhere in the fog inside my head I hear a scream. Debbie races toward me, a metal ashtray in a raised hand. Two men rise to block her entrance. Another leans over, grabs my jacket and nearly pulls me out of my seat. "You know I got a car parked out back. I put you in the trunk. You wouldn't be the first guy I put there."

Another puts his face so close I can smell his aftershave lotion. "You punk. I ought to dump your naked ass in the barn area so the other stealing jockeys will know we don't play."

Racing through my mind come photos and TV news clips I'd seen of bloody bodies squeezed in car trunks or sprawled on city streets. But none was naked. Did he really say naked?

Debbie is fighting to get through the two men at the door, and they finally have to hold her back. "You hit him again," she screams, "and so help me God I'll put you all in jail. I've seen every one of you and I remember good."

153

My mouth drops open, and I struggle for words to get everyone to calm down. Words always worked, and they're all I've got. I don't know if I'm more shocked at gangsters hitting me and threatening to kill me or at Debbie, who may be creating more of a problem. "Please guys, let's be reasonable here. We can work this thing out."

I stand up to get to Debbie and hands push me back to my seat. "Hon, I'm all right. Nobody's hurt me. Calm down before you get us both killed."

I raise open palms, still believing I can find the right words. "Let's talk about this. I told you I'll make it up. I just had a good meet at Rockingham. I can give you some of the money back you lost. And honest, I'll give you a winner."

I look at the man in the porkpie hat who before seemed friendly. I concentrate on him. "You'd better control your wife," he says dryly.

I turn to Debbie. "Look Hon, we're just having a business discussion here. Go back and sit down. They're just working off a little steam here. I'll be all right."

"I got family back in Rochester," she says coolly. "They're connected, and they're going to hear about this."

Every eye is on her. I shake my head, fighting to think. I sit back in my chair, trying my best to look casual. Trying to show I am not rattled. As if I know what I'm doing. Like this is something that happens to me every day. My ears ring. My vision is blurry. A screaming wife is not something they expect, especially one with enough brass to say she has relatives in the mob. I'm thinking they probably don't want to kill us both. But I later learn that one of the men likely in that room had shot to death a young woman who happened to be with a man who was considering testifying against the group, one of the some 20 people he admitted to killing.

But at that moment they know they have a choice: kill us both or let us walk. If they beat me, she'll rat them out. They have to be considering killing us on the spot. I can see the Cadillac dumping my naked body in the Suffolk Downs barn area.

I keep rattling on. "I promise I'll make it up to you. I'll give you a winner. You can get your money back. No heat on anyone. None of this ever happened."

"Shut up," the fat guy beside me says. I do, noting I'm breathing in shallow gasps. All is quiet. No one seems to know what to do. "Eight thousand and a horse we can bet it on. And we don't want a favorite," says the fat guy. "You call us when you got one. The horse loses, we're back to square one, you understand? Anybody hear about this and we're going to be mad on you. You understand what that means?"

The guy that wanted me killed is shaking his head. "No way he should walk out of here. Let me handle this, and everybody will know we don't play. He's making a chump out of us."

The guy in the porkpie hat shoots him a glare. "This is handled." He looks at me. "You need to hang around Suffolk for a while. One of our jockeys might tell you to hold another horse you ride. We're not done with you."

I nod my head, wanting to reach out and shake hands to seal the deal. No one looks like they want to shake on it. "I will. I will. I give you my word. This one was a fluke. It won't happen again. And the horse I'll give you will win. I guarantee it." I keep nodding, forcing a smile and wondering if the side of my stinging head is going to have a visible lump. But I'm glad my teeth are still in my mouth and my legs still work.

We arrange the deal. I'm to give the cash to the jockey who originally bribed me. We work out the time and place. They get up, and I rise with them. Debbie is by my side. They stare at me like a cat staring at a mouse. Debbie glares at them. They look smug as if a business deal went their way. I'd been around long enough to know that anger has little to do with mob hits. My death or even our death would be a thought-out business decision. It would contain no more emotion than a chain store rep ordering dolls from China. Logic would be the deciding factor. If they thought the possible harm we could do them outweighed any good we could do for them, my naked body might indeed be found in the Suffolk Downs barn area. Debbie's body would likely never be discovered.

I keep smiling and nodding like a bobble head doll. The boss in the porkpie hat glares at a spot behind my eyes. I know he isn't jiving. His trunk had actually held bodies. He leans forward. "I own you."

He rises and I get up with him. He nods at me and I take Debbie's arm and turn her toward the door. "It'll work out," I say. "It'll work out fine. I guarantee it."

We scurry out. Debbie has her chin in the air. I inhale the outdoor air like I just came to the surface after being underwater for a week. It's raining hard now. I don't care. My mind is still seeing my body sprawled on the horse path between two barns, backstretch workers looking at it in panic. Death is severe enough but being found dead and naked is even worse. We use long strides to get back to our Subaru hatchback. We glance at each other. "Don't look back and don't run," I say. Yet as I say it I realize that running is a motif we may have to live with.

We pull out of the parking space and drive back to the track.

"God, am I glad that's over," she says. "The guy who threatened to kill you is right. No way we should have walked out of there. They're Irish, you know. The Irish mob. Worse than Italians. They got no honor."

"One thing. You were so high on going together. Well sweetheart, be happy. We're in this until death do us part and that might be sooner than later. I think we both better pray they don't get busted. We saw a half-dozen guys both of us can testify are involved in race fixing. We know enough to put them in jail for years."

Debbie looks out the window, her face pale. "That's another reason we had no business walking out of there. They know that too."

Aided by adrenaline surging through my veins, I win a race on a long shot that afternoon. Debbie stands beside the horse when the track photographer takes the win photo. I remember little about the race or the horse. But the win winds up being a miracle.

156

(D) LIFE TODAY

PREACHING OR HELPING?

24: Venice Beach California, August 2009

I walk to the center of the high stage, remove the mic from its stand and look out at the crowd. Some 1,000 people look at me, nearly all of them homeless. Though the Venice Beach Gospel Rally had gone on for years, I'd won a "Salvation on the Sand" grant from Foursquare Foundation. It helped pay for the 23 buses we rent to bring the homeless to watch gospel bands and choirs, including the famous Mass Choir from the West Angeles Church of God in Christ. That afternoon we'll feed some 1,500 a hot meal and baptize some 100 people in the waves just beyond the grassy rises. Four ministers, including me, will preach.

Venice Foursquare Church, where I am assisting pastor, is a few blocks away, and our church often sets up a sidewalk stand where we play Christian music, hand out tracts and talk and pray with some of the thousands who walk past each weekend day. In between songs, I'd take the mic, recite John 3:16 and tell them Jesus loves them. No hellfire and brimstone. I just want to give them hope. I've talked to tarot card readers, fortune tellers and crystal sellers, and offered the hundreds of homeless

157

youth who come here to party, panhandle and sleep on the beach a chance to reset their lives at Hope for Homeless Youth at the Dream Center.

But today, I'm to speak. I'd given my testimony in churches, halfway houses, homeless shelters and recovery conferences. My story of redemption had been in *Chicken Soup for the Recovering Soul* and *Evangel* magazine. I'd been on several radio shows and been the subject of a video shown to several thousand at our denomination's convention. Pat Robertson's "The 700 Club" had done a feature on me titled "A Jockey's Wild Ride." After it aired, they sent an email saying 287 people called to either accept Christ as Savior or reconfirm their faith. I'm comfortable speaking to crowds, yet I'm not sure this is all God has for me.

I never thought I'd be a famous evangelist. Billy Graham preached a variation of the same sermon for seven decades and I believe his success had to do not as much with oratory skill or passion or content as with the Holy Spirit. Only He can move people to make a decision that will give them life into eternity and radically change their lives.

I'd always thought of myself as stronger on paper than in person. Yet I'd fasted for days, marched with teams to spiritually claim one of the most demonic areas in the world and spent all night locked up in a tiny church in South Central praying for today. I doubt there's anything more valuable than leading someone to Christ. I'm happy to come clean on all the dirt in my life if God can use it to clean one soul.

I speak softly at first, and after 15 minutes my voice raises and my passion shines through. I finish minutes later and ask people to come forward to acknowledge their acceptance of Christ as Savior, renew their faith or pray with our workers for divine healing. As soft music plays behind me, well over 100 make their way to the altar.

The Holy Spirit has used me to bring hundreds if not thousands to Christ. The Apostle Paul said, "I can glory only in the cross," so I cannot do otherwise. I say it now only to confirm the power of God, something Mary Ellen also believed in on that day when I sat on the lawn of my Crystal Beach home overlooking the canal and she said, "Son, God is going to use you in a mighty way one day."

After a day of speaking, talking and praying with scores of mostly homeless persons, Sandi and I go home and she turns on our phone's voice mail. I have a message from Orlando Forbes. In 1992, the Virgin Islands native was a top exercise rider, galloping horses for such famous trainers as New Yorker Lefty Nickerson. On a summer morning at Delaware Park, he started to gallop a feisty two-year-old. The colt bucked, throwing Orlando onto his back. He severed two vertebrae and was made a paraplegic. He used his workers' compensation payoff to buy a home near Savannah, Georgia. But Social Security drastically reduced his payments, leaving him with a $740 house payment and a monthly income of $1,100. He had to declare bankruptcy to keep from losing his home. But the bankruptcy is holding up his efforts to refinance. Fiercely independent and rightfully proud that he only needs a part-time nurse, he is considering giving up the only home he'd owned and moving to an assisted-living facility.

These are the kind of situations track chaplains deal with every working day. I'd helped Orlando write an appeals letter he circulated to hundreds of people in racing. I'd made a score of phone calls on his behalf, written several letters and filled out a myriad of forms for his mortgage company. While only jockeys are eligible for the Permanently Disabled Jockeys Fund, the Jockey Club Foundation agreed to pay him an extra $200 per month, something that had tipped the scales and finally caused the mortgage company to refinance. Still an avid racing fan, I enjoyed talking racing with him, and I prayed for him nearly every time we talked.

Orlando's phone message is as simple as it is profound. "Chaplain Eddie. I just got a letter from the mortgage company. They refinanced, and I only have to pay a little over $300 a month."

My heart swells. Orlando will not lose his house. It's been an incredible day. I don't profess to understand the theology involved, but I feel that what I did for Orlando is at least as valuable as my altar call at "Salvation on the Sand." I often say of my riding career that I'd started at the top and worked my way down. Maybe it's the same with my ministry. Maybe that's good.

As Sandi puts a roast in the oven, I say, "I think God is trying to tell me something here."

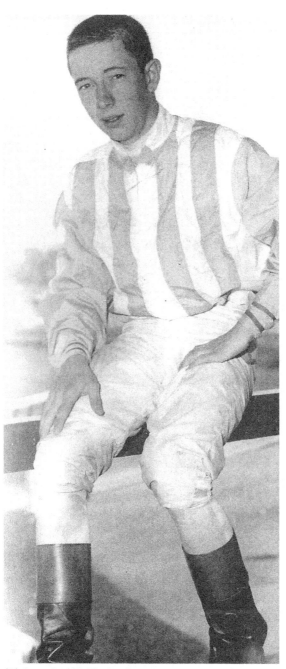

Taken in 1963 during my apprentice year.

Walking onto Aqueduct Racetrack aboard Angel Fish for my first race in C.V. Whitney's famous Eton blue and brown silks on September 4, 1962.

LUCILLE CARROLL's "Prince Jacopo" E.C. DONNALLY up
Florida Downs, Fla. W. COMBEE, trainer
February 1, 1975 Wigg's Superstar-2nd
6 furls. 1:13:3 Licorice King - 3rd

Prince Jacopo, as consistent as construction on the way to work and a favorite horse. Second from left is Debbie, my first wife.

CHURCHILL DOWNS
E. L. Berry & John Fischer, Owners
4 1/2 furlongs-54.1-sloppy

"THINK SWAPS"

Edward Donnally, up
John Fischer, Trainer
May 5, 1978

Winning at Churchill Downs on the day of the Kentucky Oaks, run the day before 1978 Triple Crowns winner Affirmed took the Kentucky Derby.

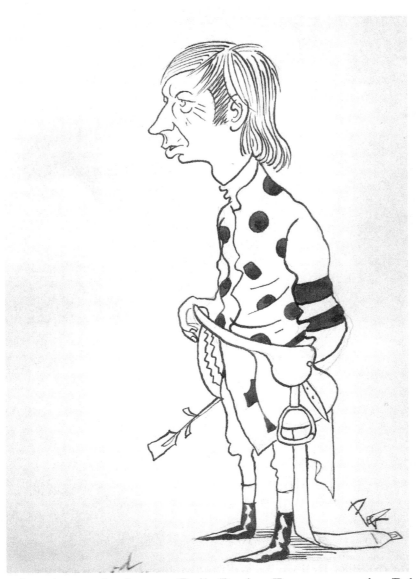

A caricature by famous Daily Racing Form cartoonist, Peb.

Accepting the 1984 Eclipse Award for Outstanding Newspaper
Writing for *The Dallas Morning News*

Hosting one of the 175 editions of his weekly horse racing TV Show, *On the Right Track,* at Criterion Productions in Dallas.

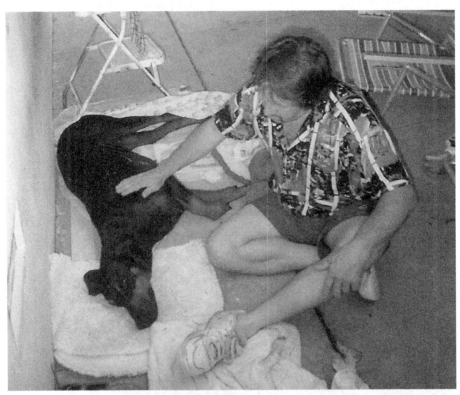

Jack, injured at a vet clinic in 1996, is being nursed back to health.

Praying after taking the final step in Foursquare licensing and being
ordained in 2007.

Four Riders: From Left Pat Day, Eddie Donnally, Laffit Pincay Jr., and Russell Baze. The four have won over 31,000 races. Never mind that I added about 1,200 to that total.

Praying for a man's healing on California's busy Venice Beach Promenade

Preaching during the Venice Beach Gospel Rally in 2009

In November 2012 ministry partner Carol Bluejacket in light blue jacket and I pray with a family in Staten Island, NY who lost their home to Superstorm Sandy.

(A) CHILDHOOD TO ARREST: RACING AND REALITY

EGGS AND TOUTS/TALES OF THE TOUGH

25: Baltimore Maryland, Fall 1969

"Here, I got this for you," says the blue-uniformed police officer as he hands me a bag of marijuana.

I'm 26 and standing at the Pussycat Club bar. I'd come to collect a bag of grass from "Gabby" Hayes, the club's manager who loves to take strippers to nearby Pimlico, have them hang out with jockeys and show them how to bet on winners. Not sure what I should do, I stand there with my mouth open. Hoots go up from behind the bar and Gabby bends over, crippled by his own laughter. Even the cop laughs at me.

At the time, I'm one of the top five riders at Pimlico, live in a high rise overlooking the Baltimore Harbor, have a cadre of girlfriends and spend a lot of nights in the city's nightclubs and the nearby red-light district known as the Baltimore Block. Gabby supplies grass and coke and parties where anything goes in exchange for betting information. In the world of horse racing, he is known as an "egg." I, as one who supplies betting information for gain, could accurately be termed a "tout." The touts and the eggs have a relationship that is truly symbiotic. Tracks are filled with gamblers who're convinced jockeys not only know the name of the unknown soldier, but where he was born. They are willing to provide drugs, women and hard cash in exchange for the name of the next "sure thing." I'm a kid from small-town Covington, Virginia, where the only action is in the pool hall when baseball scores come in over the ticker tape. Here, there's a party every night. Syphilis at 19 and 40 shots of Penicillin hadn't slowed me.

Despite the partying, I'm given to melancholy and often sit alone in my apartment late at night and pen short stories and poems. None are good, but on the written page I meet a part of me I don't allow to exist anywhere else.

Sleepwalker:
Sleepwalker walking in the dead of night
Senseless moving in the artificial light
Looking for peace, finding none
He'll have to wait for the morning sun

In the mind disturbing quiet
Of a damp and dismal dawn
He walks the streets, seeking relief
From the grief that fills his hollow, shallow mind
He's the universal soldier
In the war of success
A champion of status and of quo

He fights the good fight
In the everyday light
But at night
His battle is himself

175

And he'll wander on alone
Tired and weary to the bone
From the guilt upon his back
And the hate within his heart

And somewhere in the beyond
He'll stop and start to weep
And failing, finally fall asleep

My pain and rage are still there, just below the surface. They've turned inside to haunt a hidden place only my unconscious musings can touch. Like a festering wound it's destined to fester and erupt. A part of me knows I'm dangerous.

Realizing there is healing in recording my thoughts, I decide to study journalism, a decision that gives me new life, something I spread around. One evening I walk into an already underway creative writing class at the University of Maryland, jerk a pen from my leather jacket pocket and watch my baggie of marijuana fall to the floor.

If the teacher notices, he doesn't let on. I scoop it up and look around to several knowing smiles. After class, a tall girl I chatted with previously sashays over wearing a sly smile. I learn that her name is Sunday. We date for a time and I discover she's an artist, poet, flower child and like me a Bob Dylan fan. We have several romantic evenings and wind up sharing more than grass. Being a jockey has its benefits. And also drawbacks.

Not long after, I'm on an examining table with an orthopedic specialist poking my exposed knee, something that causes me to jerk and squirm. "You have to stop riding for at least a month and give the knee time to heal," he says.

"Just one more shot of cortisone and I'll stop. I promise."

He shakes his head. "Sorry, but I'm not going to aggravate your injury. You've damaged the cartilage. You keep on riding and you'll need an operation. That would keep you out for months. Ignore it and keep riding and you may wind up crippled."

Bowie Race Course, the now defunct track near Washington, D.C., where I won my first race, had a circular enclosed jogging ring. During inclement weather, riders slow-galloped their horses on a narrow track bordered by cement walls and covered by a roof. It had a single entrance and exit, and when a rider slowed to turn right and leave the ring, he had to shout "leaving" so those behind him wouldn't run up his rear. During a recent winter day, a horse I was on decided to leave prematurely. He propped and wheeled to the right, hurling me into a block wall. My knee took the brunt of the blow.

I'd gone through three doctors who injected cortisone into my knee. Like the last, I'd burned them out. That day I go home determined to find a fourth. I no longer have my first-year apprentice weight allowance that induces trainers to put me on their horses. I owe the IRS several thousand dollars for last year's taxes. The pain in my knee makes fully concentrating during races impossible. I'm in a slump and finding mounts is getting hard. I can't keep from limping as I shuffle through the barn area. If anything scares a trainer more than a sore horse it's a sore jockey. With boxers, the legs go first. With jockeys, it's knees. Both live in a chicken today, feathers tomorrow world of "No ticky, no laundry." No ride, no pay. A month without a paycheck while waiting for my knee to heal would have me bunking on the backstretch.

I hobble into my tiny apartment, these days in a far tamer and blander Laurel, Maryland, site of Laurel Park Racetrack and halfway between Washington and Baltimore. I carry a tub of chicken and a two-liter bottle of Coke. The soda's carbonation makes it easier to regurgitate the chicken. I'd lost my bout with not eating to make weight long ago when I found myself walking up and down the aisles of grocery stores, looking at food I couldn't eat. I took the next most efficient route: bouncing or heaving. I am so conscious of my weight that at any time day or night I know what I weigh within a pound. Cocaine and other forms of speed dim my appetite, but a steady diet of them is worse than heaving. The huge amount of food I put into my stomach and then hurl out of it has enlarged it so much, I'm hungry 30 minutes after I throw up.

I sit in silence gobbling down the chicken and gulping the soda. When I had the money, I'd spend an entire weekend afternoon in some of the area's best seafood restaurants eating $150 worth of hard shell crabs. In a local Howard Johnson's, where an ice cream sundae was $2.50, I spent $35 on ice cream in a single evening. I'd gotten kicked out of several all-you-can-eat, or what I called "pitch till you win," restaurants. I ask my friends, not in complete jest, to invite me over when they defrost their refrigerators.

Filled to bursting, I enjoy the full feeling for only a few minutes. I have to heave. I'm so dried out that food quickly absorbs, and tomorrow instead of losing my usual three pounds in the hot box I will have to lose four, something that takes over an hour of sweating. Being overweight will damage my already limping career.

I get up and hobble to the commode. I'm so experienced no nausea is involved. I don't need to stick my fingers down my throat to get started. I can stand in a restaurant stall and throw up while carrying on a conversation with an unsuspecting person a few feet away.

I bend over to upchuck the chicken. Up it comes, a feeling I've grown to like. My knee buckles. It gives way. I collapse to the bathroom floor. Pain shrieks through my senses. I think for a second I've broken it. I bend over to rub it. The gag reflex hits again. I throw up pieces of chicken over both thighs.

I sit there in gobs of Coke soaked chicken and try to remember where I'd put my phone book. I need to look up another bone doctor.

(B) BATTLING ATTRACTIONS AND ADDICTIONS

ONE DAWN IN MY DARK NIGHT OF THE SOUL

26: Inglewood California, November 1994

My well-used hatchback is filled with my clothes and belongings when I check into a tiny motel across the street from Hollywood Park, a few miles south of downtown Los Angeles. I'd driven straight through from Houston, stopping only for water and naps in rest areas. My stomach is in no mood to be bothered. Time and distance from my addiction to crack cocaine have come slower than the miles across West Texas.

It'd been three days since I left the chaplain's office at Sam Houston Race Park and headed back to California. I can feel the drug oozing from my pores. I smell like Coca-Cola souring on a sunny sidewalk. As a person who's earned my living for several decades with my body, I know mine is weak and getting weaker. I walk into the dingy motel room and sit on a creaking bed. I hold my hands out and look at them. They quiver like a leaf in a stiff wind. I feel like I want to throw up but know if I do, it'd only be bile. I'm restless, can't sit still and feel like taking a walk, though I know the area is one of the worst in the city. I get up and walk to a phone booth next door. Hollywood Park's parking lot is across Prairie Avenue and beyond it looms the massive grandstand.

In its prime, it was one of racing's crown jewels. I'd spent time in its Turf Club, chatting with Mickey Rooney and Merv Griffin, a pair who'd bet on more races than most jockeys will ride. In 1984, *The Dallas Morning News* sent me here to cover the first Breeders' Cup, and I'd stayed in the Marriott. These days I'm a mile down the street in a motel whose name is mounted on an iron pole.

I call Jack Van Berg. He seems happy I'm in town and asks me to meet him at the stable gate at 4:30 a.m. We hang up, and I swallow the nasty taste in my throat. I was hoping to start as an exercise rider, but Jack said groom. Hard to argue. I weigh 150 pounds and haven't ridden a racehorse in years. It's after Christmas, and I'll be rubbing babies who'll officially turn two in a few days. They had first been ridden and groomed a few months earlier and are still largely wild. It's like I was still at Patchen Wilkes Farm and starting all over, this time not even as a rider.

It's dark now, and as I walk back to my room I spy two young men standing outside their rooms as if waiting for someone. I know they are dealers. I try not to stare, but I'm stunned. They have rock. I can get enough to stop hurting and settle my stomach. That way I'll be able to work tomorrow. I walk up to one. "You holding?"

The young African-American looks me up and down. "Look," I say. "I'm way too short to be a cop and that car over there is mine. It's got Texas plates. "

He looks at the car, seeming satisfied. "What you want?"

"Rock and a pipe."

"You got cash?"

I look over my shoulder at the car. I have less than $50 to my name. "I got a Sony stereo, cost $300 new."

"I'll take a look."

"I'll be back."

I hurry back inside my room and realize my whole body is shaking. It's the first time I've seen my knees shake. The dealer is there. I can trade for some rock and a pipe. I can get high right here, right now. Nothing, absolutely nothing is standing in my way.

"Oh God, I don't want to do this."

I listen to my words as if they come from something outside me. My life as bad as it is, is about to get worse. One toke and I'll never stop. I'll die in the streets. I see T.C., tubes connected to his near-dead body, me at his grave lamenting a wasted life. Randy's prayer for me rings in my head. Pain like an arm being twisted sears through my brain. My mind is bent. It hurts. I don't want this. I don't want to die.

Breathing in short huffs, I rip off my dirty T-shirt and sink to the linoleum floor. The chill cools my heated body. Drops of sweat peel off my face and fall a few inches to the floor, forming tiny puddles. The high races across my mind like a runaway racehorse. My mind mounts up and charges. Off to the races. Acceleration. Acceleration. Like breaking from the starting gate and going from zero to 40 in two strides. The white horse of cocaine high I had ridden for months rears up and races in an explosion of joy. It ends. Fear smacks me. The dealer could leave. I'd be left to hurt.

I struggle to my feet, stagger to the door and lean against it. I refuse to look at the dealers and make my way to my car. I rummage through the clothes piled in a lump on my back seat. There it is; my old brown Ryrie Bible.

I make it back to my room, sink to the cold floor and lie on my stomach. I'm still breathing in short gasps. The Bible is before me. "You got to give me a verse, God," I call out. "You got to say something to me, or I'm going to die."

The Bible falls open to the 43rd chapter of Isaiah. I search up and down, and my eyes fall on verse 19: "Behold, I will do a new thing. Now, it shall spring forth: Shall you not know it? I will even make you a road in the wilderness and rivers in the desert."

I didn't know it at the time, but the great prophet was prophesying the return of the Israelites from captivity in Babylon 200 years into his future. I realize now that he was also prophesying about my return from Babylon some 6,200 years into his future.

A calmness falls over me like a heated blanket inside an igloo. I'm breathing slower. A fatigue, as great as any I've experienced seems to descend from the ceiling and engulf me. I grab a pillow off the bed, place it beneath my head and am still.

I hear a persistent knocking. My watch says 4:00 a.m. I struggle to my feet, thinking one of the dealers is looking for me. Instead, I hear a feminine voice. I open the door. A woman, tall and slim, cocks an elbow against the door frame and cups her chin in a hand. She grins at me. "Hi, Honey. How about a little company up in here?"

"No, thanks," I manage. "I got to go to work."

(C) LIFE AS A JOCKEY

MAKING NICE WITH THE MOB

27: Churchill Downs, Louisville Kentucky, Spring 1975

I stand in a phone booth on Third Street near the track and with sweating hands make a call that can send Debbie and I into hiding and possibly get us killed. The same Boston jockey that paid me a bribe to lose the race I'd won quickly answers.

"Tell your friends to get down on this one," I say, naming the horse and race.

"You sure about this?" he asks. "You wrong, some of the boys going to come down and pay their respects."

The words "pay their respects" stuns me. That's what you do to dead people. The threat to leave my naked body on the Suffolk Downs backstretch as a warning to other jockeys gallops across my mind. Worse, there is no such thing as a "sure thing." Horses can get sick minutes before a race. Another horse can slam you leaving the gate, or a rival jockey can run you into a "blind switch" and trap you behind other horses. The best horse doesn't always win. I clear my throat and try to sound confident. "This is as good as it gets."

That afternoon I ride only a few horses and the horse I told the Winter Hill Gang leader to bet on is in a late race. A jockey friend sees me pacing in front of my locker and asks if something is wrong at home.

"Not at all," I say, realizing that he, too, rode at Rockingham Park. I sit on the bench beside him, lean close and quietly ask, "You ever heard of the Winter Hill Gang in Boston?"

"I used to think Raymond Patriarca ran New England. Now I hear the Irish are going all over, giving out money and a ton of coke to fix races."

Though not surprising, this was something I hadn't expected. "You heard that, huh?"

"Somebody said they're doing races at places like Aqueduct and Saratoga, passing out big money along with blow." He gives me a questioning look. "You did business with them?"

"Nothing major," I say, thinking now they might have been too busy to call and ask when I was going to tout them on a winner. I get up and start polishing a set of goggles. "Not enough to talk about, anyway."

It's a brisk spring day in Louisville, but I'm sweating as we approach the starting gate. I know the horse well and have been thinking of him as the horse to get me even with the Winter Hill Gang for a week. He had a particularly rough trip in his last race and should have finished much closer. I also know he tired in that race and came back to give a solid workout in which he could have gone faster. He looks good physically, and I have taken the time to personally exercise him every morning for two weeks. I know he is a happy, sharp horse, full of himself and ready for a top effort. I also looked hard at the *Daily Racing Form's* past performances for the race. My horse is dropping in class and seems to have hit an easy field. I have even gone by the barn, looked at the horse and talked to his groom. The horse had eaten well the night before and has no leg problems.

The groom knows more about the horse than the jockey, trainer, vet, and blacksmith combined. In halting English he tells me the horse could not have been doing any better. I told him I was placing a $50 win bet for him. Knowing all this is only slightly reassuring. A hidden virus can hit a horse at the last minute. He can kick the stall wall in exuberance and injure a back ankle or hock, something that would only show up under the tremendous pressure of racing. How could the race set up? The horse has enough natural speed to get a good position early, but what if his back legs slipped or his front ones stumbled when he broke from the starting gate? What if he got an even rougher trip in this race?

I once had an apprentice rider veer into me so sharply during a race at Philadelphia Park that my filly went over the inside rail. I broke my hand in several places. Oddly, I had met the same young man standing outside the stable gate at Florida Downs a few years earlier, signed him into the track and helped him get his first job exercising horses. No good deed goes unpunished.

It might seem otherwise, but I'd bet less often than many other jockeys. I went home a lot of nights after winning a race at good odds, knowing the horse had been an overlay or had a better chance than the odds indicated. When I later picked 10 winners on an 11-race Louisiana Downs card while handicapping for *The Dallas Morning News*, I'd bet on none. As a jockey, and perhaps as a professional handicapper, I was one of the few who should have bet more often than I did.

I understood first-hand the vagaries inherent in any horse race. And on this day I am considering each and every one. I'm not into religion, yet I often say the Lord's Prayer during the post parade. But I did it as a ritual to ward off the lingering fear I kept neatly tucked in the back of my mind. This day it seems to have new meaning. I want—as much as anything in my life—for this to be over. I've learned my lesson. Despite being offered bribes since, I never even came close to pocketing the money.

The horse breaks well from his outside post and is in the middle of the pack down the backstretch of the six-furlong race. Several horses are stacked up on my inside and in one of those vagaries of a horse race, my horse starts to lug in toward the inside rail. Horses don't always run straight but often resemble autos with a variety of problems that cause them to lug left or right. I'm left-handed, making it possible to whip stronger with that hand. My specialty is heavy-headed horses that need a jockey to help hold up their heads while running, and those that lug in. Still, I'm taken by surprise.

I'm fourth straightening for the stretch, about three lengths off the lead. But the horse is lugging in toward the rail so badly I'd have to fight him to keep him outside and take the safer overland route. I'm also not sure the horse is good enough to lose the ground and still win. And muscling or fighting a horse in a race depletes the animal's strength. I can't go outside and win.

But the three horses in front of me are packed as tight as fat men riding the same motorcycle. Seconds pass. There's an eighth mile left and I'm still fourth. A small space begins to open. But not enough.

The horse is aching to run but has no place to go. My nightmare is coming true. What will I do? Leave the track and go on the run? Rat myself out to racing authorities? I'd decided to face the Winter Hill Gang in Danny's Bar because I didn't want to spend my life running. Now I will have to. Debbie and I expect the birth of our first child in a few months.

I'm going through the hole, large enough or not. Yet even if I bully my way through, I could bump my rival and risk a disqualification. But that is better than finishing fourth with my hands in my pockets. One thing about holes on the rail: if the horse is willing and can get his head in, the body will follow. But if my rival on the right veers even slightly toward the inside, I'm going to mow the infield grass with my face.

My fear of falling is not close to my fear of failing. I give him slack, chirp in his ear, and he starts for the space. Halfway in, he stalls. He's still lugging in and inches from the rail. Bouncing off it and back into my rivals would mean losing or being disqualified. I raise my whip in my left hand, and hit this animal as hard as I have ever hit a horse. Like Stepin Fetchit when he sees a ghost, my mind is saying, "Feet, don't fail me now."

And they do not. I'm gaining ground. Yet I'm running out of track. The wire is just ahead. I stop whipping, lift the horse's gradually lowering head and pump.

We cross the wire. I look to my right. By the length of my mount's head, we win.

While the name of this Thoroughbred that might have saved my life has been erased in the span of over 37 years, I look at the tote board and see a $16.40 win payoff. The boys in Boston will be happy. I'm off the hook. Or so I think.

Saratoga Springs, New York, August 1975

"They offered me $10,000, but I turned it down," jockey Mike Hole tells me over dinner at a plush Saratoga Springs steak house. "You think they'll come after me?"

That summer I'd ridden at New Hampshire's Rockingham Park but had driven a few hundred miles to ride a horse at the famous upstate New York track, only to learn when I arrived that my mount had been scratched. But I'd gone to dinner with my old friend and told him about my encounter with the Winter Hill Gang, which I know is still in the race-fixing business.

"I don't know," I say. "I didn't think they'd come down on me in the first place because I kept believing they wouldn't want the heat. Found out I was wrong."

I tell Mike what had happened to me and the stories I'd heard of riders and trainers being badly beaten. "It's nothing personal, just a business decision for these guys. If it helps business to kill you, you're dead. Simple as that."

I'd met Mike several years earlier at Long Island's Belmont Park shortly after he'd stepped off a plane from England filled with racehorses. He arrived with $90 in his pocket and a dream burning in his bosom. We'd ridden at the same Maryland tracks, and a few summers earlier Mike, Maryland trainer Billy Christmas, his wife, Mary, and I had rented a spacious house on one of the lakes near Rockingham Park. Besides racing together, Mike and I water-skied over a jump and skydived in nearby Orange, Massachusetts. That summer, I'd met a leggy English girl, Yvonne, whose family ran a small motel across from the track's entrance, and we had dated casually. I introduced her to Mike and sparks flew. I graciously

187

bowed out, and Mike soon escorted her to the wedding chapel. Now he is one of the leading jockeys in New York, one the toughest circuits in the world. But 10 grand is still a lot of money. Mike looks up from the steak he's eating and gives me a dead-cold glare. "I'm going to turn them in."

I stop eating and glare back. "Mike, you thinking straight? That would give them a real reason to kill you. They think you're going to put them in jail, and I don't care if you're Eddie Arcaro reincarnated, you're dead meat."

"I hate people who think they can buy anything. This world's not just about money."

"You're right, Mike. And you and Yvonne just had your first baby. You want to see him grow up, right?

"This is an ugly world. Sometimes I'm not sure what I want."

Mike, like me, had grown up in an ugly world. He'd talked of his father drinking and beating his mother and him. Like me, he left home early to become a jockey.

"Mike, you got more self-discipline in one finger than I got in my entire body. Just look at you. You never smoked, never did drugs, and when we lived together in that big house on the lake, you used to limit yourself to one candy bar a week. Not many folks that strong. I know you're able to get over all that stuff in the past."

He lifts his drink, the third of the evening. "It's not that easy."

"Mike, you got a family, a farm in Maryland, houses in New York and Miami, and you got to drink to get you through the day. Sorry, Mike. You used to get on me if I smoked a joint. Now you're going to let booze do you in."

I put my linen napkin beside my plate and try to remember if I saw the men's room on the way in. I can't keep the steak I just inhaled inside me for long. "Mike, you're riding some of the best horses in the world. And now you're going to let alcohol get to you and you're ready to go rat out a bunch of killers. You ever try a shrink?"

His look is sullen and dark. I go to the bathroom.

Keeneland Race Course, Lexington, KY, April 1976

"You hear about Mike Hole?" a fellow jockey asks me in Keeneland's Jockeys' Room in Lexington, Kentucky the following April. "They found him dead on Jones Beach. They think gangsters killed him."

I'm standing in front of my box (locker) cleaning my goggles with Windex when he walks up and makes the announcement. I'm fighting the urge to throw down the goggles, race from the track and call Debbie. These are the days before phones are allowed in tracks much less yet-to-be-invented cell phones.

"When'd it happen?" I manage.

"Just yesterday. It's all over the papers. I heard some say they stuffed paper in his tailpipe and ran a hose through his floorboard. The fumes killed him. But the papers are all talking about how he didn't take a $10,000 bribe and ratted out some of the New York riders. Those guys from New England are smart. They know how to kill you and make it look like suicide."

That evening when I get back to Louisville and the motor home we're living in, Debbie takes our one year old daughter, Dawn by the hand and we walk around the corner to a phone booth to call Yvonne, Mike's widow.

She's distraught but tells me Mike had been seeing a shrink, was depressed and they had talked about divorce. "He left two short notes, but they were mainly just apologizing."

We're both too stunned to talk about other details. I put Debbie on the phone, and she mostly listens. Whatever the reason, injury and death are never far from the thoughts of jockeys' wives. The phone booth is outside a bar, and the street is brightly lit. Yet I can't help but look around. My heart feels like it's slipped down to my kneecaps. I figured it was over for me with the Winter Hill Gang. But a few weeks earlier, I heard about jockey Pete Fantini at Atlantic City Race Course. He'd taken a bribe from Anthony "Fat Tony" Ciulla to hold a horse, and it looked so obvious track

189

stewards called him in. He had caved like a thrift store suitcase, telling them about Ciulla. Word had it that Fantani had worn an FBI wire the next time he met the fat man at his motel a few days later. Fat Tony, who was in that Somerville bar with me, had been busted.

Debbie gives me the phone, and I tell Yvonne how sorry I am. I get up the guts and ask if she thought Mike had been killed. "I don't think so, but I'm honestly not sure. I'm not sure of much of anything right now." We soon hang up.

Walking back to our place, I have a revelation. Mike and I were alike in many ways, but in the end decidedly different. We'd both had ugly childhoods and were victims of abuse. Our wounds had been scarred over in the intensity of race riding, but never healed. Mike's pain had surfaced in depression and alcohol abuse. Mine is still buried. Debbie and I are getting along. I drink a beer or two each day and smoke grass regularly. But unlike Mike, I haven't turned to a psychiatrist. And in the end, Mike had turned down a whopping bribe, disclosed a famous jockey who had offered it and is now dead. I had taken the money, cost the Winter Hill Gang a monster bet and seen their faces up close. Yet, unlike Mike, I'm still alive. Something seems odd about that picture.

(D) LIFE TODAY

OH BOY, I'M A REAL CHAPLAIN NOW

28: Humboldt County Fair, Ferndale California, August 2006

They're in the track's parking lot just like the jockeys told us. A girl no more than 18 slouches in the cramped back seat of a rusted-out Pontiac Firebird. In her arms, a baby is curled up in a pink blanket, sleeping soundly. Piled in every vacant space are clothes, blankets and tools. It's cold and early morning, and the girl looks up and flashes an embarrassed grin. I glance over at my wife, Sandi, and put on a warm smile. Not far behind us in the barn area is the baby's teenage father. I'm thinking I should have brought him.

After working as the Race Track Chaplaincy of America's Director of Development and Communications for five years, I get a two-week vacation. When a track chaplain friend calls and says the usual chaplain for the tiny track in far Northern California can't make it this year, Sandi and I decide to be real track chaplains. We've driven 600 miles from Los Angeles to the county noted for giant Redwoods and pot grower. We walked into

191

the backstretch that morning for the first time, quickly meeting an older jockey and two others who told us about a young couple, who were broke and living in their car with a young baby. The riders want my help in taking up a collection to get them a place to stay.

The girl cranks down a back window and Sandi leans in, smiling broadly. "Sorry to surprise you. We just wanted to come see how you and the baby are doing."

"We're okay, except it's kinda cold."

I bend closer. "How about we go someplace warm and have breakfast?"

Soon, we're in a nearby diner booth where she's shoving down bacon and eggs with one hand and holding the baby in the other. She tells us her name is Lisa, and she met her "fiancé," Ralph, when he came from Idaho to ride here last year. She became pregnant and had her baby, Sarah, while living with her mother who won't allow Ralph in her house. When he returned this year, she hopped in his old car with their baby, not yet a year old, and came to the track.

"She's real healthy and eating baby food fine," Lisa says. "It's just that Ralph blew the transmission in his car on the way here. We don't have much money, but he's named on two horses tomorrow, so we have money coming."

The irony hits me. I too had once showed up to ride at Rockingham Park, busted and with a five-day-old baby, depending on coming paychecks to keep us going.

"Some of the jockeys are taking up a collection to get you a place to stay," I say. The baby is awake now and looking around. Sandi starts making faces and tickling the baby's stomach. Sarah starts laughing.

Well, I'm telling myself, I wanted to be a track chaplain. This is exactly what they do. The work is rarely neat, usually filled with dangling ends, and how to help is not always clearly defined. It's far colder than Sandi and I expected, and we're staying in a donated garage-top apartment no bigger than a motel room, so staying with us is out.

"It's in the 40s this morning," I say. "It's dangerous for your baby, and if someone notices and calls social services, they might take little Sarah."

"I'm not going home. I love Ralph, and we're going to get married one day."

I want to tell her she's being shortsighted and selfish, but I'm not into sermons. "Great. But we need to get you and Sarah a place to stay."

We stop at a grocery store, and I pay for diapers and baby food. When we take her back to the auto, she starts the engine for heat, but explains she can't leave it running long or it will overheat.

It's the first day of racing, and at the outside rail we watch horses train and introduce ourselves to trainers, jockeys, grooms and owners. It's like they're all kids and it's the day before Christmas. Many of the trainers and riders work at other racing jobs as exercise riders and shed row foremen but leave during the summer to race the California fair circuit. It starts in early June with the Alameda County Fair in Pleasanton, moves to the California State Fair in Sacramento and the Sonoma County Fair in Santa Rosa and ends in August at the Humboldt Country Fair. Like the rest, this one has livestock shows and contests, flower and craft competitions, and a midway with rides, sideshows and rows of win-a-stuffed-bear vendors. Racing is for Thoroughbreds, Quarter Horses and mules.

Unlike typical racing, there is room for non-rich owners. Successful owners of small businesses and companies buy a half-dozen or so horses in the spring, take a hiatus, gas up their motor homes and for a few months enjoy live horse racing. They help at the barn, park beside each other in the track's RV lots and maintain a friendly but competitive camaraderie. After the races, they gather on lawn chairs under their portable overhangs, barbecue, have a few beers and rehash that day's victories, defeats and the enthralling peculiarities of racing. Humboldt is the last in the circuit and some say the best, kind of a Saratoga for poor folks.

Sandi and I find Ralph outside one of the ramshackle barns and wait until he ends his conversation with a trainer. We introduce ourselves and tell him we just had breakfast with Lisa and little Sarah. We learn he's a part-time cowboy who each summer reduces and rides the fair circuit. But this year there were problems and he'd just arrived. He's at least 5'7", and while lanky, I wonder how he makes weight, though the weights seem higher than at the larger tracks. I explain about the riders planning to take up a collection to get the baby a safe place to stay. He seems accepting and explains he'll have a paycheck in a week.

"We're in love, you know. We do plan to get married."

"You met her last year?" Sandi asks.

"I left before I knew she was pregnant. I wanted to take her with me, but she wasn't 18 yet and her mother hates me. Now she's of age, and we can get married without her mom's permission."

"That's one sweet baby," Sandi says.

"Yeah, she's something else."

"You need other accommodations," I say.

"This is the season here, and motel rooms are high," he says. "Some of the jocks are so broke they have to sleep in the jockeys' room. Don't know how much they can help."

"We'll figure out something," I say, having no idea what it might be.

*****

The racing secretary's office and adjoining jockeys' room look like a tool shed built in the 1930s. Their decaying wooden slats painted a fading red tilt slightly and have places where the boards don't meet. It's nearly noon when I walk into the jockeys' room. Filled with at least 25 jockeys, no valets are in sight. It has three rooms lined with dark boards that show daylight. Its wooden benches sag and the walls are lined with cupboards the size of microwave ovens for the jockeys' gear. No showers or reducing facilities are in sight. On the floor of an adjacent room, I see several rolled up sleeping bags.

Yet, conversation and laughter flow. As in all jockeys' rooms, there is a sense of fellowship, community, and we're-all-in-this-war-together attitude. I chat with a couple of the riders proposing the collection and with the clerk of scales' permission, ask loudly if any would like to gather for a pre-race prayer. Every person in the place stops and comes forward.

I've said pre-race prayers in several jockeys' rooms. Usually, a handful or a dozen show up. Never have all wanted prayer. I later learn why. I recite the 23rd Psalm and say a prayer for everyone's safe return at the end of the day and close with a petition for Ralph, Lisa and little Sarah. I announce the collection and riders step forward, a few with $20 and some with change. I count it in front of them: $127.43. I add another $20, possibly enough for two nights in a motel.

Ralph clears his throat. "I'd rather use it to pay for part of a new transmission. We're okay for now in the car."

I stiffen, but hold my tongue.

Ray, the older rider who wanted the collection, takes a step forward and faces Ralph. "Kid, you're not thinking clearly. That baby needs to get out of your broke-down car. Like today."

Ralph's face reddens. He takes a deep breath, and I use the pause to jump in. "Is it all right if I ask some of the owners? They understand things like this. They'll help."

"Do what you want," Ralph says and walks off.

On my resume is a history in raising funds for the national RTCA office and a Certificate in Fundraising from UCLA. Asking people for money is what I do. I go into the saddling paddock with the riders and trainers who saddle their own horses, identify the owners, and after the horses are saddled, I introduce myself. I tell the story, trying not to be maudlin. Some donate on the spot, others promise to later. An older man there with his wife seems genuinely shocked. They talk privately for a second.

"Look, we got a 42-footer with an extra bedroom in the back," he says. "She and the baby can stay there as long as they like. Just tell her to stop by after the races."

I learn he's a retired RV dealer who fell in love with racing decades earlier. I thank him, go back and give Ralph the money I collected. He seems pleased. He's not only got his wife and baby a place to stay, but over

$200 toward getting his transmission fixed. That evening I take Sandi out to dinner to celebrate.

In the next two weeks, I organize and make the chili for two backstretch cookouts that feature hymns played on a guitar, singing, and a short message. I remind all that Jesus loved having dinner with those not loved by society and is always ready to have a deeper fellowship with anyone. Later, several ask me to pray for specific needs. That week, a woman who runs the midway asks Sandi and me to hold a Sunday morning service for the carnival workers beneath a giant Ferris wheel.

I learn why the riders love prayer: mule racing. The mule Black Ruby won fame when she won 57 races, earned $175,000 and even raced at classy Del Mar. This meeting's richest race is a $5,000 winner-take-all match race between mules Smokin Joe and Sarah Nelson. In it, Sarah smokes Joe. A hybrid cross between a female horse and a male donkey, a mule is not easy to train. While intelligence is a trait attributed to mules, it is not evident here. In their defense, some at Humboldt do not seem to be trained to race. Many refuse to load in the starting gate, rear in the air once inside and in the first turn bolt to the outside. Several run through or jump over the outside rail. Worse is the immediate stop. After the race ends and riders rise in the stirrups, many mules dig in their front feet and in one stride prop to a stop. Rider after rider is propelled into the air like circus acrobats. Mule riders are falling like soldiers at Gettysburg. A few are hospitalized, treated and released. I don't know that I ever prayed harder for safety.

But it is a spider that kept Sandi and me busy at the local hospital. A few nights into the short season, Ray is sleeping in the jockeys' room when he's bitten by what a doctor says is likely a Brown Recluse. In about half the cases, the bite is not serious. Not so with Ray. He is so sick on our way to the ER that we have to stop several times to allow him to throw up. I watch as a doctor lances and medicates the ugly red wound on his lower leg. The painful wound grows and does not respond to antibiotics.

We visit daily and help him contact long-lost relatives and collect information needed to become a Medicaid patient, something that seems necessary if he is to remain hospitalized. A cowboy and former bull rider, he has a face of shriveled rawhide. He tells us of herding cattle in a blizzard and outrunning a Montana Grizzly on horseback. He's ridden the summer fair circuit for decades and lists his broken bones like combat metals.

Each afternoon at the track, a fog bank rolls in from the nearby Pacific Ocean like an arctic dust storm. The temperature falls as fast as the mule jockeys. Sandi and I go to a thrift store and buy coats. One morning we're late getting to the track because a fence has come down and the road is clogged with Guernsey cows. I tell Sandi, "We're in the big time now."

On the final day, we throw a farewell chili dinner. The poor folks' Saratoga is over. None of the riders have been injured. I think the prayers helped. Ray is still in the hospital, but I've found an owner willing to file a worker's compensation claim on his behalf, one that allows him to get paid while he recuperates. Ray is talking regularly with the formerly estranged daughter I'd called for him. I think she even listens to his tall tales. Ralph won a few races, making and collecting enough money for a new transmission.

Outside one of the barns, the long August day lingers. The group, which includes the horse owners who housed Sarah and Lisa, use plastic spoons to dip into Styrofoam cups and put away the chili Sandi and I made. Most of the riders and trainers will go back to their more mundane jobs. I'll go back to my RTCA office in the bowels of Hollywood Park. Sandi will resume a job for an inner-city charity. Like the owners who will drive home in their RVs to jobs in ordinary businesses, we leave to face a life not nearly as enthralling as the Humboldt County Fair.

But for a few more hours, fair racing is our universe's center. Earl Baze, an Outrider and member of the same family that includes famous riders Russell and Tyler Baze plays his guitar with a new gusto. We sing songs into the night. Ralph, with Lisa beside him carrying Sarah, amble up to Sandi and me.

"We're going to get married up in Idaho," Ralph tells us again.

"In a real church," says Lisa.

197

"Congratulations," I say, thinking I should suggest pre-marital counseling but don't.

Lisa puts an arm on Sandi's shoulder. "Would you two pray for us?"

We do and at the end share hugs. Sandi holds Sarah to her shoulder, rocking her from side to side. Ralph looks at me head on. "Thanks chaplain."

I savor the word "chaplain." I was officially endorsed as a chaplain by my denomination the previous year, and many people call me chaplain. Tonight it has new meaning.

Behind us, the music starts anew. The smell from the big pot of simmering chili wafts into the cool air. With it comes the heady aroma of celebration. I remember diving joyously onto a muddy track following the last race at a Florida Downs meeting. It's a celebration I understand.

Hollywood Park, Inglewood California
One Year Later

I'm in my little office at Race Track Chaplaincy of America when the phone rings and a female voice asks if I'm Eddie Donnally.

"Did you go to the University of Maryland in 1969?" she continues.

"I did. But what, that was almost 40 years ago. Why?"

"Did you once walk into a creative writing class and a bag of grass fell out of your pocket?"

My jaw goes slack. I had all but forgotten. "Who are you?"

"I'm your daughter."

My first instinct is to tell her she's wrong. A picture of my grown daughter, Dawn, pops into my mind. I realize this is something I hope I never have to tell her. But these days I'm an ordained minister and chaplain. I strive to live a transparent life. My past is past, and I've talked about it all in a variety of ways and at a wide assortment of places.

"Who is your mother?" I ask.

She explains that I met her mother in that classroom and that we dated briefly. I do remember her but, sadly, not well. I'd left Maryland to

198

race at Green Mountain Park in Vermont that summer without knowing she was pregnant. I later learned her mother's efforts to locate me had been unsuccessful. The woman on the phone tells me her name is Amber Ricci. She lives in Hawaii and is a professional singer and yoga instructor. She also says she's not yet married but someday wants to have children.

A few months later, she comes to Los Angeles and my wife, Sandi, and I have dinner with her and a boyfriend. She not only looks like my daughter, but has the identical habits of twirling bits of her hair and popping her knuckles. She says she grew up the stepdaughter of a Lutheran pastor and had a lifelong love of singing and dancing. She speaks proudly about using her talents to raise funds for charities. She seems intrigued that I'm a chaplain.

Her initial reason for looking me up is to learn if I have any genetic abnormalities I might pass on, and otherwise curiosity. Today, she's married to Canadian Eddie Riggers who owns a construction company, and they have a son, Dakota, my only grandchild as of this writing. In May 2013, they come to Disney World in Orlando, and Sandi and I go up and spend a wonderful week with the three. Incredibly athletic, Dakota can already swim.

The phone call, as shocking as it was, is one I'm glad I received. And I'm also glad I decided to be transparent.

(A) CHILDHOOD TO ARREST

STUPID IS HARD/ ELECTRIC JOCKEY WITH A JUICE MACHINE

29: Latonia Racetrack, Florence Kentucky, March 31, 1973

The motor home is purring. Debbie and I make our way across Northern Tennessee and cross into Kentucky. It's spring. We're in a great mood: it's a momentous day. We're on the way to Latonia Race Course, now Turfway Park, in Northern Kentucky. This evening I'll ride the three-year-old Bootlegger's Pet in the $15,000-added Latonia Spiral Stakes. That winter, we won the prep and then the $10,000 Eastern Air Lines Tri Star Stakes at Florida Downs (now Tampa Bay Downs), setting in the latter a track record of 1:09 for six furlongs. Supposedly bred by actual bootleggers in far Eastern Kentucky, the smallish bay is a runner and in top form.

Near Valdosta, Georgia, the boxy motor home broke a U-joint that attaches the axle to the drive shaft, something it has done several times. We had to get a wrecker to tow us to a truck repair shop and wait nearly all day for it to be fixed. "Trucking" is a way of life. Each year I've put some 40,000 to 50,000 miles on a car traveling on day trips between tracks for a single race. Each spring we leave Florida for Kentucky, move on to Chicago or New England for summer racing, then back to Kentucky in the fall and go home to Florida in the winter.

For now, our vehicle's short-stroke Chevy engine is humming, and we're making good time. Arriving in time is so assured that when we pass a field filled with violet wildflowers, we stop to take pictures. Our children are not yet born, and Debbie sits among the flowers, leans back on her hands and poses.

It's nearly 5:30 that afternoon when we pull onto the track's parking lot for jockeys and stop. I know the stakes race is scheduled late in the evening card because I rode on the same card the previous year. I have plenty of time, but decide to check in with the clerk of the scales to let him know I'm here. I walk into the jockeys' room. My mouth gapes open.

It's full of people. Valets are scurrying about getting their jockeys' tack ready for the next race. Several riders are returning from showers. Others are dressing. The clerk of the scales is standing before the scales, checking the jockeys' weights as they stand in line and in turn step on to weigh out for a race.

"Where on earth you been?" The clerk stops putting check marks on his racing program and glares at me. "You could have called if you weren't going to show up. The stews called, and they want to hear from you."

The riders turn to look at me. Some smile, some show sympathy, others seemed puzzled.

I shake my head in disbelief. "So I missed the stakes race?"

"Was run 20 minutes ago. When you didn't show, the trainer put Mickey Solomone on him. He won in a gallop, 15 lengths. What happened you didn't make it?"

I drop my tack bag to the floor. My legs feel like spaghetti. I can't answer for a moment. Bootlegger's Pet had won what would have been my richest race to date. I missed a $1,500 payday, the biggest of my career. Had he won narrowly, I could have consoled myself with the thought that

I might have blown the race. But 15 lengths for heaven's sake. All I had to do was keep a leg on each side. And now, Mickey would keep the mount, and I'd miss out on riding what may be the best horse I rode.

The work in the room goes on, but the older, gray-haired clerk of the scales walks to me. "You miss a plane, car break down or something?"

I shake my head and exhale loudly. The pit of my stomach churns like the inside of a washing machine. "I thought it was a night card. Rode the same day last year, and it was at night."

"We switched to day racing on Saturdays. Too bad. But you'll still have to call the stewards."

I follow the official to his office and make the call. I see Mickey getting dressed a few yards away. I don't want to talk to him, much less congratulate him. The stewards understand, and it's obvious they're not going to fine me. But when I explain for the second time I feel even dumber.

Outside the jockeys' room, I see Debbie standing at the saddling paddock rail. "I heard the news," she says. We blew it."

"Big time. He's a great little horse. A real runner. And now he's gone."

We stand there in silence. I hate the pain I see on her face and realize my face must look the same. I finally mouth the words I detest. "I feel so stupid."

Anger I can do. A year earlier at Florida Downs, I won the first four lifetime starts aboard the Robert Van Worp-trained Proud and Bold that included a division of the Florida Breeders' Futurity and the Success Stakes. He'd moved to the "bigs" at Gulfstream Park. I never again rode him. That was anger.

I've missed riding some good horses because of injuries and while being suspended for careless or rough riding. My agent and I had been forced to pick between two mounts running in the same race, and I watched from the saddle the horse not picked glide past me and cross the finish line in front. But those are simply a part of being a rider and happen to us all. They rank as disappointments.

202

This is different. I can fault no one but myself. This is sheer stupidity. Stupid is the hardest.

Debbie and I finally hug, hold hands and walk away.

Bootlegger's Pet will win 16 races, including 10 stakes—one of which is graded and earn a total of $208,910. Proud and Bold will win 25 races, including the then Grade II Donn Handicap at Gulfstream, and earn $319,899. Both horses will earn enormous sums for horses racing in the early 70's. They are probably the best horses I rode. Though I never lost on either, I never got to ride them very long.

Four Years Later: Churchill Downs, May 7, 1977

It's the day before the Kentucky Derby, and its sister race for fillies, the Kentucky Oaks, is less than two hours away. Nearly 47,000 fans are there to watch the field for the fourth race, a $4,000 claiming race, line up in front of the massive grandstand and twin spires. I'm astride Jubilist Jude as we near the starting gate parked 1/16 mile from the track's famous finish line for the 1 1/16 mile race. Folded inside my right hand on the grandstand side is a machine.

As machine horses go, this one is the real thing. He's a grandson of the great Citation, with decent conformation and is healthy and fit. But he's extremely lazy. Suspecting as much, I'd ridden him in a workout without the trainer knowing it and touched him once with the machine. He had responded with a burst of new speed. He'd raced at lowly Beulah Park his previous race and I believed his odds would be high. I glance at the odds board and am disappointed to see him only five to one. In the grandstand Debbie had bet $400 to win and $400 to show. At Churchill Downs, Oaks and Derby Day are best for insider bettors. The mutual pools are so large that massive bets go undetected and barely lower the odds. While my bet is insignificant, except to me, Oaks and Derby day betting coups are the stuff of racing's wagering legends.

Once behind the starting gate, an assistant starter approaches to lead the horse into the starting gate. I watch in horror as my mount spits out his "tongue tie," the thin cloth strap that in the saddling paddock the trainer had wrapped around his tongue and tied beneath his chin. Some horses have a habit of nervously darting their tongues back and forth during a race. On rare occasions, they manage to get their tongues over the bit; something trainers believe inhibits horses' air flow, even though as far as I know horses breathe solely through their noses.

The assistant starter holding my horse sees the dangling tongue tie and calls it out to the starter, a racing official. My stomach sinks. In Kentucky at that time, only the trainer can put on or fix a tongue tie. I'll have to wait with the other horses and riders until the starter calls the track announcer who will ask over the PA system for the trainer to come to the starting gate. I might have to dismount, something I don't want to risk with a machine in my hand.

The assistant starter leads my mount around in circles a few yards from the prying eyes of thousands of fans and God only knows how many cameras. While the machine is tiny and wrapped in flesh-colored tape, the end containing the two metal prods falls below my hand by less than an eighth inch. While it's unlikely any of the fans lining the rail will intentionally look for something in my hand, I envision one taking a photo and noticing. I'd be at a stewards' hearing as they and Thoroughbred Racing and Protective Bureau agents, perhaps the same ones who searched me at Florida Downs ask me to explain. It's possible the assistant starter leading me can see it or even the starter might spot it from his stand a few yards away.

Riders caught with machines are usually suspended for five years or more. I'd ridden 16 years, broken a dozen bones, thrown up over 10,000 times and watched several tons of my sweat run down some 54 "hot box" drains. I wasn't a top stakes race rider and knew I would never be one. Five years on the ground and my riding career was as dead as Man O War. Go out this way and no newspaper is going to hire me as a writer. Instead, to support my kids, I'd wind up delivering newspapers.

Sweat gathers under my helmet. I consider standing in the irons as if to rest my legs and deftly dumping the machine into my pants. I'd placed it prongs-out in top of my jockey strap inside the jockeys' room, and in a move my pony rider never saw, retrieved it a few seconds earlier. But once dropped into my pants, retrieving it would be far too obvious. My $800 bet would be toast. Worse, I might fumble and drop it to the track, something sure to be noticed.

The Kentucky Derby, to be run on the same track in some 27 hours, is known as, "The Greatest Two Minutes in Sports." I'm undergoing the worst two minutes of my career.

After being led in several score circles by an assistant starter and what seems like hours, the trainer shows up and reties the tongue strap.

I hold on to the machine, noticing that when we are loaded my hands are shaking. Early on we're fourth. Going into the last turn, my mount is ready to pack it in for the day. I slap his shoulder underhanded with the stick in my left and at the same instant touch the right side of his thick neck with the machine. He finds new energy and takes the lead the last eighth-mile. He begins to loaf. Rivals start to close. I cock my whip, swing with my left hand and again touch the right side of his neck with the machine. He again stretches out to full stride and wins by a half-length.

He pays a disappointing $10.80 to win and $4.20 to show. We make $2,200, not counting the $260 I earn for winning the $4,000 purse. I vow to never again use a machine. A vow I keep.

(B) BATTLINGS ATTRACTIONS AND ADDICTIONS

RUBBING GRETA AND GLORY

30: Hollywood Park, Inglewood California, Winter 1994-95

"I remember you," says Mary, one of trainer Jack Van Berg's exercise riders. "You used to be a jockey and a reporter."

She's standing outside a cinderblock barn cleaning her saddle stretched out over a wooden sawhorse. It's my first day on the job, and I'm on my way to a tack room to find an extra hoof pick. I nod and keep going. I find the metal pick used to clean horse's hooves and head for the barn next door, home to the four green horses I'm grooming for Van Berg. But Mary puts her hand up, and I stop. "At Saratoga just before the Travers Stakes, aren't you the one that said Alysheba was using endorphins?"

I stop long enough to say, "I am," then walk on. "What goes around comes around," she shouts at my back.

When Alysheba ran in the 1987 Travers Stakes at Saratoga, it was billed as one of the most interesting races of the year and *The Dallas Morning News* sent me to cover the race.

The gangly, hot-blooded colt gave Van Berg his first Kentucky Derby win in 1987, then took the Preakness Stakes but finished a miserable fourth in the Belmont Stakes. Unlike most reporters, I made it a practice to spend much of the afternoon before the race on the backstretch. Real stories don't start in the press box. At Alysheba's barn, I was talking to one of Van Berg's grooms I'd known from Oaklawn Park. I saw two uniformed security officers standing in front of the horse's stall. Security guards around famous racehorses are not unusual. But to have two standing so close, wearing looks that could melt glass, struck me as a bit strange. I pulled my friend to the side and asked. What he said was so startling that at first I didn't believe him.

The men guarding Alysheba were New Jersey State Police officers, and they had received a tip that before Alysheba raced today someone was going to slip him endorphins.

"You for real?" I ask.

He nodded. "They been here all day."

I was thinking major story, possibly a scoop. "Where's the boss?"

"Was here with the owners and they left together."

Probably in the grandstand. Jack was not one to get far from his horses. I was stunned. Endorphins I knew were naturally occurring substances in animals and humans, produced usually by a rush of adrenalin or extreme pain. I saw a horse who'd broken a leg in his stall casually munching hay on three legs. A vet had said it was because the injury had caused a release of pain-killing endorphins. If someone could synthesize endorphins, they'd have the perfect "hop." It would be a powerful painkiller and, because it naturally occurred in a horse's body, likely impossible to detect.

I slinked away and called Jack on my cell. Voice mail. I said nothing. I called the desk editor at the paper, the one who decided what made it into the paper. I told him what I had, and he told me that's peachy, but I had to have more. I gathered my thoughts and went back to the barn and arrived at a different part. A man who wore a trench coat and a glare had to be a detective and was standing at one end of the barn, a few feet from inside the broad entrance now closed with a low sliding gate. I strolled up and introduced myself.

His thick Italian eyebrows shot up when I said "reporter," and he stepped back. I could practically see his mind regroup as he developed an I-know-nothing stare. I plowed on. "It looks like a couple of your guys are standing outside Alysheba's stall. Why you guys way up here?"

"We'll have no comment."

"You are from the New Jersey State Police?"

"I can't comment."

"You're a police officer and you can't identify yourself as a police officer? If I write this, and you are a police officer and you refuse to identify yourself, your whole group is going to look bad. Can't you folks put people in jail for lying to you?"

He turned and walked down the shed row, likely knowing I was not permitted to follow. I hurried back to the grandstand, showed my press pass and got on the elevator to the stewards stand. The situation's irony was not lost on me. Here I was, all but kicked out of horse racing for race fixing, waltzing into the stewards office to pin their backs to the wall with questions I know they wouldn't want to answer.

This is a spectacular story, and so far I was the only one who had it. I could quote an unnamed source and report that two officers wearing New Jersey State Police uniforms are posted at Alysheba's stall. If I can find Van Berg in the grandstand, I can flat-out ask. But I could hear him say his famous words to me: "No, Eddie."

I had a reputation for asking trainers and riders hard questions when they gave interviews in front of a crowd of reporters. I knew the game better than most of the writers, and I suppose I was showing off. Several times during the 1987 Triple Crown races, I'd asked Van Berg a series of tough questions. Other writers, especially Jay Privman of *The Daily Racing Form*, kidded me about Van Berg's stock reply: "No Eddie."

In the hall outside the entrance to the steward's office overlooking the track, a Pinkerton's security guy stood guard. I introduced myself. "I need to talk to the stewards about some race-fixing information I've developed."

He looked at me like I crawled out of a sewer, but disappeared behind the door. In 20 seconds he was back, and I went in to talk to the three stewards. I told the three what I learned, but when they asked me to reveal my source, I refused.

"Gentlemen, this is going to make the news sooner or later. A 'no comment' is not going to help racing's credibility. Don't you think the racing fans deserve to know?"

The three looked at each other and one of the stewards admitted to what I had found. My reporter's notepad was out, and I was scribbling like crazy. It was all on the record. The state police had called, saying an informant alerted them a person or persons unknown—not necessarily connected to the stable—was going to give Alysheba endorphins before he raced. "Apparently your source knows as much as we know," he says.

Another asks, "When will your story run?"

There's no Internet in those days so I have no means to broadcast it immediately. But I understood where the stewards were going. They didn't want the public to know before the race and for good reason. Fans might bet on the horse, thinking he has an edge. Or they would shy away because they thought the guards and the whole thing would hurt his chances. Many might not bet the race at all. In any case, the betting will be determined by something other than past performances. The horse was being guarded so the stewards are off the hook. My immediate fear was that they would call a press conference and tell everyone.

"Tomorrow morning," I answer. "But I'm not saying jack squat to anyone until it makes the paper."

"Want your scoop, do you?" one steward comments. "Something I'd expect from an ex-jockey."

I had my scoop, right under the noses of some of the best sportswriters in the nation and in many of their own backyards. The next day, my story ran on the front page of the sports section and was highlighted on the paper's front page. It was a Sunday when we sell over a million papers. A slew of papers around the nation also ran the story on Monday. Java Gold and Pat Day won the $1.1 million Travers Stakes with Alysheba finishing up the track as the favorite. It made the story all the more compelling. To this day, nothing more is known. However, the story didn't exactly endear me to Van Berg, who refused to be quoted in the piece I wrote. But here I am at Hollywood Park, working as one of his grooms.

As God would have it, I'm assigned four fillies about to officially become two year olds, but in reality had been on earth some 20 months. Among trackers, horses' official names are the last thing remembered. Instead, pet names and personalities are what we recall. Of the four, I remember two, Greta and Glory, and not oddly those two went on to become stakes winners. Greta was a gangly dark bay with a narrow head, white-rimmed eyes and a dislike for mankind that rivaled Brahma bulls. She is a Greta Garbo who wants to be alone. Glory is a bulking, light-skinned chestnut with undesirable white legs (topical leg medications often irritate their pale legs). She has a way of raising her wide head, which has a near perfect white stripe running down its middle, and looking off into the distance, her round intelligent eyes seeing and sensing things far beyond mere human comprehension. I believed she was looking at Glory.

With racehorses, personality has little to do with ability. Often the most unlovable of horses are the most talented. In general, racehorses learn through repetition. Anything new is a challenge. From the time they are turned out in paddocks with their mothers and even before they are weaned, they are handled. Workers put on and take off halters, pat their necks, brush their manes and comb their tails. One early and crucial lesson is allowing their handlers to lift each leg in turn and use a hoof pick to remove muck from their hooves. After accepting this, they can be shod by a blacksmith. At two, the time they generally reach a racetrack, it should be nothing new. For three of my charges, it is not.

As I run my hand down the side of Glory's leg to signal my intention, she lifts each leg in turn. When I do the same with Greta's back legs, she often lashes out, trying to kick me. Unlike most horses who seem to enjoy looking out over their stall's webbing and into the shed row, Greta likes to face the back wall and ignore the world. Often when I entered her stall, she'd turn her rump to me and threaten kicks. Once or twice she'd delivered. All missed, so far. In 23 years of being a jockey or learning to be a jockey, I've been kicked once. I remember it vividly.

At this point, I have been thrown a hundred times, horses had broken legs beneath me in a full run, charged over fences and while walking past a stall one had bitten my shoulder so hard it turned a blackish shade of blue and ached for weeks. But working close quarters inside a stall with a horse who wants to injure me is something new.

In all my years on the track, I'd seen someone get mad and genuinely abuse a horse only once or twice. Yet we all know we sometimes have to get a horse's attention. Sometimes a jockey's light strike with a whip will be all a reluctant horse needs to walk into the starting gate. A groom's hand slap under a horse's belly is often enough to stop the horse he is grooming from trying to cow kick him.

On the second morning, I walk into her stall as she faces the back wall. She lashes out with both hind feet, with one narrowly missing my face. I retreat under the stall webbing, my heart pounding and my throat dry. I remembered seeing a female groom at Oaklawn Park with her head misshapen and bloody after being kicked. I was standing with a trainer when he received a call telling him his wife, while working on their horse farm, had been kicked in her chest. Both died.

Mary is standing outside the stall with saddle and bridle draped over an arm. "Looks like she loves you. I can hardly wait to take her to the track. I bet she's a doozie."

"At least she can't kick you if you're on her back."

"I imagine she's the kind that will figure out something else."

"I hear Alysheba was the same way."

"I wasn't his regular exercise rider, but I was around him enough to know he'd bite or kick you just for fun. He'd also run over you. Jack had to handle him a lot himself."

I wish Jack were here now to help with Greta. He'd hardly questioned me about why an ex-jockey and horse racing writer had called, looking for a job. I'd told him about my addiction and that I thought I could put it behind me. That was enough for the hard-nosed Nebraskan who was born into a famous racing family but worked longer and harder than anyone he ever hired. I didn't expect coddling. I was on my own.

Mary glances at her watch. "This set is going out in 10 minutes. We need to get going."

Greta is in one of the six or seven sets of horses that will have to be on and off the track when it closes at 10:00 a.m. The production line is moving. Slow it down and a foreman will have to help me. There'd be a story circulating that the ex-jockey is over the hill, incapable of even being a groom.

I remove a six-foot lead shank from the wall and wrap the chain part around my stronger left hand. Watching Greta's back hooves, I duck under the stall webbing and into the stall. Her rump lifts, and she kicks with both back feet. I duck to one side and lash out with the leather shank. It lands on her backside, closer to her back than I would have liked. But the resounding crack lets me know it hit hard.

She turns and faces me, ready to charge. I cock the shank, ready to strike again. She hesitates. That's all I need. I walk forward, take hold of the bottom of her halter and snap it to the metal chain attached to the back wall. Once secured, I use the rub rag in my back pocket to wipe her down. She turns once to bite, but I utter a warning and she stops. Mary joins me in the stall, and I put on the saddle. I slide off her halter, slip the bit into her mouth and put the head stall over her ears.

I leg up Mary in the stall and we walk in circles until I unsnap the webbing and lead them into the shed row. "I got her from here," she says as I unsnap the lead shank while keeping an eye on Greta's back legs. Mary looks back and smiles.

"Good job, Big Ed," she says, giving me a nickname that will last throughout my stay on the Hollywood Park backstretch. "You're going to make a helluva groom."

212

"Oh boy," I shout after her. "My dream has come true."

I settle into a routine. Up at 4:30 a.m. Coffee and a donut in the track kitchen. I brush and tack each horse and clean their stalls while they're at the track. After the track closes at 10:00 a.m., I brush them again, pick out their feet and remove any fresh muck from their stalls. I kneel beside their front legs and rub in Bigeloil Liniment, put thick standing bandages on each leg for protection, mix their feed and set their feed tubs inside the stalls. I finish by neatly raking the shed row in front of their stalls. Somewhere around noon I go back to the track kitchen and eat, go to my room and collapse. I'm back at five p.m. to feed, pick out the stalls and rake the shed row.

It's hard to sleep at night, and I sleep better in the afternoons. My head aches often and sometimes my ears ring. But I'm not sick, and I don't have cravings, at least not for crack. I'd read that kicking crack will cause tremors, depression, loss of appetite, nausea, vomiting, constipation and cravings that can last up to a year. I drink a few beers a day, and smoke a joint or two at night to help me sleep. But I am not undergoing withdrawal.

Maybe it's the hard physical labor. Maybe God performed a real miracle with that Bible verse. I keep the Bible in my room and try to read it, but nothing much seems to make sense. I sometimes pray too, but mainly I think about God and how I failed. There are two porn video arcades down the street on Century Avenue. It's a fight to drive past without stopping: a battle I don't always win. Other than not being addicted to crack cocaine, I'm no better off than I was when I left Houston. My most frequent prayer is "God don't let me get AIDS."

My sleeping room on the second floor above the shed row is small, has a roll-out window and four concrete block walls. A previous occupant had bored holes in two cement blocks in a corner, inserted stretched-out coat hangers in two blocks and attached a wire line between them. This is where I hang my clothes. A foot locker for the rest of my clothes, a stand for my boom box, books piled in a corner, a plastic chair, and a soft, squeaky cot make up my furnishings.

213

Living in a barn inside 30 acres populated by 1,500 horses has its own set of peculiarities. At night, I constantly hear horses neigh, nicker, whinny and blow out of their noses as they move about in their stalls and seem to talk to their neighbors. If I open my window, the muck pile below makes my room smell like a dirty stall. About 70 percent of the some 800 residents are Hispanic. While friendly, open, and constantly helpful, most of them speak little English, and I speak only pidgin Spanish.

I read a lot, mostly Dick Francis mysteries. Perhaps one day, I muse, this ex-jockey might also publish a novel. Mostly, there is talk before, during and after work. Each stable has a close-knit crew of workers, and there is always competition with other stables and camaraderie among each team. Ninety percent of the conversations are about horses. The race tracker's Bible is the *Daily Racing Form*, some 40 pages of racing news and Thoroughbred past performances. On the front overleaf are some five paragraphs of news. Events like landing on the moon, the assassination of President Kennedy and 9/11 maybe get two.

On the backstretch, fame, fortunes and funerals come and go while horses take on immortality. They're an island of consistency in a sea of vagaries. Here you are who you've rubbed, exercised, shod, shipped, treated, trained or rode in races. Every race tracker has an ever-ready litany of stories about their charges. Over time, horses' winning margins, pari-mutuel payoffs, money won, bravery, meanness and kindness all enlarge. All here live vicariously off their horse's artful grace, raw power and unswerving courage, traits that almost always exceed their own. Racehorses are the gladiators and lovers we all want to be. Their battles become our battles; the races they run, the races we run. Sadly, this unholy joining becomes so strong that negative human traits inherent in us all—be it greed, a need for recognition and acceptance or the conquering genes of maleness—are projected onto the horses in their care. Horse racing itself becomes a golden altar on which horses are sometimes sacrificed to appease the failings of those who so readily identify with them.

On the Hollywood Park backstretch, some like Mary remember my past. I laugh my way through the moments when I'm recognized. Most don't ask how I came to be a groom. The backstretch is full of has-beens. Stories of past glory are passed around like the peppermints I give my horses. Unless I'm helping another groom "run a horse," or take them to the saddling paddock for a race, I never go to the grandstand. Unlike others on the backstretch, I refuse to talk about the golden moments of the past for fear that reliving them will acknowledge the bleakness of my future. A slew of former jockeys park cars in the track's valet lot or work inside the jockeys' room as valets, massaging the egos, cleaning tack and shining the boots of a new crop of celebrity jockeys. Some find jobs as exercise riders. There's nothing wrong with any of this. I'm just not ready to accept that as my future. There's a fence surrounding the backstretch's perimeter. It's there to keep the unlicensed from entering, but the race trackers joke it's there to keep them in. I'm determined to break out.

I get two days off every two weeks, and on my first I head to see Pam O'Neill, who lives in a condo in upscale Irvine, about 25 miles from the track. We had met in Laguna Beach on New Year's Eve in 1992 and became friends—real friends, no sex involved. Pam divorced a wealthy businessman, won an impressive condo in the proceedings and made gold-leaf cakes for a living. She'd sent me the $200 to get here from Houston. Classy, well-mannered and well-read, she and I talk for hours on end about our lives, current events and our mutual love for literature. During my visits, she allows me to sleep on her posh white sofa in front of a roaring gas fireplace. It's a memorable treat.

"What is it about homeless people and dogs?" she asks after I say I want to get a dog. "Something about people having a hard time taking care of themselves wanting to take care of something else. What is that about?"

"I'm just tired of being alone," I say. We're in her small living room, drinking a glass of wine. "All I do is work and sleep. I've gotten to know one or two people, but they work in the day and go home at night. "

"You can't make friends? When you lived in Laguna Beach, you had a hundred friends. Everybody knew you."

"They weren't actual friends. I just hung out with them. Did a lot of partying I should have avoided. Things are different now."

"You spent most of your life on the track. Now it sounds like you're too good for them?"

"Pam, it's not like that. Outside of horses, we have nothing in common. I want to get out of there. It's like my soul is drying up."

She takes a long look at me, her round brown eyes crinkling with sadness.

"Don't get me wrong," I say. "I love the people on the backside. I'm just not ready to believe that's where I'm going to be the rest of my life."

"And if you hang out with them, that's what you think you'll become, a has-been?"

"Something like that." I lower my head and shake it wearily. "At least I'm done with crack, and if I lose 10 or 15 pounds I can start exercising horses."

"You're going to make a comeback?"

I grin. "I wish. But I'm too old, too soft, too scarred ant too scared. Besides, I weigh 150 pounds. The only way I'm ever going to weigh 110 again is if I have terminal cancer. But exercising horses, I'll be done every morning at 10:30 and I'll at least double the $250 a week I make now. I can pay you back, get a little place off the track and start to get a life back. Maybe start writing again for racing magazines."

"Go for it. You back on your meds?"

I'd taken Lithium for six years and Paxil for two. I'd stopped while I was doing crack in Houston, but I'd found a free clinic near the track and am back on both. "Yeah, but I hate that I have to take them."

I'd told Pam about God giving me a passage from the Bible to give me the strength to get off crack. Yet here I was taking psychotropic medication, smoking grass in my room and drinking wine with her. Pam was a go-to-Midnight-Mass-on-Christmas Catholic, but we'd had long conversations about God, and she is a believer.

The next morning, my car won't start. Pam promises to have it fixed then drives me to the track. "I know it's great to have a friend like you," I say as I get out. "But I feel so stupid."

"Get yourself a dog," she says with a grin.

*****

"All right," Van Berg says to all the grooms he has gathered in front of his barn office. "It's time to line them up."

He is going out of town for a few days, and he wants to do one of his famous "show and tells" before he leaves. I head to the barn next door, put a shank on Glory and lead her back to the main barn. Van Berg stands in the middle of the shed row as grooms line up their horses. As each horse is led to him, he gives it a once-over to check the gloss on their coat, the brightness in their eyes and sometimes gently opens their mouth and runs his fingers along their gum line, looking for cuts or teeth too sharp. Yet with racehorses it's all about the legs.

Looking away he runs a hand down each front leg, he feels knees and the fronts and backs of each ankle. "Do this one up in Absorbine. Mud his knees. We need an X-ray here." He calls out the orders as his assistant takes notes. Some of the grooms make comments and ask questions to clarify the instructions.

I lead Glory, and he feels her legs and looks in her mouth. She is unperturbed. "I like this one," he says. "Got a great body and a mind to match."

"Smarter than I am," I quip.

"That's not hard," he says.

In the next round I lead up Greta. He gives her his once-over and when he starts to pick up her hoof to look at her feet, she jumps sideways. I snatch on the metal shank across her nose and get her back in line. This time he tries a much more dangerous back leg. She jumps away and lets out a cow kick at the same time. Her back hoof whizzes past his leg. He slaps her under her belly, causing her to lunge forward and I step aside and again haul down the shank.

"Can't you hold the damn filly?" he shouts. The young foreman puts down his clipboard and takes the shank I'm holding. He holds her while Jack manages to lift a back leg and get a quick look at her hoof. "Dirty as hell," he says. "You picking out her hooves regularly?"

"As much as I can. She's still green."

"I don't care. You're supposed to teach her. Get somebody to hold her for you. Put a twitch on her if you have to. She's gotta learn. Way you going, she's bound to get thrush."

The foreman hands me the shank, and I lead her off. "Teach her," I say under my breath. "Be easier to teach a mule to play chess." Seven years earlier, I was asking Van Berg snooty questions in front of a crowd of other reporters. Right now, I'm hoping he doesn't fire me.

(C) LIFE AS A JOCKEY

HELLO U.S. MARSHALS/ TAKEN FOR A RIDE

31: Rockingham Park, Salem New Hampshire, July 2, 1978

It's 5:30 a.m. Sunday when I guide my Subaru into the track kitchen parking lot and park. Behind us in our small utility trailer are all the belongings we brought from Florida for the seven months we are on the road. Curled up in the back are my 3-year-old daughter, Dawn, and Debbie's mom, Marge. Debbie is in the passenger seat and like them, asleep. Awake, but quiet in her arms is our son, Derek. He is five days old.

I bend over and smile into his face. Taking out my wallet, I look again. It still contains $200. Thank God, several months earlier I paid the $700 first month's rent on a small house to reserve it. We have a place to stay for at least a month. Gas and groceries are another matter.

The spring meeting at Churchill Downs had not been kind. I'd won enough races to keep us afloat, but the Jockeys' Guild insurance didn't pay for births and the $3,500 I'd paid the hospital had busted me out. Derek chose to wait it out inside his mother's womb a bit too long. The Churchill meeting had ended. Most of the stables I rode for fairly regularly there as well as those I'd successfully ridden for the previous summer at

219

Rockingham Park were already here. The meeting opened on the Fourth of July, two days away. My agent had called from the track to say if I didn't arrive soon, I'd lose several mounts the first few days. If those horses won or even ran well, I wouldn't ride them in their next race. Trainers are as fickle as pregnant wives and seem to suffer from the what-have-you-done-for-me-lately syndrome. I might easily lose my best horses and entire stables to other riders. With $200 to my name, that would make life difficult.

The preceding Wednesday, Debbie and I sat in a Louisville doctor's office and made the decision to induce labor. With me watching, Derek took his first breath five hours later. We left Saturday morning and stopped in Rochester along the way to pick up Debbie's mom, who is going to help for a while. This time I'd driven all 1,000 miles. Entries for the opening card will be drawn in about three hours, and my bearded face will be solace to my agent and the trainers who want to make sure I'm there before they list me as the rider in their entries. Also, I'd promised trainer Troy Lane, who had stuck with me through feast and famine, that I would work one of his best horses that morning.

I look over at Debbie. "You awake, Hon?"

She nods, still mostly asleep. "I gotta find my agent," I say. "Let him know I'm here. Then I'll drive you to our new place and come back after I work a couple of horses."

She nods again and goes back to sleep. I walk inside the track kitchen.

"Well, look who finally showed up," deadpanned a beanpole of a man in a padded down vest and white cowboy hat. It's not my agent, but trainer Troy Lane.

"Just got here. I got our new baby in the car, a boy we named Derek."

"All righty now. Got that extra mouth to feed. We best be riding hard."

Peaches, my agent, walks up, a pen stuck behind his curly, sandy colored hair and a condition book in his hand. The condition book contains a categorical list of upcoming races. To book a jockey, the agent circles the chosen race and the trainer initials it. It's a binding contract. There's an ongoing joke about horse owners putting up sometimes millions of dollars, the trainer investing thousands in setting up a stable and even a jockey buying his own tack. All an agent needs to earn 25 percent of a jockey's gross salary are a free condition book and a 29-cent pen.

Peaches flashes one of those sales smiles agents seem to have painted on. "We been waiting for you. Got a lot of business opening day."

"I got three in myself," Lane said. "Ready to blow them out."

A blowout is a short, fairly fast workout that supposedly opens a horse's lungs for a race no more than 48 hours away. I nod, thinking I'd have only one and say, "Sure thing. Give me 30 minutes to drive the family to our new place, and I'll hustle right back."

Peaches sees my frown and jumps in. "How about I drive them? I'll help unload some of your gear and be back by scratch time." Scratch time is 8:30 a.m., the appointed time in the racing secretary's office when horses are scratched or withdrawn and their replacement determined by drawing numbered pills from a pill box normally used for pool. My agent grins, his personality cheery even before dawn. "I want to see the new one, anyway."

I go with him to the car, show him the new baby and retrieve my helmet and riding boots. I'm bone tired, but I've been on racehorses in worse shape. I go with Troy to the barn and work the first two horses without incident. I'm dead fit and Debbie once told me my butt looks like two boiled eggs in a condom. But I'm tired and want to go home. The third is a two-year-old filly who in two days will race for the first time. A groom gives me a leg up. With Troy on the pony beside me, we walk to the track. It's daylight now, and the track is filled with horses.

Jogging on Churchill Downs track two months earlier, she'd wheeled out from beneath me. In the world of Thoroughbreds, the most unpredictable of all is a two-year-old filly, and this one is white-eyed wild. Horses with white rims around their eyes are particularly excitable. On the track, proper protocol is to have your mount stand and face the passing horses, then turn counter clockwise with the flow of traffic, walk and jog and then ease into a gallop. While just starting a gallop a few weeks earlier, she had pulled a move on me. She planted both front legs during a gallop, propped to a full stop in one stride and wheeled right, all in one move. I was hurled to the track. There are some moves a moving horse can make and you're on the ground, simple as that. As the adage goes, "Never was a horse couldn't be rode; never was a rider couldn't be throwed."

I had slightly sprained an ankle, nothing unusual. Much of the time I, like most riders, am nursing a strain, a bruise or stiff joint. Jockeys have a way of listing their injuries and ending with, "I was lucky." I understand. I broke 13 bones and consider myself lucky. As Troy leads me to the track, I lower my stirrup irons below normal for breezing to give my legs more surface grip. I shake my head to clear it. Troy is talking about some of his crew, and I'm fighting to listen.

This would be a bad time to get hurt. The meeting is about to start, and I'm already playing catch up. No doubt some of my regular mounts have been committed to riders already here. Even a few days on the sidelines nursing an injury could ruin the entire summer. Riders get paid only when they ride, and a badly pulled muscle or broken bone means no racing for weeks or even months. My house rent is paid for only a month, and the meter is ticking. If injured, I'd collect a whopping $200 a week from the Jockeys' Guild. Once, on the last day of racing at Florida Downs, one injured rider had just returned to riding after a three-month recuperation and didn't have shipping money. He hadn't won a race at the entire meeting and was as they say in horse racing, "On the Duck." He rode a favorite in the meeting's last race and after taking up a collection for him, some of the other riders in the race, so I heard, made sure he won. Taking charity is not my style.

I walk onto the track. Troy cuts me loose. My green, bug-eyed mount watches horses go past like a shoplifter eyeing a security guard. She ducks to the left, dropping a shoulder and scooting sideways. With two fingers wrapped in the mane, I lose my right iron. Somehow I hang on.

Troy and his pony jog near. I turn her around to go with the traffic flow, using both feet to kick her ribs. Standing still aboard a frightened racehorse is worse than moving in almost any direction. Standing still, they can rear, fall or just do a back flip. Getting out from under a horse falling over backwards is an inexact science.

An Outrider swoops beside me. These expert riders on fast horses regulate racetrack traffic and this one takes my left rein in his right hand and ushers me down the track. I kick her again, this time squalling at her like a scalded pig. She breaks into a fast gallop. I snug up the reins to slow her, feeling assured when she pulls to go faster. The outrider cuts me loose. Less than a quarter mile later, I guide her toward the rail, tuck into a monkey crouch, and smooch.

It's obvious she has real ability. I'm constantly amazed that often the fastest horses are the craziest. She whips off a brisk three furlongs, and I allow her to slow gallop to the backstretch. Once past the entrance and exit gap, I pull her to a stop. She's snorting and blowing vapor into the crisp morning air. I walk her back to the gap and stand her out, facing horses who gallop past. She starts to sidle back and turn to the right. I've figured out her move by then and kick her right side. She straightens, and after she faces out again for a few seconds, Troy puts a thin lead strap under her bridle's chin strap and escorts us home. "Thirty-six and change, looks like she can run a bit," he says, smiling.

"Sideways, too," I say, keeping my two fingers wrapped deep in her flowing mane.

*****

I arrived nearly broke and with a new baby but by August I'm winning races, water skiing on the lake we live beside and bouncing Derek around on my knee to burp him. All is well. One morning at the track, the PA system announces the track stewards want to see me. When the "Stews" call, you go. I suspect the worst.

I heard Tony Ciulla was convicted of racing fixing and in jail. Mike Hole named several famous riders as fixers in New York and racing is riddled with rumors. I'd sold articles to a host of racing publications and newspapers, including *The New York Times Sunday Magazine*, and the *Baltimore Sun* ran my article on race fixing and the susceptibility of exotic wagers to manipulation. The article depicted selecting one horse to win and trying to stop all the others as tricky, if not impossible. However, it noted that trifectas, picking the first three finishers in order, are vulnerable to fixing, and worse were superfectas or doing the same with the first four finishers. Tony Ciulla may have perfected the science of fixing horse races, but he didn't invent it.

For instance, in a nine or 10-horse field, keep five or six from winning through a variety of means, then box or take all possible combinations of the remaining horses and winning becomes far more likely. Even with up to a 25 percent takeout on some exotic wagers that go to the house, use this method over a period of time and the statistical probabilities will be on the side of the fixer. Ciulla knew it, I knew it, and while I wasn't about to tell on myself, I wanted the racing world to know the inherent dangers of exotic wagers. As I walk into the track's white administration building that houses the steward's offices, I somehow hold out hope that this is what they want to talk about.

Instead, once inside the office of the lone steward on duty, he introduces me to two well-dressed men then politely leaves. I'm reminded of the crowd of diners who mysteriously walked out of Danny's Bar, leaving me alone with the Winter Hill Gang. They flip open badges and identify themselves as U.S. Marshals. If anything, I am expecting TRBP dicks or maybe the FBI. Why U.S. Marshals? We sit in facing chairs at a small table. The younger one in a tight, blond crew cut takes out a notebook and pen. "You nervous?" he asks.

"What's the difference between a regular FBI agent and a marshal?" I ask.

"For one we oversee the Federal Witness Protection Program."

The other one, older and with a broad Irish face, leans in, smiling. "Look, I think you know why you're here."

I shrug my shoulders, faking stupidity.

The other one stares, his face drawn and serious. He cites a date in 1974, which is incorrect. But he names the correct horse, Society Boy. "You won on a horse you weren't supposed to. You took $800. You remember Tony Ciulla, one of the men who beat you up the next day in a bar in Somerville?"

"Nobody beat me up in any bar."

"Then why did you grow a beard? You're the only jockey I saw with a beard. Must be hot, riding in that beard."

"I started when my daughter Dawn was conceived. I had it at the time before the time you're talking about."

"Then you're saying you don't know Anthony Ciulla?" says the smiling one with slick hair.

"I don't live in a cave. I know who he is."

"Maybe you know this guy, too," he says, shoving an 8"X10" glossy in my face. On it the man's face looks like it was cut by tiny knives. His jaw and forehead are massive lumps. Both eye sockets are reddened and his eyes swollen nearly shut. I recognize him. Paul Whiteman. He's a Pennsylvania jockey who migrated from Eastern Europe with a name with too many syllables to pronounce, causing him to take the name of a famous bandleader he saw advertised on a nearby poster. I heard he'd messed up a race, and the boys from Winter Hill met him in the track's parking lot. Flashing through my mind came an 8"X10" glossy of my naked bloody body lying between two Suffolk Downs barns.

"Whatever these guys did to you that day in Somerville is nothing compared to what they'll do to you now." He leaves the photo on the table, and I know I can't hide the fear on my face. "There are a lot of people whose bodies we don't even know where they're buried who couldn't have damaged Howie Winter and his pals like you can."

They have to see the fear on my face. The younger one cocks his head and smiles, a shade of compassion filtering through his eyes. I realize they're doing "good cop, bad cop." "Mr. Donnally, you're a dead man walking."

The older agent reaches over and gives one of my shoulders a buck-up shake. "Look, Eddie, we're here to help you. Save your life actually." He leans closer, so close I can smell his breath mints. "We know what happened, how Ciulla beat you with a blackjack, how one of them told you he'd put your body on the Suffolk Downs backstretch as a warning to others. They were serious. They'll find out we talked to you. They have people all over the place, on this track even. They're going to get worried. We think there was one guy who was in that barroom that morning named Jimmy Martorano. We have good reason to believe he's already killed at least eight potential witnesses."

Sweat rolls down the bridge of my nose and my throat is as dry as a desert rock. They're right. Killing me would be no more personal than swatting a pesky New Hampshire mosquito. It would be a business decision. I could see them sitting around that same table in that same bar, saying Eddie Donnally had to be whacked. They'd all nod their heads and toss back a shot to seal the deal.

I clear my throat and shake my head. "So Ciulla's talking." I say, instantly wishing I'd said nothing.

"So you remember him, then?" the young bad cop asks as he jots down a note.

"I'm not saying anything without a lawyer present. Is that what this is about? Me testifying against the Winter Hill Gang?"

The young one continues writing. Older Mr. Nice Cop sits back, looking relaxed as if this is a conversation he has every day. There are too many thoughts to sort out. I want out of this room more than I wanted out of the Somerville bar. It's as if someone has turned a page on my life and nothing will be the same again.

"Something to think about, huh?" says the old one. "You got young kids, right?"

"Australia," says the other. "You ever been to Australia? We can send you and the family there. Get you new identities, Social Security cards and everything you need. We'd help you get started."

I know Australia has lots of racing but I'll still look the same, new identity or not. At 5' 4," I'll be easy to spot. "No way I could race again or even go to a track. Somebody would have to recognize me."

"We know you went to college, can write articles and stuff. You'd be fine. "

I shake my head and stare at the hardwood floor. The word "fine" ripples through my brain like a sentence of life in prison. I see myself walking down an Australian street, looking over my shoulder, sure I'm being followed. The Winter Hill Gang can get on a plane just like me. They wouldn't forget. I'd seen the movies. Them walking into restaurants with guns blazing, blowing up cars when the mark turns on the ignition, bloody bodies in the trunks of cars and lying on sidewalks, blood seeping into the concrete. But this is no movie. The two federal marshals are as real as paraplegic former jockeys.

I look up. "I'll take my shots here." The two rise and look down at me. Mr. Friendly Irish face pats me on the back. "Talk to Debbie. We know she was with you. If they kill you, she's dead, too. Go home and take a long look at your kids. They'd both be orphans. This guy Jimmy Martorano is at large, and he's already shot a girl to death along with her boyfriend. They'd think nothing of taking you both out."

"They tagged him 'The Basin Street Butcher,'" the young one says. "He's got bodies buried all over the place, some of them people who couldn't put as many of them in jail as long as you can. You don't cooperate; we can charge you with race fixing. You're looking at five years. You'd be dead meat in a jail cell."

The older one hands me a card. "You both are going to have to appear before a grand jury. Call any time if you want to talk or have questions. We don't want to see you in jail. Even more we don't want to see you dead."

My head is hot and my hands holding my helmet are shaking. I take the card. A steward comes back into the room, and I wonder how long it will take for them to bar me from racing.

"We're done for now," the young one tells the steward. "We'll keep you posted."

The stern-faced steward nods with approval. Even a charge of race fixing is enough to end my career.

*****

A month later, a trainer I know slips me a piece of paper with the name and phone number of Boston attorney, Al Farese. Debbie and I visit him in his office, and he takes our case, asking me to write a check for a fee that seems too low. However, we have not been charged but know it may be coming. He says that despite the legal client/attorney privilege, he wants us to tell him only what he specifically asks. Nothing more.

That summer, every time I look in the rearview mirror I see a gray Plymouth with a tiny antenna in the middle of its roof. We're staying in a little cabin on one of the nearby lakes. Dawn is three now, and Derek is only a few months old and doing well. Debbie's mom has gone home. The tiny home has a phone and every time I use it, I hear an intermittent beep.

It's late August, and the meeting is about to end when one night we hear a firm knock. I peek out the curtains to see the gray Plymouth. I still have my unlicensed pistol and a machine, though I hadn't used it since the tongue-tie incident in Kentucky. Dandy, our one-eared Doberman, growls softly. I take one end of his choke chain in one finger and open the door. The two marshals eye Dandy, clearly uncomfortable. "We'd like to come in."

"You have a search warrant?"

"Just some information you need to know," says the young one with the crew cut. His partner smiles as always. I nod and step in. I put Dandy in the bedroom and am glad Dawn and Derek are sleeping.

"We don't have to talk to you at all," Debbie says. "You got questions I'll give you the name of our attorney."

"We already know Mr. Farese," Crew Cut says. "Bet he's giving you a great deal."

I bristle. "Look, I know you two didn't show up to discuss attorney fees. What's up?"

"Your time on earth," the smiling one says, no longer smiling. "We've developed some information from an informant. He says there's a hit out on you two. Could be any time."

If they want to see fear on our faces, they're pleased. federal marshals are supposed to be good guys who save other good guys and put bad guys in jail. Now two men with shirts and ties, badges, pistols and the full weight of the Federal Government are telling us we're about to be killed by a group that has a history of murdering its foes.

"You know your buddy, Fat Tony Ciulla, is in jail," says Crew Cut. "He's a tough guy, but he's so afraid of these guys he entered the Witness Protection Program. You two were in a room with him and other members. We know it just like they know it. I'm amazed you two walked out of that bar that day. Now they know you've talked to us, and they'll think you're going to corroborate Tony's testimony."

Crew Cut steps closer. "You're both bright people. You must know there's no way they're going to let either of you walk into that courtroom."

I glance at Debbie. "We've got nothing to say."

Crew Cut glares at me. "I told you a few weeks ago that you're going to have to appear before a grand jury. But I don't think you'll make it that far. You come into the program and you're an unindicted co-conspirator. We'll keep you in a nice safe place until the trial is over. Be with you every minute when you come in to testify. After it's over, you both get new Social Security numbers, financial help and a chance to start a new life. "

"I know, in Australia," I say. "The other side of the planet."

"It's the only way you two are going to stay alive," the friendly one says. "We can take you right now. Spend the night in our headquarters in Boston, sign the papers the next day and all of you can be on a plane to California, where we'll guard you until the trial. "

We both shake our heads. Dawn and Derek are in the next room sleeping. As scared as we both are, entering the Witness Protection Program is something we'd decided against.

*****

It's not yet 7:00 a.m. and I see the green Cadillac drive slowly through the Rockingham Park backstretch. I'd been told by a trainer friend I trusted that the man would be there, and he wanted only to talk to me. I was assured that the man would be alone, and I told my friend that if I got in the car, it would be in the back seat. I told Debbie I was going to meet with a man I believed to be Howie Winter, the leader of the Winter Hill Gang. She'd taken the kids to a friend's house, saying she'd check for a tail on the way. If I didn't get back, she'd know what happened and call the marshals. At least they'd be safe. I don't want to enter the Witness Protection Program and spend the rest of my life worrying about being killed. So far we'd refused the Fed's offer and I want Winter to know it.

The green Cadillac stops and I hop in the back, scooting to one side so I can see his face. Why I feel more comfortable sitting in the back seat makes no sense. It's not like he can't turn around and shoot me, or pull a gun and take me some place else to kill me. It sounds strange and perhaps dumb, but I feel more comfortable with him than the marshals. Wearing the same porkpie hat he had on in the Somerville bar, he turns and smiles at me. It's a warm, engaging smile. If the guy is ready to whack me, he could win an Oscar.

"How's it going?" he asks. "The Feds on your case?"

I know my life could depend on what I say. I had given them $8,000 and a winning horse. I'd done my part. I was even and, I hoped, on good terms. "Big time," I say. "They're following me everywhere, tapping my phone. They came to see us. They want Debbie and me to enter their protection program."

"Why don't you?"

"I don't want to spend the rest of my life running. Figured I'd take my shots with you. I've stood up so far. Thought you'd honor that."

I can't tell what he's thinking, but he smiles again. "What'd you tell them about meeting with us?"

"Told them it didn't happen. They have the dates wrong. They said Ciulla told them they beat me with a blackjack. I won a race the same day. No marks in the winner's circle photo. I gave it to my lawyer. He thinks it's important. It also shows me in a beard, something they said I grew because of the beating."

"Ciulla's a liar. He lied on a couple of us. It'll all come out. You and your wife, you're both going to have to testify before the grand jury. Your lawyer can't be with you. What happens if they indict you and you wind up in jail? Somehow jail changes a lot of people's mind about testifying."

"As long as I believe you know I'm standing up, I'll make it through. Look, I like being just who I am. I got two young kids. I'm not going to watch them grow up while I'm hiding out with a new identity."

He pulls over and stops the car beside a barn. The stable gate is a few yards from the car. His gall amazes me. The head of the Winter Hill Gang in the middle of the Rockingham Park backstretch. He pulls a roll from his pocket and peels off a wad of $100 bills. He reaches round and puts the money in front of me.

"Take it," he says. "No strings. Just something to tide you over for a while. Things might get rough."

I take it and shove it in my jeans pocket. One of the guards is looking over at our car. I open the door and start to get out. "Keep standing up, Eddie," he said. "You stand, and nothing is going to happen. Understand?"

*****

I call Debbie to let her know what happened. She thinks I did the right thing. That night at home, I'm cleaning up the dinner dishes, and Debbie is sitting at the table nursing Derek. Dandy, the Doberman, is reclining on the floor his legs stretched out. Dawn starts to lie down on him, but he gets up and moves. I give her crayons and a coloring book, and she starts scribbling. I know that makes Dandy happy.

I put the money I'd received on the table, and she gives the wad a dirty look. "Eddie, he could have killed you."

"I guess I got us in a little deeper. But if I didn't take it they'd get worried." I sit opposite and look at Derek. He's nursing well, gaining weight, had his shots and never been sick a minute. Not bad for a kid who rode in a car through six states before he was six days old. He's big though, and I'm thankful, lest he one day decide to become a jockey.

"Look, Hon," I say. "If they wanted to kill us, neither of us would be here now."

"They could do it and make it look like an accident. That's what they did with Mike Hole. You know it."

"I don't know it. Mike had some problems. He probably killed himself."

"That's what they want you to believe. They're killers. They think we're going to put them in jail, they don't care who they take down. We'll all be dead."

Derek is finished now and has passed off to a peaceful sleep. "Let me hold him," I say.

I scoot my chair back, and she places him in my arms.

"You know we're both going to have to testify before a grand jury," she says. "Things are going to get crazy."

"They already are. We can either become somebody else, move to Australia, or we can both get killed. Makes going to jail look easy."

Debbie is staring off at a wall. I look down at Derek, breathing softly. A new life with so much in front of him. "I got you into this, little man. I'll get you out."

She looks back at me. "It was my greed as much as yours. Even if I'd known I wouldn't have told you not to take the money."

"But it was still me who did it. I made the choice. Now we're all in a jackpot. What bothers me most is that if they kill me, they have to kill you."

Debbie has tears in her eyes, but they contain no fear. She sniffs and swells her chest. "You're right about one thing. They lay one hand on you, or I ever have reason to think they'll ever touch my babies; they won't have to worry about going to jail. I'll take them with me to hell."

(D) LIFE TODAY

TURNING THE PAGE. . .
OUCH!

32: Santa Anita, Arcadia California, October 23, 2008

Inside the back room of the chaplain's trailer office at Santa Anita I sit in a gray folding chair and face my inquisitors with a broad smile. I'm about to be excommunicated.

Dr. Enrique Torres, the Race Track Chaplaincy of America's Executive Director, sits opposite. He wears a look somewhere between discomfort and ministerial polish. Pastor Ron Fraker also takes a seat and leans in, clearly wanting to get the proceedings going. They are here to tell me that my job as development director for RTCA is as dead as Kelso's career at stud. The Breeders' Cup races at the track are two days away, and I'm expected to be civil, even polite at the sixth White Horse Award, an event I invented and developed.

I've known about the executive committee's action for a few days, but I'm determined to be dignified. Dr. Torres is my boss, and we've worked well together. During my eight years at RTCA, the number of track chaplains and tracks where they serve has doubled. Revenues for both the national office and the entire chaplaincy have increased some 500 percent.

The five years I've spent getting a fundraising certificate from UCLA have not been spent in vain. In terms of revenues produced, my tenure at the ministry is a whopping success. Therein lay much of the problem.

Pastor Fraker gives me a solemn look and hands me a letter. I read it, already knowing what it contains. My job has been eliminated. The ministry needs a person better capable of dealing with "business." I am offered three months' severance pay if I sign a second document waiving my right to sue for wrongful termination.

I can't keep from smiling. I'm sitting in a building I had encouraged a donor to give to the   Southern California RTCA division. I led the way in restarting the division when I lived at the Los Angeles Dream Center and started coming to Santa Anita on Sundays for pre-race prayer with the riders. The person handing me the letter is a fellow Foursquare pastor, one I had served as assisting pastor at his nearby church for several years. I got him involved in RTCA, so involved he's now an executive committee member and had voted on my job's elimination. How he voted, I don't know.

"I'm not planning on suing anyone, much less a ministry I helped build," I say, handing the waiver back. "But I've made it a rule to never sign anything I haven't thought about. Besides I'm speaking at a fundraiser in a few minutes, and Sandi is waiting in the car."

Dr. Torres leans over and places a fatherly hand on my shoulder. "You've done a good job, and we'll write you a letter of recommendation. This has nothing to do with any moral breech or ethical violation. It's all true. Times are getting hard, and the executive committee simply wants to restructure."

"I understand," I say, remembering that despite the sinking economy, the last financial report I gave the executive committee reported a revenue increase of $60,000 over the same quarter a year earlier. I get up and walk out, trying hard to keep my nose out of the air. I explain to Sandi on the way to the event. She already knows but is deeply angry. I've traveled cross-country and was gone at least a week each month. The recession is taking hold, yet the organization is in the best financial condition in its history.

Our chaplains have grown from 35 to 70, and for the first time we have a significant presence internationally. The White Horse Award has brought a slew of major donors and earned us new recognition and respect.

Still, a few local division leaders feel I raised funds for the national office at the expense of their local chaplaincies. I did my best to adhere to the protocols for donor fund sharing and taught a lot of councils how to raise money. Still, the home office is perceived as being wealthy while some local chapters suffer financially. My fundraising is to blame.

During a breakfast meeting in Lexington five years earlier, Ben Walden Jr., a prominent breeder, told me how his church wanted to start helping the area's thousands of largely immigrant horse farm workers, and I'd suggested we start a chapter for the Lexington, KY area farm workers.

Ben wrote a check for $20,000. Dr. Torres and I traveled to Kentucky a few times, enlisted some well-known Christian breeders and trade organization executives, and formed the most influential council within our organization. About the same time, I called Mary Lee Butte when I saw her name on one of the checks made out to the home office. I also knew her husband, Don, was an executive with the Lexington, KY based Fasig-Tipton sales company, so I invited her to a luncheon we held each spring in Lexington a few weeks before the Kentucky Derby. She came, we met and, realizing her verve, exuberance and organizational skills, I easily convinced her to work for RTCA's Blue Grass Farms Chaplaincy Division, of which she later became executive director.

A few weeks before my position was eliminated, Libby Jones, a lovely and classy lady whose husband is former Kentucky Governor Brereton Jones, attended a fundraiser Mary held in Lexington. Apparently she told Mary she thought the $10,000 check Brereton Jones gave to Dr. Torres and me when we attended the Kentucky Derby had gone to the local chaplaincy. The home office had given the local organization $1,000, or a tenth as protocols prescribed, but this apparently displeased Mary. She never picked up the phone and called me so I took it upon myself to call Brereton Jones and explain the problem. To his credit, he promptly wrote a check for $9,000 to the local chaplaincy, giving them a $10,000 donation, which was more than the home office had received. I called Mary, gave her the news and apologized, though I had done nothing outside the prescribed protocols. Still, I knew she had become my competitor.

During the same time, Dr. Torres came under fire from the board for a variety of reasons. A meeting of the executive committee, much like a board of directors, was hurriedly called in Lexington, oddly at night. I'd attended every executive committee meeting but was not invited. When Dr. Torres returned, I knew without his telling me that he had survived and I had not. He would make it another three years. But for me, my time at RTCA had come to a close.

Once in the car with Sandi, I say, "I think God has something else he wants me to do."

"Like what?"

"Maybe be a real chaplain. Maybe write more. I think he wants me to write a book, talk about all the things that happened to me. Tell the truth about a lot of things I did in horse racing. No way can I do that working for RTCA."

That evening at the nearby fundraiser for a local crisis pregnancy center, I take the stage after Martin Luther King's niece, Alveda King, speaks eloquently about the evils of abortion. I face the 200 attending and speak briefly about the local Crisis Pregnancy Center. "I want you all to know that a few minutes before I drove in the parking lot tonight I was informed that the job I held for eight years had been eliminated. I am officially out of work. I came tonight to give $200, which for Sandi and me is a significant gift. But I believe that giving is a gift God gives us and that none of us can out give God. So we decided to double our gift to $400 as an act of faith, and I'm asking all here to join me in doubling your gift."

Later, Sheila, the woman who directed the charity that had saved the lives of many unborn children, told me the take had set a record.

That week, I sign the document saying I won't sue for wrongful termination in exchange for three month's severance. I get a glowing letter of recommendation from Dr. Torres and write the press release announcing my leaving. I planned on retiring the following fall when I turned 66. Yet I am hurt. Many of our chaplains are friends and I've grown fond of many of our donors. Still, it would be a breach of fundraising ethics for me to pursue their friendships. It's like a pastor leaving a church, a situation in which is it proper for the departing pastor to step aside and give the new pastor space. My evangelistic bent must move elsewhere. Hall of Famer and former RTCA spokesperson Pat Day has been a friend since we rode together at Rockingham Park in the early 1970s. I'd won a $65,000 grant from the Foursquare Foundation, operated by my denomination, to fund "Racetrack Revival." With my leading the organizing and Pat giving his testimony of God taking away his addiction to cocaine, over 1,000 people inside racing responded to his altar calls. Today, we remain friends as I am with Dr. Torres and Pastor Fraker.

Though wounded, I feel God wants me to turn the page. During the entire process, no one told me I'd done anything wrong. The Kentucky division later withdrew from RTCA and formed its own 501(c)(3) organization. Mary Lee has done much good work on behalf of farm workers and their families. I salute her.

I promised God that I'll always work to bring the love of Christ to horse racing. That promise remains in place. On Halloween 2008, I clean out my desk and go home. Trick or Treat indeed.

(A) CHILDHOOD TO ARREST

A VALENTINE FROM THE FEDS

33: Oaklawn Park, Hot Springs Arkansas, Valentine's Day 1979

Steam rises from the tailpipe of the black Sedan idling atop the blacktop in the track's parking lot. I've just been told by someone in the Racing Secretary's office that two men in suits were looking for me. I figure they're U.S. Marshals or the FBI.

It is a cold Valentine's Day morning. I've finished exercising horses and am about to go home and take a nap before returning to race that afternoon. When I spot the car, I realize I won't be racing that afternoon or perhaps ever again. Over four years earlier in Danny's Bar, I'd decided there was little future in running. I walk to the driver's side. The window lowers.

"You with the FBI?" I ask.

Both exit the car. "Are you Eddie Donnally?" the driver asks.

I nod and both smile. I've made their day simpler. "You've been indicted for sports bribery. We're going to have to put you under arrest."

It's snowing in Little Rock early the same evening when the plane I'm on lifts off for Boston. The two agents on either side of me remove my handcuffs and start chatting with me as if they do this every day. I have a ton of questions, but I know if I start, I might say things that can be used against me. I politely ask if I can sleep. They have me take the window seat, get me a pillow and start talking with each other about Razorback basketball.

After the arrest, they'd taken me to their headquarters in the federal building in downtown Hot Springs without bothering to handcuff me. They allowed me to call Debbie and my Boston attorney, who warned me to say nothing, nothing at all about anything. Debbie didn't want to stay in the house with the two kids alone, and in the snowstorm had gone to stay with trainer Troy Lane and his wife, both friends. I sit on the plane with eyes closed but far from sleep. Might the FBI search our house? If they do, they'll find a loaded and unregistered German Mauser my father gave me years earlier and a tiny jewelry box containing a machine, something I don't use anymore. I'm far more concerned about the machine.

Once in Boston, another agent arrives and, with me in handcuffs, drives me downtown to the federal building where I'm placed in a cell and fed dinner. The following morning, wearing the same jeans and boots I had on when arrested, I'm escorted downstairs and arraigned. My attorney pleads not guilty. Within 10 minutes, I'm released on my own recognizance and that afternoon, Farese puts me on a plane back to Little Rock. I don't remember paying for the ticket.

In one way, I'm relieved. Debbie and I both appeared before a grand jury the previous spring and answered questions. Neither of us had to actually lie because the government had a lot of the details wrong. They denied the husband/wife privilege and Debbie had to testify. It's obvious neither of us will be friendly witnesses. My lawyer told us last year that the grand jury had met for three six-month periods, the maximum allowed. Had the prosecutor designated made me an unindicted co-conspirator, he could have granted me immunity, charged me with contempt for not testifying and sentenced me to jail for the 18 months the grand jury convened. Why the government did not, I never understood. Perhaps they were afraid of my lying on the stand, something that could have genuinely hurt their case against the 19 others who were indicted with me. According to newspaper accounts, Boston's Who's Who of organized crime were indicted, along with two Las Vegas casino executives who allegedly made bets for them in their casino horse parlors.

When I get on the plane home, I have several newspaper accounts my attorney had collected. If my memory is correct, my lawyer had called a week earlier and said I'd been indicted but never asked me to turn myself in. For my own protection, he may not have wanted me to seem friendly to the FBI.

I sit on the plane and think about the upcoming trial and read accounts in *The Boston Globe* and the *Boston Herald American*. The indictment said that Howie Winter and William Barnoski had "beaten jockey Edward Donnelly (they misspelled my name) in Danny's Restaurant in Somerville because Donnelly's horse had won a race at Suffolk Downs, Oct. 16, 1974, after Donnelly had accepted a bribe to hold his horse out of the money." It also reported that Joseph "Joe Mac" McDonald said, "Donnelly should be killed and his body placed in the backstretch at Suffolk Downs as a warning to other jockeys."

It also said that Barnoski and two others indicted had beaten up trainer Vernon Ewalt in a Pennsylvania motel and jockey Vernon Gallup outside a bar in Pennsylvania's Pocono Downs. As the marshals had told me, one of their top hit men, John Martorano is at large.

Joe McDonald, whom I later learned was an original member of the gang and described as a "hit man," is on the FBI's Ten Most Wanted List. He is also at large.

I still have the business card of one of the federal marshals in my wallet. I buckle my seatbelt, listen to the engines rev and watch the frozen Belle Isle salt marshes pass beneath me. How will the authorities react? On one hand, I'm technically innocent until proven guilty. On the other, I've been indicted for sports bribery along with some of the nation's most notorious mobsters in a scandal that has become the talk of the sports world, especially after Bill Surface had written a cover article in *Sports Illustrated* naming Ciulla as a "Master Fixer." However the authorities react, I face up to five years in a federal prison.

In jail, Ciulla became so scared of the Winter Hill Gang that he became a relocated witness. One of the marshals told me if I were in prison, something the mob thought would make me turn, I'd be "dead meat." On top of that, two guys who make a living killing or beating those who can harm them or other gang members are out there somewhere in the darkness. Debbie and I and our children aren't hard to find.

Australia doesn't look so shoddy.

Tampa Florida, March 21, 1979

Tampa Stadium is packed. The crowd isn't here to watch the three-year-old Tampa Bay Buccaneers. No, on this night Billy Graham is in the house. There's an old racetrack saying that "hard times will make a monkey eat red pepper," and I'm gasping for water.

The lights blaze down on the seats occupied by Debbie, my wife of seven years, and me. I sit there wondering if anyone here has a problem as big as mine. No state racing commission has lifted my jockey license, but we returned to our home in nearby Crystal Beach to learn that Florida Downs, where I've raced many years, had, like Oaklawn Park, denied me "permission of their grounds." I have my license but can't come on track grounds. I am sure other tracks, if I try to race there, will do the same. I've found a job exercising horses on a farm, but it isn't enough to support the family, so I've found a second job delivering the *St. Petersburg Times*. I get up at 2:00 a.m., throw over 150 newspapers in nearby Tarpon Springs, drive to the horse farm, get on a dozen green two-year-olds, go home at noon, collapse then get up and get ready to again pick up my newspapers. I haven't called the federal marshals, but often while delivering papers on darkened streets at 3:00 a.m. consider how easy killing me would be. As I wait to hear Dr. Graham preach, I realize I need a miracle.

Debbie sits there, staring out in space and smoking a cigarette. "It'll work out okay," I squeeze her arm and say. "One of these days this will be something we can tell our grandchildren."

She gives me a hard look. "Not sure I'd want them knowing. I got more important things on my mind. Everybody in the world knows where we live. You can't ride here. We need to leave."

"And go where?"

"My folk's house."

I laugh. Her last name had been Bonazza and she came from a family in Rochester, New York, who had relatives who were supposedly "connected." I shake my head. "It would take the guys in Boston about 10 minutes to figure out where we were. If these guys want to find us, they'll find us anywhere we go. I don't want it to look like we're running."

That night Billy Graham gives an altar call as Cliff Barrows sings "Just as I Am." Debbie and I are among the thousands who make their way onto the field. I don't feel much of anything but I do want to change. I promise God that if he gets me out of the mess I've made of my life, I'll always work to bring the love of Jesus to horse racing.

*****

A few months later, my dad is in the ICU unit in Alleghany Regional Hospital in Low Moor, where I grew up. He has silicosis (black lung) as a result of working in the coal mines and is near death. Debbie, the kids and I drive from Florida. I get there in time to be alone with him. He's on a ventilator to help him breathe and has a drugged look on his pale and drawn face. We've talked by phone, and he knows I've been indicted for sports bribery. I put on a false smile and tell him I think it's all going to go away. He can't talk, but he gives a weak smile.

I talk about all the trips we made together and the time early in my career when he came to Boston to watch me race. He seems pleased, but I know it's time to talk about now. I was told that my Mom was a Christian, but I never saw my dad inside a church or heard him talk about religion. I tell him about my decision at the crusade, and he seems ambivalent. I take my New Testament from my back pocket and read all of John 14. Several times I read the first few verses where Jesus says, "In My Father's house are many mansions; if it were not so, I would have told you. I go to prepare a place for you. And if I go and prepare a place for you, I will come again and receive you to Myself; that where I am, there you may be also. . ."

I take one of his rough hands, hands spent mining coal, hopping on and off C&O freight trains and cabooses, and working in the gardens he loved so much.

"Can you believe that, Dad? That Jesus is God's only Son and can give you eternal life?"

He nods and squeezes my hand.

A few hours later, Debbie, my three sisters and my half-sister, Libby, circle his bedside after the respirator he hated had been removed. We hold hands and I say a prayer. Within five minutes he is dead.

We hug, cry and talk about the man they called "Big Daddy." I share with my sisters the decision he had made. That brings comfort. But for me there is unfinished business. My father had not lived long enough to learn the outcome of his only son's upcoming trial.

(B) ATTRACTIONS AND ADDICTIONS

JACK THE TRAINER MEET JACK THE DOG

34: Hollywood Park, Inglewood California, Spring 1995

The bulky, flop-eared Doberman drags me across the street when we leave the Torrance Animal Shelter. Pulling like a racehorse, my new 99-cent leash digs painfully into my hand. But I have my new dog. Something every homeless person needs.

Back at the barn I show the dog to Jack Van Berg, who stands outside his office to supervise the evening feeding. He is a quintessential teacher, and successful trainers Bill Mott and Frank Brothers once worked as his assistants. He's the first trainer to have strings of horses at multiple tracks around the country, and he grew as famous for his constant travel as for training over 100 horses at the same time. He'd won a then record 5,000-plus races and was enshrined in Thoroughbred racing's Hall of Fame.

"I'm naming him Jack after you," I say.

"Eddie, that's exactly what you need. You got no place to live, nowhere to go, so you get a dog, a giant one at that."

244

"I could have named him Alysheba."

Jack the dog sits on his ample haunches. That he shows little interest in the horses around him makes me feel better, as it likely does Van Berg. Most racetracks, including this one, allows dogs on the backstretch. Horse people, being hopeless animal lovers, fill it with dogs, cats to keep the rodent population in check, parrots, ducks and a herd of goats. The latter is especially useful as Thoroughbreds' calming stall mates. I think that's what I'm looking for in Jack.

Van Berg lifts one of Jack's long drooping ears and looks inside. Like polished shoes on a businessman, the inside of an animal's ear says a lot. The ear is clean, free of mites and ticks. "Looks like they gave him a bath at least."

"He's got his shots, and they neutered him. How old you think he is?"

Van Berg pats Jack's head and with both hands, peels back the dog's lips. "Eight or nine at least. He's got a few good years left." He lets go of his namesake's head and looks up at me. "You don't start taking care of yourself, he'll outlive you."

*****

I wish I could write. It always helped. I'm getting better; starting to think about something other than getting high, something other than me. I bow my head, feeling tears well up in my eyes. Feeling might be healthy, but right now it hurts.

A few nights later I can't fall asleep. I sit in my lone plastic chair, the bare light bulb glaring overhead and read a Dick Francis novel. I can't get interested. Jack is curled up in the corner, fast asleep. He's great company, except he can't talk. I give up and take out my yellow pad containing an unfinished short story. My mind is getting better but it's still hard to write a coherent paragraph. But I'm capable of having thoughts outside myself, something I know is healthy. Yet, it's painful. I keep thinking about missing Dawn's high school graduation, something I can never get back. She and Derek are growing up 1,600 miles away and I'm living in a backstretch tack room.

Derek at nine had walked to my door, lugging a suitcase as big as he was. Dawn had practiced acrobatics on the practice bar I'd built in the garage. I'd been there when both were born. I want to go home, give my kids a hug, go have a pizza, maybe go roller skating. But that's impossible. I have to first save enough money to get an apartment, get fit and start exercising horses. Make a lot more money.

It's nearly midnight, and I have to be up at five. Greta is waiting to kick my head off. But feelings keep flooding back. After all I'd done in racing, I'm sitting in a cement-block sleeping room on a racetrack backstretch at midnight and nobody cares. I glance out the window at the blackness. If nobody cares, do I really exist? I want to exist. Somebody has to hear me and let me know I exist.

I find the roll of quarters I keep for calls, bounce down the steps and stand in the shed row. It's raining. A hard wind blows it sideways. I consider going back upstairs, but I need to hear a human voice, one that knows me. I just need to tell somebody I'm not dead on the backstretch of some racetrack.

I run to the row of three phone booths. Rain pelts my face and runs down my hair. My jacket and jeans are soaked. I shove a quarter into the phone and dial Pam. I wait until an automated voice tells me to deposit another five quarters. I shove them in. No answer. Not even voice mail. I get out my little book with numbers and dial Janet, a former girlfriend in Los Angeles. We have talked recently, and I know she'll talk to me. Voice mail. I don't leave a message. I go through my book, finally trying Chaplain Randy's number in Houston. It's nearly 2:00 a.m. there, but he'd understand. Voice mail again. I hang up and leaf through the tiny book. I see names but realize none will want to talk to me. My bridges are now ashes. I don't even have Debbie's number or I might have given in and asked about the kids.

I look again. No one is there. No one to prove I exist. I'm a tree falling in the forest, crumbling to the ground with no one around to hear it. There's no noise if no one hears it. Feelings have to reach out and touch someone or they're not feelings, just sad musings. I don't exist anymore. I drop the book and to retrieve it sink to my knees in the mud. It's soaked, the numbers ruined. It's my connection to the world. On my knees in four inches of dirty water, I turn my face to the heavens and welcome the rain beating onto my face. At least I can feel it. I must be alive. I scream into a peal of thunder, "God, you gotta help me here."

(C) LIFE AS A JOCKEY

LIVING ON THE Q-TEE

35: Rochester New York, May 1979

There's an old gangland saying, "going to the mattresses," referring to the sleeping accommodations when mobsters war with rivals. Debbie, the kids and I have "gone to the mattresses," sleeping on two pushed together in the second bedroom of her parent's modest two bedroom apartment. I get a part-time job manually tallying employees' work hours at a hospital. On the way home every day, I stop at a newsstand to buy my usual *Boston Globe*. The paper is covering the upcoming race-fixing federal trial like it's the second Tea Party. The aging Italian owner in his black toboggan fishes out the copy he reserves for me. He gives me a wink and knowing smile.

My mind goes on high alert. No one except Debbie's immediate family even knows why we're here, staying with her folks. I look at the paper. There I am front-page center, a headshot photo of me beside a photo of Howie Winter.

"I read the article," the Italian says. "Sounds like they want to make a rat out of you."

At that moment, I'm not sure if I'm more rattled by matching front page photos of me and the leader of the Winter Hill gang or a complete stranger who knows where I am. "Something like that," I mutter as I put a dollar in his hand and turn to leave.

"You act like a clam and you'll be all right," he calls after me.

Rochester is a reputed mob town. Even a guy who runs a newsstand can be connected. Running my name up his flagpole wouldn't be hard. By tomorrow morning the mob here could know that Eddie Donnally, the guy with enough information to put in jail most of the entire Winter Hill Gang, is living in Rochester. If Boston's largest newspaper thinks I'm significant enough to run my photo beside the photo of the gang's leader, it isn't unrealistic to believe the mobsters think I'm significant enough to kill.

I get to the car, and after glancing around, read the complete article. Howie Winter has skipped and joined Joe McDonald, (who wants to put my naked body on the Suffolk Downs backstretch) on the FBI's Ten Most Wanted List. Add John Martorano, who has killed more people than Audie Murphy and you have three gang members who have ample reason to see Debbie and me in our graves.

I drive around awhile, trying to think. I don't want to appear this nervous when I go home and see Debbie and the kids. My eyes keep straying to the rearview mirror. I'm one of three jockeys scheduled for trial. I haven't officially skipped because my lawyer knows where I am. I haven't seen any FBI or federal marshals, but I still have one their business cards. After a while I drive home, say nothing to Debbie's parents, play with the kids a few minutes, then call her into our bedroom and show her the story. Her face goes ashen. She lights a cigarette and reads it. "I don't think anybody but our lawyer knows where we are," she says.

"For God's sake, the Italian who owns the newsstand saw the picture and made me. He told me to act like a clam. By now the man's every gumba who runs numbers or books bets in the whole city is going to know I'm here. They could be connected with Boston."

"I can talk to my uncle. He knows everybody. He can find out."

I sit on one of the mattresses and rub my forehead. This is getting crazier all the time. Debbie is going to talk to her uncle to learn if the locals want to take the contract to kill us. Like they'd even tell her uncle.

"I just need to think this out," I say. "Maybe we need to go somewhere else. The trial is next month."

"And what, not tell Al where we are? That might really get us killed."

"We don't actually know he's talking to the mob," I say. "One way or the other, I think we're taking a bigger shot staying here."

"Eddie, you got in the back seat of Howie Winter's car one day. You're still here. Besides, it wouldn't be fair to the kids to just pack up and go live someplace else. They like it here. They're with their grandparents. The only ones they have."

I get up and resume pacing. "I don't want to see your parents having to raise them. You told me once you thought Howie Winter had Mike Hole killed. But when Yvonne visited us up in New Hampshire she said she didn't think so and she was his wife."

I keep walking. "But who knows? Who know anything?" And now on a day I don't need to remember Mike's death, it sticks in my mind like a Beatles melody.

Debbie gets up and grasps my arm, forcing me to stop pacing. "I just think if they wanted to find us, they could," she says. "And if they wanted to kill us, we'd been dead a long time ago."

We sit on the mattress, silent for a time. "I lit a candle at the church yesterday," I say.

"You make a novena?"

"Don't even know what that is."

"You pray for nine days for something special."

We both walked to the field during the Billy Graham Crusade in Tampa months earlier but Debbie and I never went to church in Rochester. We'd gone to a small church in Crystal Beach a few times before we left. Now coming home from work each day, I'd stop at a Catholic church and because it's always open sit down, enjoy the silence and try to pray.

"Jesus," I say now. "We need you to protect us right now."

We're quiet again, sitting there holding hands. We get up and walk to a phone booth to call our lawyer. It's after five o'clock in Boston, but an assistant answers and puts us right through.

I tell him about the newspaper article, and he chuckles. "Don't worry. I got good news. I got a letter today from the prosecutor. I'd made a motion for a separate trial based on what is called 'prejudicial joiner,' meaning that to try you with the others would be tantamount to prejudice. You'll have a separate trial. They're sure to schedule it after the main trail."

I feel God already answered our prayers. "So I just wait until this trial is over?"

"Listen, Eddie, they don't want to try you. They only indicted you so they would pressure you into becoming a witness. Where are you calling from anyway?"

"A phone booth."

"Good. The marshals didn't talk to you again, did they? They know they got to go through me."

"After that time at our cabin, we haven't heard from them." I look at Debbie and smile. "Then all I have to do is wait until my trial?"

"It might not even happen. Ciulla is the only possible witness and he's in the Witness Protection Program. I doubt he'd want to come back to Boston for your trial even if they'd let him."

I feel like a 200-pound jockey just dismounted from my back. All this paranoia had gotten me crazy. "So I'll just sit tight and wait for your call?"

He clears his throat, and I hold my breath. "Not exactly. I got a subpoena for you. You're going to have to testify at the trial."

"My Lord, that's just what I don't want to do."

"Don't worry. You have an upcoming trial so you can invoke your Fifth Amendment rights and not say anything that might incriminate you. I'll go over it when you get here. You can fly in the day before and leave after you show up in court. A piece of cake. "

We hang up, and on the walk back I explain to Debbie.

She seems relieved, more than I. It's almost dark and I can't help but look down an alley we cross. Regardless of what Al said, out there somewhere are three killers, one of whom already said he wanted to kill me. All face long sentences. How can they know for sure that I'm not going to sit in that courtroom and, when the federal prosecutor asks about what happened in that Somerville bar, point them out?

If I were them, I'd be nervous. That makes me nervous.

(D) LIFE TODAY

SACRED SPACE/WHAT IS GOD SAYING?

36: Time and Place Anonymous

The gentleman lies in the ICU hospital bed, his mouth gaped open, his breathing raspy and labored. His wife sits beside him, holding his hand and looking into his eyes with an intensity I later learn is born of over 60 years of marriage. The man is in his eighties and his wife had requested a chaplain.

I pull up a chair on the opposite side of the bed to be at eye level. She explains that minutes earlier at her request his ventilator had been removed, and he is about to die. I'm fairly new at hospital chaplaincy, but I'm honored to share this sacred space.

"There's something I want you to understand," she says softly. "We talked about this a lot, and we both know that there's a time for this."

"A time," I muse.

"Life doesn't stop for any of us. Time moves on. Dying is just a part of living."

"Yes, it is."

We're silent for a time. She's right. Words can get in the way.

253

"Don't get me wrong. I'm going to miss him a lot. Death is never pretty. It's just necessary. I wish we'd had more time. He seemed to be fine but then he fell away quickly. I suppose it will be that way with me. I hope so. I know he's going to heaven, and one day I'll be with him. He was a great man of faith . . ." Her voice trails off, and she delicately wipes away tears.

We're silent again. "Heaven awaits," I finally say. "A wonderful thought. Does it help now?"

"It does." She brightens a little. "Would you say a prayer for us, that he'll have peace and then maybe read a verse or two?"

I stand, put my hand on his shoulder and, as she reaches out, take her hand. I've long believed that even comatose people have a soul that can be reached. "Fred, I know you two love each other very much and Joyce asked me to pray."

I pray, first for the peace that the Bible says passes all understanding for them both. I verbally note that Psalm 139 says that God and not man know the number of our days.

"God, If this be his time, I ask you to send angels, just like the ones in Luke 16 who carried the beggar Lazarus to heaven. I pray for strength for Joyce and all their family."

I close in the Name of Jesus and see tears trickle down both her cheeks. I get out my pocket Bible and read the third chapter of Ecclesiastes: "A time for every purpose under heaven. A time to be born and a time to die. . ."

I hear a soft gasp and look up to see Fred take a frail, halting breath followed by silence. Like a spring-wound clock gradually slowing to its last tick, Fred's time ran out. I'd seen people near death and I'd seen many people dead, but this is the first time since my father died that I've been with someone who takes their final breath. But his eyes do indeed have peace. I don't see the angels, but I've seen glimpses of them since, and that day I felt their presence. Joyce is crying softly, and I know it's time for her to be alone with her husband.

"I know your being here at this time meant a lot to him," I say.

"You being here meant a lot to me."

Death, as she says, is never pretty. Yet at that moment I feel a presence, an awe of God. I hear chimes, ones from a floor below us that signal the birth of a new baby. I sense a mysterious wonder of the infinite, one that defines death by life and life by death. It's a cycle I can never fully comprehend this side of heaven. Yet at that moment, I know I'm standing on holy ground. In sacred space. I know I'm right where God wants me.

LIFE AS JOCKEY

BACK TO BOSTON

37: Boston Massachusetts, July 1979

The skyline appears as the plane cruises in over the salt marshes and lands at Logan Airport. I get off, glancing around at every person inside the huge corridor, and walk toward the sidewalk. My small satchel contains by best suit, shirt and tie and little else. Tomorrow I testify near the end of what is to date the longest federal trial in history.

Danny's Bar where Debbie and I met with gang members is a few miles away. I have no way of knowing if they are certain I'm going to invoke my Fifth Amendment Rights and refuse to testify against them. Two U.S. Marshals insisted that the Winter Hill Gang already "had a hit out on me." At this point, I'm trusting a group of known killers more than I'm trusting agents from the U.S. Government.

An hour later, I pull up to a three-story brick house in the upscale area of Chelsea. It's nearly dark, and I know I'm not being followed. Still, I drive around the block a few times and check for suspicious delivery vans or men waiting in cars. I'm greeted at the door by my niece Elizabeth and her husband, Tim. Elizabeth is holding their infant son. They let me hold the baby, a large boy. I attended their wedding at the University of Virginia chapel. Elizabeth, who grew up in tiny Covington, Virginia, is the daughter of my oldest sister, Patsy. Elizabeth graduated from the state's most prestigious college, the University of Virginia, and married a young intern at the university's hospital. Tim, tall and lean, comes from a wealthy family, is a Harvard graduate and now an oncologist at Mass General.

They'd ordered Chinese, and I ask if I can call Debbie and my lawyer before I eat. I call Al, assuring him I'm in town and will meet him at the courthouse at 7:00 a.m. I mention that I'm staying with my niece but don't say where. He goes on assuring me and going over the procedure for invoking the Fifth Amendment.

"Can we talk more tomorrow?" I ask, thinking he might be keeping me on the phone to trace my number. I hang up and call Debbie. She's glad to hear my voice, and I'm glad to hear hers. "All this is going to be okay after tomorrow," I say. "We won't have to look over our shoulders anymore."

"Just be careful. Does Al know where you are?"

"I called, told him I'm staying with my niece. He can't know who she is."

"Eddie, don't be stupid. They can find out anything they want. They got cops in their pockets."

I didn't know it at the time, but two gang members, including the notorious killer Whitey Bulger, a Winter Hill Gang leader, was working in concert with the head of the city's FBI agency. "I'm fine here. Nobody followed me. Even if they know where I am, I don't see them breaking down the door of a doctor in swanky Chelsea."

I hear her gasp. "Look, you're giving out things on the phone you shouldn't," she says. "Call me tomorrow when you get off the stand. And don't think you're in the clear until then."

It seems odd to me. Debbie doesn't want to leave Rochester in fear but seems to fear for me now. I hang up and join Tim and Liz for dinner. Their son is upstairs, asleep. We make chitchat about Deb and the kids back in Rochester. My family has followed my career as a jockey, and they know that Patsy was the closest thing I had to a mother. We switch to talking about Patsy, and halfway through the chow mein we run out of ways to avoid talking about the reason I'm in Boston.

Tim breaks the ice. "You said you've got a flight out tomorrow night, but if you'd like to stay longer, see some old friends or spend some time with Elizabeth, you're entirely welcome."

They know why I'm in Boston. They read *The Boston Globe* just like I do. When I called to say I was going to be in Boston for a short appearance at the trial, they had readily invited me. I like them both and wanted to see their new baby. Yet somehow I felt it was safer than a motel. In my haste to protect myself, I never stopped to think I could be jeopardizing them. "Thanks, but I really need to get back."

"Don't you still have a trial?" Tim asks.

"Maybe, maybe not. Not soon anyway. I don't think they want to convict me as much as they want me to help them convict the guys on trial."

I look down at the table, trying to gather my thoughts and say something to let them know I'm not a gangster. Debbie had been saying that an article I wrote on race fixing was the real reason the feds are trying to convict me. "I just want to ride again and put this behind me," I say. "I did something stupid. It was wrong. It's probably going to cost us our house, and if I don't get reinstated, I'll be exercising horses on a farm somewhere the rest of my life."

Elizabeth stops eating and in a grave tone asks, "How are you holding up, and what about Debbie and the kids? Are they all right?"

"She's handling this just like I am. And the kids don't know any different. It's been crazy lately, but I think after tomorrow things will be better."

Tim leans in. "That man who said he wanted to kill you and put your body on the Suffolk Downs backstretch— you think he's serious?"

I put on a brave smile. "If he is, he wouldn't have to take me far. But I think he's on the Ten Most Wanted List. I doubt he's in Boston."

Elizabeth's eyes pinch in frustration. "So none of this scares you?"

"If they wanted to kill me, I'd been dead 40 times."

"Eddie, you don't know that," she says.

"Look, maybe I should have stayed in a motel. I don't know, but I get the feeling my lawyer has told the Winter Hill guys I'm here to take the Fifth. That I'm solid. I've stood up this far." I look around at their faces, amazed that fear could have spread to this upscale couple. "But yeah, I've been scared. We both have."

I slide my chair back, rise and glance at their solid oak door. "But I got no right to expose you and your little boy to my stuff."

Tim rises with me, shaking his head. "No, Eddie. We talked about this and we asked you to stay. We still want you to."

My niece gets up and gives me a hug, holding me for a long time. We separate and I can see her eyes are milky. "There's no way we're going to let you walk out that door tonight."

Tim gives a soft cough. "And I meant what I said. Stay as long as you like."

*****

I'm up at five, make up my bed, write a note thanking them, grab my bag and drive to the John Joseph Moakley United States Courthouse on Fan Pier in South Boston. I find a spot in the huge parking garage and watch from the car as two men walk toward me. They pass by, toting briefcases and joking. I exhale loudly.

I hop out of the car and scurry until I'm right behind the two lawyers and follow them into the courthouse. I find the courtroom and see its hall is full of people I believe are spectators and probably reporters. The trial has been going on for weeks and Fat Tony Ciulla has been rattling off names, dates and details of over 40 fixed races. In my indictment, he detailed the events in Danny's Bar fairly accurately. However, he said I was beaten with a blackjack and had grown a beard to hide the scars. I was only slapped, and I won a race the same day. The winner's circle photo shows no marks on my smiling face, one with a thick beard. But there is no doubt some of the men on trial are men I saw in that bar with Fat Tony.

Originally 21 people, including me, had been indicted. Jockey Guy Contrada and six others had pleaded guilty. Howie Winter was already in jail for extortion and four others, including Jimmy Martorano and Joe McDonald, are fugitives, with the latter on the FBI's Ten Most Wanted List. Charges were dropped against another, leaving seven on trial, two of whom were Las Vegas hotel executives and jockey Norman Mercier. A December race-fixing trial in New Jersey in which Ciulla testified resulted in convictions of five jockeys and two trainers.

Al Farese is waiting for me outside the courtroom and scurries me around the corner to an empty hallway before even saying hello.

"The place is crawling with reporters," he explains. We go over exactly what I'm to say on the stand, and I already have it memorized.

"Their calling you is just a formality. They want the jury to see you scared so they'll think you did what Ciulla testified to. Just get up, be serious but not scared, okay? Just state your name when he asks and answer every question with your line. Don't change it and don't say anything else. Got that? O'Sullivan will get tired after a while, and you'll be done."

Neither of us is allowed in the courtroom until we are called and Al seems to know when it will happen. A reporter comes up, and he tells the man I have no comment and will have none after I testify. The reporter grins but saunters away.

A uniformed bailiff comes out to get us, and we go in. Al sits at the front table, and I take a seat. I look around to see the two U.S. Marshals who kept trying to get Debbie and me into their Witness Protection Program. Several men are sitting in the front beside their attorneys. All turn to look, but I can recognize only Mercier, a jockey I casually know.

Within two minutes I'm called to the stand. I take a deep breath as I sit in the raised box and look out over the faces of the defendants. I think I recognize a couple, though I doubt in a legitimate lineup I could pick them out. All wear ominous looks and I get the feeling they are not sure how I will testify.

I turn to look at a court worker who holds a Bible and swears me in. Jeremiah T. O'Sullivan, who questioned me during a grand jury appearance, appears in front of me, wearing a look that belongs on the guy who flips the switch on an electric chair.

I state my name when asked, and he goes into questions detailing the race Society Boy won and the events in the bar the following day. He asks if I won the race on October 16, 1974. He gives me an expectant look as if I might actually answer. I glance over at the two marshals, who give me a look that I know means their offer is still open.

I glance around at the serious black-robed judge, the eyes of 12 jurors and the room's stately mahogany walls. I concentrate on keeping my voice firm and confident. I look at Farese, who has the eyes of a football coach, and say, "I respectfully invoke my Fifth Amendment Rights and refuse to answer on the grounds that the answers may tend to incriminate me."

It goes on and on, questions intended only for the jury to hear. Some make incorrect assumptions, but I recite my line like I'm starring in a Shakespearian play. O'Sullivan gives a knowing look at the jury that says this guy is guilty and we all know it. Finally, it ends. I'm dismissed.

Farese walks me to the car and tells me that my case will likely be dismissed a few weeks after the trial ends. It's obvious I am not important enough to engage the huge federal machine of jurisprudence. And perhaps testimony at my trial may aid appeals by some convicted. It's the last time I see the suave Italian attorney who only wanted me to tell him what he explicitly asked. It's several hours before my flight, yet I drive to the airport. I'd seen enough of Boston to last a lifetime. To this day, I've never again set foot in the city.

*****

Ironically, my life may have been saved by FBI agent John Connolly Jr., his boss, John Morris, along with the case's prosecutor, Jeremiah T. O'Sullivan. The first two had convinced O'Sullivan, who supposedly met with Whitey Bulger, not to indict Bulger and his partner, Steve "The Rifleman" Flemmi in the race-fixing case though they were members of the Winter Hill Gang and almost certainly took part. Bulger and Flemmi were longtime FBI informants, mainly ratting out the Raymond Patriarca crime family. Fat Tony Ciulla named the two as race-fixing partners, and when they weren't indicted, the mastermind-turned-government-witness was angry. He'd told *The Boston Globe* reporters he'd fear the pair less if they were in jail.

Whether Bulger and Flemmi were among the group Debbie and I met in the Somerville bar I honestly don't know. It's certainly possible.

Had the two been indicted, they may have given more thought to killing me to keep me from testifying than had Howie Winter. In the realm of potential witnesses, Bulger left little to doubt, allegedly murdering 21 persons who threatened his empire. Debbie and I might have been among the bodies of three of their potential witness victims, including a teenage girl Bulger allegedly strangled and was later dug up in nearby Dorchester, Massachusetts.

Howie Winter was released from prison in 1987. In 1993, he was caught dealing cocaine. When the FBI informed him that Whitey had been a snitch all those years and offered Winter a deal if he would inform on Bulger, Winter refused, telling the FBI he was no rat, though he faced another decade behind bars. He served his time and was released in July 2002. At 83, in June 2012, Winter was again indicted for extortion.

Bulger, who took over the Winter Hill Gang when Winter was convicted of race fixing and sent to prison for 10 years, kept killing, actually six people, according to a host of published reports. Allegedly when Bulger and Flemmi were indicted on racketeering charges in 1995, Connolly tipped Bulger off, something that caused him to flee with a $2 million reward on his head. For years, he topped the FBI's Ten Most Wanted List and was finally replaced by Osama bin Laden. Bulger was finally apprehended in Santa Monica, California, in June 2011. Ironically, I lived a few miles away in West Los Angeles during much of the 12 years he was there. We may have passed each other on the city's famous pier. In September 2013, he was convicted of killing 11 persons.

Connolly was indicted on December 22, 1999, on charges of alerting Bulger to the FBI's investigation, falsifying FBI reports to cover their crimes and accepting bribes. In 2000, he was charged with additional racketeering-related offenses. He was convicted on the racketeering charges in 2002 and sentenced to 10 years in federal prison. His boss, who was also charged with taking bribes from Bulger, testified against Connolly. Oddly so did John Martorano, who I think was the guy who slapped me in Danny's Bar. On the stand at Connolly's trial, he admitted to killing 12 people for the Winter Hill Gang, most of them about to become witnesses. In return for his testimony that helped convict Connolly, he received only a seven-year sentence. He is a free man today.

The 2006 movie "The Departed," in which Jack Nicholson plays Bulger, is loosely based on the scandal and won that year's Academy Award as Best Picture. Martorano's reportedly optioned his story for a movie, and at least two movies are being contemplated on Bulger's life. Warner Bros is reportedly making a deal with a script writer for the movie that Ben Affleck plans to direct, with Matt Damon playing Bulger. *Black Mass,* a movie based on the non-fiction book by former Boston Globe reporters Dick Lehr and Gerald O'Neill, is also a movie possibility. *Black Mass: The True Story of an Unholy Alliance Between the FBI and the Irish Mob,* is a good read, as is *Not by a Long Shot* by T.D. Thornton. Both mention the fixed race I won and encounter with the Winter Hill Gang, but neither is totally correct.

In the 46-day Boston trial, seven of the eight were convicted with the jury finding only Mercier not guilty. My testimony would not have involved him, and in the end my refusing to testify did not affect the outcome. My attorney was a gift from God or the Winter Hill Gang or both. I will never know.

Why the federal prosecutor never chose to try me first and instead open the door for my separate trial after the Boston trial is something I'll never understand. Why Joe McDonald didn't make good on his threat to kill me and leave my naked body on the Suffolk Downs backstretch is also something I'll never know. Why Howie Winter the day I climbed into the back of his green Cadillac didn't just pull a gun, take me somewhere and off me remains a mystery.

O'Sullivan could have also made me an unindicted co-conspirator, and as such could have kept me in jail for the length of the grand jury, in this case 18 months. In jail and vulnerable to a mob hit, Debbie and I would likely have accepted new identities, collaborated Ciulla's testimony and with new Social Security cards in our wallets, taken off for Australia. I believe God simply decided to believe my promise made in the old Tampa Stadium to bring Jesus to horse racing and gave me a second chance.

I return to racing at Rockingham Park and win the first race I ride. I ride another year, but concentrate on my writing and by this time have sold articles to virtually every major newspaper east of the Mississippi, including the *Baltimore Sun, Louisville Courier-Journal, Washington Post, New York Times* and sold an article on Ronnie Turcotte to the *New York Times Sunday Magazine*. I wasn't sure if I was a rider who wrote or a writer who rode. My racing career had gone on long enough. I'd won several minor stakes races, ridden four winners on the same card a few times and was earning a good living. Yet, at 40, I was never going to develop into a major stakes rider. Each day I spent an hour sweating before riding and threw up an average of 10 times. Debbie informs me one day that Dawn, at eight, had already attended six schools. And unlike many other riders, I had a chance at a second career, one I liked, and one that would allow me to stay in horse racing without the risk of having my brains scrambled.

Florida Downs Manager Mike Mackey and co-owner George Steinbrenner hire me as their Publicity Director. The same track wouldn't allow me to set foot on their grounds while I was indicted. That spring I get jobs "stringing" for several newspapers and cover the Derby. *The Dallas Morning News*, while in a state that is six years from again legalizing pari-mutuel racing, likes my reporting enough to offer me a job covering races for them at Louisiana Downs and Oaklawn Park. At first I'm paid little and exercise horses at Louisiana Downs. Among my clients is J.J. Pletcher, Todd's father. I ride my last race there that summer. The horse, a bad actor no one else wants to ride, bolts in the first turn and trails the field. Seems fitting. As far as racing history goes, I'm destined to be more infamous than famous.

The closest I came to winning the Kentucky Derby was picking up my friend Ron Turcotte at the airport the day he won the race on eventual Triple Crown winner Secretariat. On Derby Day 1977, inside the Churchill

264

Downs jockeys' room, I kidded Jean Cruguet about being "overcooked," when I saw him in the whirlpool tub an hour before he won the race on another Triple Crown winner, Seattle Slew. The next year I watched 18-year-old Steve Cauthen grin and gab as he calmly played racehorse rummy with legend Bill Shoemaker the day "The "Kid" won the Derby aboard the next Triple Crown winner, Affirmed.

Yet being a jockey, even a minor one, was part of my destiny. Along with painful injuries and the realization that the profession I chose could kill or maim me on any given day, I daily swallowed the bitter pill of defeat. Along this dangerous road were brief stops where winning races flooded my soul with a buzz far greater than any drug. While I recall many struggles, I remember best what it feels like to win. To this day I still dream about a half ton of roaring muscle gliding along between my calves as if on wings, crossing a finish line in front.

Still, being part of racing history eluded me. Shortly after Hall of Fame Jockey Pat Day's retirement in 2005, I was with him at a Derby breakfast at Churchill Downs when he encountered Hall of Fame trainer D. Wayne Lukas. Together and separately they'd made racing history. Lukas chided Day that in retirement, he would become no more than one of racing's "asterisks." Day was one of the best jockeys ever, a volume, not a dot. Yet, in the storied history of racing that is what I was, an asterisk. Yet I ate, heaved, breathed and sweated horse racing for most of my adult life. The victories more than paid for the hard times. For me, an asterisk will do.

I often say the most significant thing about my career was that I outlived it. Perhaps my best known victory will be in a race I was paid to lose. Yet, I was exonerated. Debbie and I lived without having to fear a mob hit. Dawn and Derek did not have to grow up in a strange land. God had given us the miracle I'd prayed for while standing on the Tampa football field during a Billy Graham Crusade. It's never a good idea to make a conditional vow to God but even worse to renege on one. I've tried to keep my promise, even today.

Too bad, the miracle in Boston didn't change my lifestyle.

BYE BYE BACKSTRETCH

38: Hollywood Park, Inglewood California, Summer 1995

In a horse race, just as in a bullfight, there is a moment of truth. It's the moment the matador has danced his way as close to the edge as he dares. In that second, the matador knows he and not the bull is going to walk out of the arena. For a jockey, it's the same spit-into-the-face-of-caution crystallized second that you have overcome your fear, gone for that tiny hole on the rail and know you've won the race before you reach the finish line. As a matador turned groom, I am approaching that moment with Greta.

After Van Berg derided my lack of attention to her all-important hooves, I knew I had to either learn how to clean out her feet without getting kicked or end my job with the famous trainer. His mercy will extend only so far. If I don't have a job, my room will be taken, and the next step for me will be a Salvation Army program. The day after the Van Berg inspection, the blacksmith comes to shoe Greta. When she keeps trying to kick him while I hold her, he sends me to get a twitch. The instrument is a sturdy pole much like a straight axe handle with a short length of circular rope embedded in one end. The rope loop captures the tender top lip of the horse and the handler twists until the lip is secured. Grooms all say it

266

doesn't cause serious pain, and perhaps it doesn't, but it's certainly distracting enough to cause a horse to stand still.

Greta stands still long enough for the blacksmith to change her four shoes and trim the inside of the hooves or "frogs." For the next few days, I have a foreman twitch her morning and evening while I clean her feet. She seems to have calmed down and twitching her can't go on forever. One morning when there is no one to help and I have to clean Greta before I tack her, I decide it's time for our own personal moment of truth.

Tied to the back wall with a chain attached to her halter as normal, she seems docile, and I start from her more comfortable left side. I stand facing her rear and run my left hand down the side of her left front leg. She fails to raise her foot. I push her shoulder and at the same time put my left hand inside her leg and try to lift the hoof. She raises it. Using the hoof pick in my right hand, I quickly pick clean the hoof. I try the left or near side back foot, and she's accommodating. The time spent with the blacksmith and the twitch may have helped. I walk around her to the offside. With little help she raises the front hoof. Confident now, I raise the back hoof and have it in my hand. She jumps to the right.

Her rump sends me into the wall, crushing me. She jumps the other way. I collapse onto the straw, holding my side and moaning. Two workers appear in front of my stall, delicately walk in, lift me by my armpits and help me out. Once outside the stall, I sink to my knees, gasping for air. Ribs might be broken, but I'm breathing without pain. My helpers leave, and I sit in a chair in front of the stall and stare inside. She's calm again. Going back inside is like mounting a horse after it's thrown you. Not easy but in most cases necessary.

I get an exercise rider to hold her on a shank and stand on the side I'm working. I clean the missing back hoof without incident. That night I'm sore but realize it could have been worse. I'd been rubbing horses a few months, and after the races each day I put on my sweat clothes and run at least once around the outside rail of the deep 1 1/8-mile track. I've lost about 10 pounds and am down to about 138. It's a bit heavy to breeze horses but light enough to give them regular gallops. Van Berg knows I'm trying to get fit enough to gallop horses, and when I ask about working for him he tells me he has all the exercise riders he needs and reminds me I signed on a groom.

A few days later, I'm talking to Van Berg in his barn office when a block of a man walks in. He's wearing sunglasses beneath a shock of curly hair, brown safari shorts, sneakers and black socks. Jack introduces me to Mike Mitchell. I know the name. The "Michael Master," as he is known, is a master at claiming cheap horses and turning them into instant winners. He doesn't yet train the crème de la crème, but he wins a lot of races on the tough Southern California circuit. I shake his massive hand.

"I don't know how good a jockey he was, but he covered Alysheba during the Triple Crown and he didn't even know the horse when he saw him," Van Berg says. He tells of shipping the horse in secret to Louisiana Downs to run in the track's $1 million Super Derby a few months after the horse had won the Derby and Preakness. I'd gotten a call that the track was going to hold a press conference the following day. Suspicious, and wanting a story before the rest, I went to the barn area. Sure enough Van Berg was standing in the shed row of the barn housing horses shipping in for stakes races and turned when he saw me coming. I asked him, "Is Alysheba on the grounds, Jack? Here for the Super Derby?"

"You know I can't answer that. Why don't you just wait for the press conference like everyone else?"

"Then he's here?"

"Want another scoop, I guess? What did the one at Saratoga get you?"

"Points with my sports editor."

"But it wasn't true. He was tested. Nothing."

"I just wrote he was being investigated. That was true."

A long-headed colt popped his head out of the stall and reached for his back with bared teeth. Van Berg jumped out of the way. I moved with him. "So you're telling me Alysheba is not going to run in the Super Derby?"

Van Berg broke into peals of laughter. "You dummy. You cover the entire Triple Crown, and you don't recognize Alysheba."

I was only a little embarrassed. My story on Alysheba running in the Super Derby—which he wins—ran on the front page of the sports section the next morning. Took a little of the pizzazz out of the press conference. Oh well.

This day, when Van Berg tells the story to Mitchell, they both break up in belly-shaking laughter. Mike starts to go. "Look Mike," Van Berg says. "He's had a run of lousy luck. He's been rubbing horses for me, but he wants to start galloping."

I pipe up. "I don't want to leave until Mr. Jack finds somebody to replace me." At that, I see Jack grin. Mitchell looks me up and down, no doubt seeing I'm still pudgy and soft and near the weight limit for exercise riders. "Come on around when you get loose. I got a few you can get on."

In a week, Jack hires my replacement and I'm exercising horses for Mike Mitchell. True to his word, he hires me as a freelancer, paying $10 a head. But unlike other trainers I recruit—mostly small-timers with a few horses and unable to hire full-time riders—Mike only allows me to ride horses in his shed row. He's a born-again Christian and soon on Sunday after the track closes, I get dressed in my best and go to his church in nearby Redondo Beach. Oddly, it's a Foursquare Church, a denomination I will later join. I'm down to a few beers a day and only smoke a joint on my way to Pam's. Visits to the porn shops are weeks apart. Mike often talks about his faith, but he's my boss and I certainly can't open up.

I'm exercising six to 10 horses a day, galloping for Van Berg when needed and I even get on a few for Hall of Fame trainer Richard Mandella. I make enough money to get my car fixed, and I'm no longer stuck at the track 24 hours a day. Things are better, but I'm still looking for my ticket out.

*****

Pam O'Neill and I are jitterbugging to a 1960s band at the Taste of Irvine event in Orange Country near her home. It's Sunday afternoon, and we're at a fair that features sample foods from a bunch of swanky South

Coast restaurants. Pam has visited the White House several times and is a graduate of the famous Le Cordon Bleu culinary arts school in Paris and has a catering company, Le Cake, which sells cakes made from edible gold. I sometimes help her deliver her cakes and even dress up in a white tux shirt and cummerbund and work as a waiter at several of the events she caters. Visiting her is about intelligent conversation and spending the night on her plush sofa in front of a roaring gas fireplace. Her Orange County condo and world view are in a different galaxy than my barren tack room and constant talk about horses. Around her, I'll drink a glass of wine or two, but any kind of drugs is out of the question. But this sunny afternoon I read something in the woman's face who watches us dance that is as dangerous as the life I am desperately trying to outlive. I hate it that I'm attracted. But at least she's a woman.

She is short, buxom and with rich brown hair. I ask her to dance and she does a mean jitterbug, shaking and jiggling while she shoots a hand into the air for emphasis. We stop to pant and with enough enthusiasm to launch a spaceship, she tells me she is the daughter of a San Joaquin Valley farmer and owner and founder of a wellness company that sets up health fairs for corporations.

I introduce her to Pam, whose friendliness seems fake. I arrange to meet Kate for lunch near the track. We meet at a hotel where we have lunch and get a room. All in the middle of the day. We're far from being in love, but she's intelligent, energetic, laughs easily and often, and could sell encyclopedias to aborigines.

"You need a girlfriend like I need a raid by the IRS," Pam tells me later at her place after I give her the details. Pam's former husband now has a new wife and past relationships are a conversation staple.

"She's got to be better than Debra," I say. She lowers her eyebrows and shoots me a hard look. Debra, my second wife, had moved to the Los Angeles area, and we recently started to see each other. But our relationship is as twisted as ever. One day she stole my cell phone while I was visiting and called the company holding my car loan, which was two months overdue. On a following visit, they repossessed my car while I

270

watched. I called Pam, who came to pick me up. At this point, I have the car back, and I'm not even talking to Debra.

"I just want the insanity to end," I tell Pam. "Maybe one day I can have a healthy relationship."

"You just met this Kate woman, and you're talking relationship. What's healthy about that? You sleep with her the first time you go out, and you'll probably be living together in a month. And will it be real or just a ticket to get you out of living on the backstretch?"

All she says is true. But I am doing better. I'm going to church with Mike Mitchell, and I've cut back on the beer and grass. But there are still a few porn shop visits and 10-minute encounters. Though Pam and I have this unspoken vow to keep our relationship purely platonic, we've developed a deep affinity. I've shared with her some of my battle with same-sex attraction and even mentioned my sibling sexual trauma.

I fidget around on Pam's fluffy white couch and crack my knuckles. "So what's wrong with a little quid pro quo? It's not like she's hard to look at. And frankly, making out with her reminds me I'm still a man."

"You tried that with that woman in Houston, and you got addicted to crack."

"Kate's a businesswoman. Probably has a drink here and there and maybe does a little grass, but she's no addict. You know, when you live on the backstretch you're technically homeless. I'm tired of being homeless. If I couldn't come down here and have an intelligent conversation with you now and again, I'd be in my third psyche ward."

She sits beside me and looks over. Her eyes are glassed over with compassion.

"I'm getting better, Pam. I honestly am."

She gives me a sideways hug and pats my back like I'm one of her close girlfriends.

"You're not ready, Eddie, but you're going to do this anyway. I'm sorry, but I just think it will end badly."

A week later Kate visits me at the track, and I get her in the backstretch to watch as I gallop a horse around the swank Hollywood Park track. We meet later on the track kitchen's veranda overlooking the track, have breakfast and watch other horses gallop past. I learn she's a natural salesperson with a lot of business savvy. We talk about my being a writer, hosting TV shows and being a jockey.

"Riding races is like selling vacuum cleaners barn to barn," I say. "Jockeys all get paid the same rate. I've been selling myself all my life."

"Then come help sell my company," she says. "I truly believe it's on the verge of being franchised nationally. We can make a lot of money."

"The best part is I get to sleep with the boss," I say, grinning. She lives in a nice house in San Pedro, site of the Port of Los Angeles and a few blocks from the beach. It's tempting, but I'm reluctant. I want to get my own place, gallop horses and freelance for horse publications. At Criterion, I made a lot of money. But I was far from happy.

*****

We start going to the legitimate theater, taking walks on the beach, drinking wine and even smoking grass. Though fun-loving, she's a dedicated and highly aggressive businesswoman. If she's addicted to anything it's the art of the deal. She sells her business to everyone she meets, and if she could bottle her enthusiasm she'd be rich. A longtime divorcee, she has two grown girls and an Airedale, Bucky. Taking Bucky and Jack for walks on the hills overlooking the Pacific become some of the best times of my life.

Still, there is something spiritual about riding a half-ton Thoroughbred. I'm so heavy I rarely get to breeze a horse (allow them to go into a full run). But when I do, the same magic carpet ride I experienced in a race soothes my soul. Running Thoroughbreds don't seem to move on legs but a force that flows from deep inside their chest. More like gliding than running. As when I rode races, I'm living vicariously off the inbred majesty of Thoroughbreds, and like many in horse racing have allowed their nobility to stand before the heavens in place of my flawed humanity.

I'm getting on at least 10 horses each day at $10 each, seven days a week. Mitchell still confines me to jogging or walking horses around his shed row. My body is a fairly solid 140 pounds and I'm gaining a reputation

272

for restraining tough, runaway horses. One trainer I work for calls me "Maestro," and some of the Spanish-speaking exercise riders give me their highest compliment when they call me "Vaquero" (cowboy). I'm living out the words on a 1850s ad for pony express riders. "Wanted Skinny young wiry fellows, willing to risk life daily." The days I was a jockey were the days I never doubted my manhood. I want them back.

Yet I'm far from the 112 pounds of muscle I was as a jockey. Despite the compliments, I know my reaction time has slowed. My once polished moves aboard a racehorse are now graceless. Exercising Thoroughbreds is one of the world's most physically demanding, dangerous and depreciated jobs. Not one for the Sunday-afternoon rider or even the experienced rider looking for another thrill. I fall into the category of the latter.

I realize that many of the grooms at Hollywood Park are worse than I am. They are not as well trained as in the days when I rode. Then, most were experienced, loved their horses at least as much as their wives, were brave and had a genuine feel for the whimsy inside the minds of racehorses. They were safety conscious and took little for granted. Now trainers hire workers fresh from foreign farms or even city streets. Their only experience comes on a ranch with cow horses or a few weeks spent walking hots. For many, their best qualification is being a friend or relative of someone already working on the track. When I rode races, I don't remember seeing a horse brought to the saddling paddock with a lip chain, in which the chain part of the lead shank is stretched across a horse's upper lip for control. It was not only considered poor horsemanship but cruel. I wish those same persons who advocate making jockey whips less lethal would take a look at this practice. Overall, I am not saying there are not excellent grooms today. I just don't think there are as many.

One morning at Hollywood Park, I learn the hard way. It's early when I show up to ride several two-year-olds for a small-time trainer. It's early summer and most of the "babies" have experience. Still, some have recently come from farms and know little. Normally with green horses, the groom will put a rider aboard inside the stall with a shank hooked to the bridle. In the confines of a stall, the groom will lead the youngster in tight circles, making it far harder to buck off the rider. But outside in the shed row, the edge goes to the horse. This morning, a groom leads a green two-year-old out of the stall, and I take it for granted that the horse is at least green-broken, meaning he's been ridden enough to have some notion of accepting the rider. The groom has no shank attached to the horse, something I should have questioned. But freelancers are paid by the mount and what time I can spend teaching a young horse is better spent outside the barn. I move to the left side while he holds the bridle rein with his left hand and lifts me aboard.

The second I put my weight on his back, the colt rears and lunges. The groom makes no effort to help me control the horse but instead lets go of the bridle rein. My feet aren't in the irons. I barely have both reins in my hands and the colt races pell-mell down the shed row, bucking like a bronc. Were my feet in the irons and I had a good grip on the reins, I might have lifted his head enough to control the bucking. Still, for a few seconds, I think I can stay aboard. At the corner, the colt ducks left, sending me flying. I land on the flat of my back. Air gushes from my lungs. I can't breathe. I move my legs. They're fine. But when I regain my breath and try to roll to my side, pain lights up my chest like a blowtorch. I'd broken ribs before. I know what it feels like.

Workers scramble to catch the loose horse and help me to my feet. I wave them off and sit on my rear, holding my chest with crossed arms. Within five minutes, I'm in an ambulance and on my way just down the street to Centinela Hospital.

I knew when I had broken every one of many bones while riding. By the time my jockey career ended, I had the procedure down. During a race, the ambulance followed the field. Have a serious spill and I was swept up and inside an ambulance before I could say "pain medication." But unless the injury was life-threatening, paramedics would haul me to a doctor waiting in a grandstand office. That was okay. Broken bones generally numb the surrounding area, and it took about 20 minutes for the real pain to begin. At the doctor's office, I'd peel my silks from one side of my body and extend my arm, ready for the standard shot of Demerol. Nearly always I got it. Broken ribs hurt from the start.

"Look, Doc," I say to the approaching physician inside the ER. "I been in as many of these places as you. I broke a couple of ribs, and I don't need to sit in an X-ray room with my chest screaming bloody murder while everybody figures that out."

Young, dark and skeptical, he takes a step back and stares at me. Call me a pansy if you like, but I never get used to breaking my bones. I press my case. "I'm hurting, and I'm going to be hurting worse in a few minutes. Can you give me a little something?"

He looks at my chart and smiles. "We have to examine you before we can prescribe medication."

Prescribe sounds far too complicated. "Look, a couple of times I waited outside ER X-Ray rooms long enough to grow this beard I got."

"I'm sorry, Mr. Donnally."

And wait I do. I sit in a wheelchair inside the ER as doctors and patients move in and out, all seeming to ignore me. My chest feels like a semi rolled over it. I should have faked passing out or made myself throw up. A tech finally wheels me into the X-ray room, and when I crawl on the cold table I wince at the pain. Another hour later, the doctors confirm what I've known all along: broken ribs, three of them in fact. He asks if someone I know can pick me up and I say yes, because if I say no his Demerol will not make it into my arm. He tells me to stay off horses for at least six weeks, gives me a prescription, puts my arm in a sling, and I finally get the shot.

I sit there waiting for the pain to ease before I call a cab. Because trainers often don't list freelance exercise riders as employees on the barn list they submit to track authorities, I'm not about to get workers' compensation insurance. I'm not going to get paid for weeks, and I may have to fight the trainer to keep from paying my own ambulance and hospital bills.

I get back to the track, worried that I hurt too much to take Jack for his noon walk. I hate myself already for what I'm about to do. I hobble to the bank of outside phones, shove in four quarters and dial the number. Kate answers on the third ring. "There you are," I tell her cheerfully. "Think you can come pick me up? I broke some ribs."

LIFE AS A SPORTSWRITER

HANGING WITH THE HEAVIES

39: Hollywood Park, Inglewood California, November 9, 1984

I walk around a corner inside Hollywood Park's new Cary Grant Pavilion, built next to the track's grandstand for the inaugural Breeders' Cup. I can't keep from ogling the chandeliers, buffet with lobster tails and an ice sculpture depicting the trophies the races' winners will receive. I see a woman in the center of a small crowd. It's Elizabeth Taylor. I manage to keep walking.

It's Friday night, and I've filed my story for Saturday's edition of *The Dallas Morning News*. Tomorrow is the first Breeders' Cup, seven championship races that include the Classic, the world's first $3 million horse race. It's time to party. Marge Everett, the track's head executive, knows how to throw a party. While interviewing celebrity horse owners is nothing new, I've already seen Cary Grant and Frank Sinatra, and with Liz Taylor, I'm becoming star struck. But it goes with the territory. Jack Warner of the Warner Brothers film corporation was the track's original board chairman, and Hollywood is a 20-minute limo ride.

I'm amazed that the year-end series of ultra-rich races on a single day is going to happen. First proposed by dog food magnate and Thoroughbred breeder John Gaines, the series is designed to define the voting for year-end champions and Horse of the Year, the latter an honor when won by a male adds millions in stud fees. The concept makes a lot of sense, and like a lot of horse racing writers, I love it. However, the self-made magnate Gaines makes nearly all in the industry mad with his my-way-or-the-highway attitude. But D.G Van Clief breeds his racehorses in Virginia, far away from the blue-blooded brood of Lexington, Kentucky where Gaines is a ranking member. He manages to take the helm, bringing peace and a workable plan.

A few months later, I'll return to Hollywood and the Century City Plaza to pick up my own Eclipse Award for outstanding newspaper feature writing, but this night I'm hungry for a story that will put me in a league with world's best-known racing writers, including Andy Beyer of the *Washington Post* and Steven Crist of *The New York Times*. By the end of the $3 million Classic tomorrow, the series centerpiece, I'll either be a hero or a hick. That afternoon, I ventured to the barn and saw up close a medium-sized four-year-old Wild Again. Because owner Bill Allen and partners Terry Beal and Ron Volkman have strong Texas ties, an editor requested a story on the morning-line rank outsider.

Vincent Timphony, the horse's trainer, is a former New Orleans nightclub and restaurant owner and serious gambler. He's interesting, but the field looks like a Who's Who of horse racing with the best from the East and the West competing for a record purse, and his horse looks way overmatched. In his last race, Wild Again finished third on the turf course in an $18,000 allowance race at a track in Northern California. I stood outside the shed row of one of the track's giant concrete barns and watched as a groom led in large circles a horse wearing a pink and black blanket that read "Black Chip Stables." Listed as an official dark bay, the horse looks black to me.

"So the owners put up $360,000 to get this horse in a race where he's the longest priced horse in the field," I note.

"It was worth every penny, just wait and see." Timphony's dark Italian eyes stare me down and his voice is high-pitched and intense, belonging on a carnival barker outside a girlie show. Unlike most of the other trainers in the race, Timphony, while Runyonesque, is known in the business as "a nickel and dimer," surviving mostly on claimers. But he also has a reputation for cashing large bets on his horses.

"So what happened? You shipped him to Bay Meadows his last out and he was beaten in an allowance race."

"He didn't like that kind of turf. Don't worry, he'll get the money tomorrow."

I was writing in my skinny notebook and trying not to sound sarcastic. "So you're saying this horse will win the Classic?"

"Look," he says. "I'm telling you this horse is something special. I think he's the best horse in the country right now. They won't beat him tomorrow."

I finished writing and looked up, puzzled. Wild Again was not nominated earlier at a much smaller fee, and most people think the small fortune the owners are now paying has more to do with ego than the horse's ability. And if they're planning to cash a colossal bet, why tell a reporter for a paper read by a million people?

"Then I'll quote you in the paper and pick him on top in my selections?"

"You better do more than that. You better get down yourself." He gave me a wink and a nod, and I thought this guy is either a genius or totally nuts. But I wrote a story about Wild Again, quote Timphony about his outlandish prediction and picked him on top in my selections in the paper. I finished with a short paragraph explaining my rationale, which isn't terribly rational.

At this point, I'd built a reputation as a pretty fair handicapper, and I don't want to look stupid. The day I picked in the *Morning News* 10 winners on an 11-race card, I picked a pick six bet that paid over $100,000 but I had not bet a cent on any of my selections. Being a former jockey, I know nearly all riders have considerable skills and pay little attention to riders. After I made my selections that day, I realized I'd picked jockey Ricky Frazier to win seven races, a feat accomplished only a few times in racing history. Frazier won seven.

I held pre-race handicapping seminars where bettors paid to attend and sold tapes on "trip handicapping," telling bettors what to look for in the actual running of past races, something I do value as a former jockey. But unlike my Oaklawn Park handicapping nemesis, Randy Moss, who spent 12-hour days handicapping, I can look at a set of past performances for 10 minutes and start to space out. Still, I am batting nearly 38 percent and my boss at the *Morning News* is convinced that picking winners sells more papers than writing powerful features. At the party, I eat enough lobster tails to grow claws, drink a lot of free Crown Royal and at one point see Timphony huddling with Sinatra.

The next day in the press box high above the track, my colleagues and I watch through thick windows at the manicured track below as some 67,000 turn out while an estimated 50 million watch on TV. The event is part of horse racing history, and I am part of the event.

"Who you like in the Classic?" another writer asks me.

"Wild Again. I put him on top in my selections."

"You gone crazy? You look at the race? "

I start to give my rationale, but shake it off and say, "The trainer told me he'd win."

"What else is he going to say? He talked his owners into putting up a fortune to get in the race. And that jockey of his, Pat Day, is telling everybody he just got off cocaine. Claims he's a Christian now. I think they both spent too much time on Bourbon Street if you know what I mean."

"That's why they run races. The winner is the one who gets to the finish line first. Not the one everybody picks. Talk to me after the race. You'll probably want to borrow some gas money."

I talk a good game, but I also know champion Slew o' Gold has won his last three, all prestigious Grade 1 stakes races in New York. The Jack

Van Berg-trained Gate Dancer won the $500,000 Super Derby in track-record time and won the Preakness, the middle jewel of the Triple Crown. Another horse, Precisionist, is one of the best milers ever. I go down and watch Wild Again as he walks into the saddling paddock. The just-retired John Henry, a gelding and two-time Horse of the Year who had earned a then-record $6.6 million, passes him while being led the opposite way. Wild Again flashes haughty black eyes at one of the greatest horses ever. It's time to go bet.

Back inside the press box I watch the race. Going into the first turn Wild Again is between two horses, much closer to the lead than I expect. The pace is far too fast as they reel off the first quarter in 22 3/5 seconds. "Take him back Pat," I say to myself beneath my 10-power binoculars. I've known Day for 12 years and rode with him during his early days at Rockingham Park. Randy Moss once showed me the *Daily Racing Form* charts where I beat him in three photos finishes in the same day. That looked like another of God's miracles. If we were both pro baseball players, he'd be Yogi Berra and I'd be Bob Uecker.

Day is the only jockey I personally saw who I thought had better hands than Bill Shoemaker. Of all the talents celebrated jockeys have, none is more valuable or rarer. Day is a one-man horse tranquilizer. If you took him to a zoo, the animals would fall asleep. His soft hands and calm demeanor combined with whatever else it involves—and God and not me knows what that is—has the capacity to help horses relax in a race's early stages like no one else I'd seen. Any animal only has so much energy. Saving as much of it as possible and using it at the exact time it will be the most useful is what separates the good from the great. But now that seems to have been lost. He's ridden major races before, but this was the first $3 million race in history. Maybe he's lost his poise.

"Slow him down, Pat," I coach. He's not listening. He even takes the lead, and I glance up at the tote board and cringe. The half mile is 45 3/5. Even worse, the first six furlongs go in 1:10 3/5 seconds, only 2/5 of a second slower than Ellio's winning time in the six furlong $1 million

Breeders' Cup Sprint a few races earlier. But at least he's shaken off Precisionist and is alone.

"Give him a breather, Pat. Get him to relax." In the final turn with three-eighths of a mile left, Slew o' Gold, the heavy favorite and unlike Wild Again from the gild-edged side of the tracks, approaches from the outside under jockey Angel Cordero Jr.

"He's done," I mutter. Wild Again has to be cooked, well done. Slew o' Gold reaches him but stalls. Pat has yet to draw his whip. They are in the stretch and still lead by a long neck. There's a little grit left in his gristle after all. I see a set of giant white earmuffs. Gate Dancer is making a powerful run on the outside under Laffit Pincay. Gate Dancer is famous for trying to run into horses as he passes them. Cordero aboard Slew o' Gold is famous for the same reason. Van Berg has fitted Gate Dancer with a set of racing earmuffs, based on the assumption that the colt hears the crowd's roar in deep stretch, making him constantly veer to the inside. Veer or not, Gate Dancer has the kind of momentum no horse with Wild Again's early fractions can possibly withstand. Worse, chasing him down are a jockey, Cordero, and a horse, Gate Dancer, known for bumping. This won't be pretty. Wild Again is certain to fold and finish third.

An eighth mile from the wire he still clings to a neck lead over Gate Dancer. Slew o' Gold between them is a half-length back. I see bumping. It's considered poor form to root in the press box but I scream. "Hang on! Hang on! Hang baby, hang."

He does. Pat Day is a genius. At the finish line, Wild Again's head and fiery eyes are in front. I rip out my reporter's note pad and run downstairs to the winner's circle. The inquiry sign lights the tote board. The stewards are looking at the bumpy stretch run. Wild Again could be disqualified. I stand in the winner's circle and watch the first three finishers, still on the track, walk in circles, all wanting to come in. After what seems like an eternity, actually nine minutes, Gate Dancer is disqualified from second to third, and the winner remains Wild Again. He pays $64.60 for a $2 bet.

I stand outside the winner's circle as Wild Again and Day are led in. In a moment I will never forget and one captured in a famous photo, Pat Day sits on the horse's back in his pink and black silks, raises his helmet toward the sky, looks to heaven and thanks God.

So do I. Back in the press box I cash my some $3,500 in winnings, wishing like all gamblers I'd bet more. While no statistics are kept on monster bets, it soon becomes racing lore that Timphony and the colt's owners cashed the biggest wager in horse racing history. Allegedly, they not only broke bookmakers across the nation, the trio had won so much at Hollywood Park that instead of being paid at the cashier windows, they were taken to the money room where they put towering stacks of $100 bills in large purses purposely brought by their wives. This of course doesn't include the $1.8 million purse that goes to the winner.

After interviewing Timphony, the owners and Day inside the press room, I go back upstairs and sit down to write the story. Of course, it will be highlighted on the Sunday edition front page and run in the upper left-hand corner, the sweet spot of the sports section. I get a call from my sports desk editor. He reminds me to highlight the two Texas owners. "Oh, I see you picked the winner. Do a sidebar on how that happened."

My doubting colleague comes over, grinning. "Got an extra $20 for bus fare home? The bettors in Dallas are going to think you walk on water and talk to God."

The former I never did. The latter I should have started sooner.

GOODBYE, OLD FRIEND

40: Methodist Hospital, Arcadia California, December 9, 2010

"That was some race," I say to Vince Timphony. Lying propped up in a hospital bed, he uses a pudgy hand to remove the oxygen mask covering his face. His mouth curves into a smile. I sink into a bedside chair. "You made me a hero with the bettors in Texas."

Timphony, 74, trained the nearly black stallion Wild Again to win the first Breeders' Cup Classic, a 31 to one outsider in the world's first $3 million race. After a wild stretch run in which he and two head-to-head horses slugged it out in the stretch, he won by a nose and survived a steward's inquiry. I had picked him on top in my selections in *The Dallas Morning News*, quoted Timphony before the race that the horse would win and cashed a $3,500 bet.

But going on three decades later, I'm a chaplain at Methodist Hospital across the street from Santa Anita, training to help patients and their families deal with spiritual issues surrounding illness, injury and death. When I came in to start a Sunday 24-hour on-call shift, I spotted Timphony's name on the patient census. "Lord," I said to myself, "you do have a sense of humor."

"Yeah, he was some horse," Vincent says in a Southern drawl that blends Italian and Cajun. "Pat Day said every time he was bumped he would grunt and dig in again. He might have been the gamest racehorse that ever lived. He wouldn't give up."

"Just like you," I say.

"No, I ain't giving up nothing. I want to get a motor home, park it at Solana Beach beside Del Mar (near San Diego). Get well. I don't want no more old folks homes. Last one I was in I walked out. I got some kind of pulmonary thing. When I get out of here, I'm going to have to have a full-time caretaker."

I'd seen Vince several times in recent years. He'd trained a small string of horses based at Santa Anita, and he spent time during morning training hours at the track's famous Clockers' Corner, where race fans gathered to drink coffee, eat "Bob Baffert" egg sandwiches and watch horses train in front of the San Gabriel Mountains. We'd sat down to breakfast there a couple of times and talked. Wild Again had gone on to become one of the nation's top sires for nearly two decades, producing scores of stakes race winners and putting millions into the pockets of his owners. Those mornings when I gently steered the conversation to spiritual matters Vincent talked about God in the abstract. Yet on his hospital admitting information, he'd listed Catholic as his faith tradition, something that showed up on my patient census.

"So having a full-time caretaker, what's that going to be like for you?"

"You know I love women, always have. There's one girl who said she'd come help me. But that's not something I want. Scarlet and I have been divorced for a while, and I been living with my friend, Tom."

"You've been sick for a while now, huh?"

"They say my heart's good, but my breathing just keeps getting worse. Can't hardly breathe now."

"Sounds scary."

"If I go, I go. I got the big man upstairs on my side."

I sit back a bit. A hospital chaplain's job is to learn what spiritual resources patients have and help them use those to deal with their illness.

I'm not to impose my religion but walk with patients down their path. I'm beginning to discover that my best witness may be what I do and not what I say.

"You mean God?"

"I been going to Mass a lot lately. My friend Tom takes me."

I allow silence to linger in hopes he'll continue. This is Vince Timphony. Hard partier. One of his galas featured hundreds of lit candles inserted into avocados floating in a seaside swimming pool. Here is the man who may have cashed the biggest bet in horse racing history in the world's richest race at the time. A man better known for setting up horses to win ordinary races at generous odds than winning major races at any odds. But in his heyday, a variety of race trackers would make their way up the hill to Vincent's Santa Anita barn in the very back of the backstretch and hit on Vince. There might have been a groom who needed a loan to make it home to a dead father's grave, an exercise rider who had to pay a fine to stay out of jail or a trainer taking up a collection to send a worker's body back to Mexico. Vince would whip out his roll and divvy up. And with a past like mine, who am I to judge anyone?

"So is your faith helping you deal with this?"

"Oh sure. I always went to mass back in New Orleans when I was a kid and I started going again. Father, Son and Holy Spirit—know about them all. "

"God's trifecta."

"That little Bible you got in your hand. Read me that part about going to heaven."

"I will, but I know some by heart. Like John 3:16: 'For God so loved the world that He gave His only begotten Son that whosoever believes in Him should not perish but have everlasting life.'" I stop and look into his pale face beneath a shock of coal black hair the same color of Wild Again. I fight back thoughts that perhaps Vince, a master of odds, is just hedging his bet. "What do you think, Vincent?"

"I believe in Jesus, the verse I mean, that's true."

I say a prayer for his healing, not minding that he sees my eyes glass over. "You got your ticket to heaven," I say. "They got horses up there, you know."

"Oh yeah."

I leaf through my pocket Bible and find Revelation 19. "Now I saw heaven opened and behold, a white horse. And He who sat on him was called 'Faithful and True.' Vince, that's Jesus and look here, 'He was clothed with a robe dipped in blood, and His name is called 'The Word of God.' And the armies in heaven—I believe that's us who know Jesus—'clothed in linen white and clean, followed Him on white horses.' Vince, that's when Jesus comes back to earth for the final battle and to set things right. Isn't that something? We get to follow Jesus back to earth on white stallions."

Vince looks at me, a twinkle in his eye. "Think they got a black one up there?"

*****

I visit Vince a few days later, and he's worse. We talk about his family, and he tells me about his young son, a college student and track star. "I'm training him," he says proudly. I read Vince passages from the Bible and pray for healing and peace. Mainly I just listen as he talks about his family, his former wife, Scarlet, and his life in racing. I call Pat Day in Kentucky, and the two spend time over the phone talking and praying.

Vince has a stroke and is moved to Cardiac Critical Care. Early Saturday evening, six days after admittance, I'm called from shopping to the hospital. Gathered at his bedside are Scarlet, his former wife of 24 years, his sister and brother, his two sons and his friend Tom. Vince is sedated and on a ventilator that helps him breathe. There is a breathing tube down his throat, IV needles in his arms and an array of monitors attached to sensors all over his body. All to measure a life that seems to be slipping away. The day's assigned chaplain is already there. I call her aside, and she tells me that acting on Vince's wishes in an advance directive he has signed, he will be "extubated," or have the breathing tube removed. Some time ago, Vince had decided to not live his life dependent on machines.

I excuse myself and move beside Vince's head. The previous day he was having problems breathing but was lucid and we'd spent an hour together. He talked about racing and playing in high stakes Gin Rummy tournaments in Vegas. He'd told me he had Frank Sinatra bet on Wild Again in the Breeders' Cup Classic, and talked of carrying jumbo bags of money from the Hollywood Park money room, a room that oddly became my office when I worked for RTCA. He knew he would likely never be well enough to live in that motor home by the sea, and he hated the thought of being in what he called "an old folks home." He'd talked of past wounds, including one by Bill Allen, one of Wild Again's owners who had died a few years earlier. "It's probably time for me to check out, and I don't plan to leave earth pissed at anybody," he said. "But I guess God won't be mad at me if I'm damned glad I outlived him."

Inside the Critical Care Unit, the family looks at me, and I take a deep breath and look around, knowing I'm expected to officiate here. Part of what I do is give people undergoing the trauma of seeing someone they love die the opportunity to express their feelings and hopefully help them start down that long shadowy road called grief. Vince looks amazingly peaceful, and for a time I say nothing. There are times silence says far more than I can and gives room for God to be God. To be involved in such moments is a reason I sought hospice and hospital chaplaincy. It requires more education and training than being a church pastor for most denominations. Yet the intimacy, something I missed much of my life, becomes a sacred place.

I know words are expected, and my heart swells with gratitude that I have the opportunity to frame an event this significant with the spirituality it deserves. I also know Vince is a friend and being his chaplain will take its toll.

"My heart goes out to everyone here, and I like all of you wish it were different. I do know that Vincent knows Christ as Savior and that in his faith tradition that means he will pass through a door and into heaven. In the Bible, angels came to escort Lazarus home, and I think they'll come help Vince. But I know there's going to be a giant hole left in the heart of everyone here. I believe that while he can't respond, he can hear you. So I encourage you to let him know you're going to miss him."

There is always the question of whether to pray for healing or for peace. Sometimes family members hang on to hope to the end while others have accepted the pending event. Part of what I do is to help prepare them for the death of someone they love. I pray for healing, for God does perform miracles—he performed several for me—but I also believe that in some cases death is the ultimate healing. I also pray for peace for Vince and all who know and love him. I recite verses that assure salvation, noting the Lord said He'll never leave us or forsake us. I end and read Ecclesiastes three, one of the Bible's most poetic chapters: "To everything there is a season, a time for every purpose under heaven." At its end, I stop. I'm crying. Chaplains aren't supposed to cry, I tell myself. Yet I know there will be other moments when I'll do the same.

I step back, clear my throat and look away to wipe tears from my eyes. Will others come forward to say their goodbyes? Several move closer, but no one says a word. Scarlet walks forward and stands close. She was 16 and singing in a New Orleans bar when Vince walked in. He said upon first glance he'd rolled out wads of "Grants" to give to her mother in an effort to impress her, something Scarlet maintained never happened. They were inseparable for over two decades. In a voice laced with pain and melancholy, she sings, "Amazing grace, how sweet the sound that saved a wretch like me." All join in.

During the next three days, I spend time with her, his large family and many friends. At times, the CCU waiting room looks like the Santa Anita track kitchen. I request a priest who comes and provides the Sacrament of the Sick, an anointing that in the Catholic tradition imparts God's absolution and forgiveness. I also spend time alone with Vince, offering words of faith, affirmation and prayer. I believe the Bible teaches that until death, a person's spirit is intact, and a person's spirit is present even in comatose persons.

He is moved to a private room. Family and his best friend take turns being with him. But Vince, for all his love of parties and people apparently chose to "check out" on his own. Alone, on a sunny Southern California morning at 7:10 a.m., Vince left for heaven.

Wild Again passed on his courage and talent to his sons and daughters, becoming a top sire. He died in Kentucky two years earlier. A race tracker all his life, Vincent was born just outside the back gate of New Orleans' Fair Grounds racetrack. He died across the street from Santa Anita. And he died at a time when the track was filled with training racehorses. Some wondered why he died alone early in the morning. I like to think it was time to go get the big horse to the track up in heaven.

LOW DOWN ON THE DOWN LOW

41: San Pedro California, Fall 1996

I sit my backpack on the floor and walk to the back of the small house where Kate and I live and look in the bedroom drawer where I keep my marijuana. It isn't there. A heat crosses my forehead like a hot rag. I'd had the same feeling an hour earlier, and I fought to keep from exploding again.

We'd taken Jack and her Airedale, Bucky, for a walk on a deserted beach. We usually went to the enclosed dog park overlooking Point Fermin and the Pacific but today had gone to a beach that allowed dogs. Jack ran off close to a busy road and I'd spent 30 minutes chasing him down. I knew it was not only counterproductive but cruel to call a dog to you and then punish him. But rage prevailed, and I did just that. After hooking him to the horse lead I used to walk him, I used the leather end to hit him several times.

Now I feel terrible. Kate screamed at me and a couple walking by heard it. I pushed her. That was worse than hitting Jack.

In many ways, we're doing well. Her business is successful. I'd written her promotional materials, helped find clients and set up and helped her company manage several score health fairs inside corporations. We're going to a Christian Science Church, and we've had fantastic times vacationing at Yelapa, a tiny village south of Puerto Vallarta on the Mexican coast. But I'm still on the down-low and can't totally stop.

When I'd moved in the previous year, I'd gotten an AIDS test and a doctor had restarted my Lithium and given me Paxil, a drug that mostly left me impotent. Marijuana seems to calm me and, I think, keeps me from drinking whiskey. Instead, I drink a beer or two each day.

As before, the medication eliminates those moments of manic euphoria when I am king of the world one second and crashing into depression the next. I can't stop the encounters, something that resembles manic depression. There is an intense self-gratifying thrill followed by self-loathing and guilt. Guilt or regret for individual actions has morphed into a deeper shame. It is more than the actions I hate. It is what I've become. I'm a compulsive sex addict; a bisexual. I believe God hates what I'm doing but impulses control me.

Self-hate seethes inside me, and if I don't hurt myself to absolve the guilt, I hurt others. That makes me feel pain, the twisted absolution of self-flagellation that absolves my guilt. Feeling terrible is what I deserve. Kate in many ways is good to me. I'm happy to stand in the background and watch her exuberance and people skills charm all she meets. I hate myself for what I am doing to her. I am in a cycle that is a circle with no end.

I often walk the dogs alone in a section of Fermin Point closed to the public because of earthquake damage. I stand at the edge and stare at the sharp rocks on the shore 150 feet below. I heard that a woman committed suicide in the same spot, and some days I'd stand there, trying to capture her mind and understand what it will be like to take one step into oblivion.

I walk into the kitchen, grab two Buds, sit at the table and drink both within five minutes. Kate drove back with me but had walked off with Bucky once we parked in front of the house. She had my marijuana. She sometimes smoked with me, but usually not. Lately, she says it's making me worse.

I get up and mix Jack a hot dinner with real bacon grease and start for the backyard. As I walk, I fight off tears, noting that I'm having a lot of them lately. I remember Dandy the Doberman who'd lived with my first wife, Debbie when the kids were very young. I had a vet trim his ears, but only one stood. I spent hours trying to get it to stand, even having more surgery to have a plastic strip implanted. I stroked the ear for hours at a time only to have it stand for a few seconds. It was useless. He looked odd, and there was nothing I could do.

But he was intelligent and friendly, and he'd let Dawn, then three, ride him across the living room as if he were a horse. During our nomadic life, we'd just moved to New Orleans, where I would ride for a few months before going to Oaklawn Park in Arkansas. We'd spent all day moving into an apartment in Metairie. We'd kept our tiny Poodle, Yo Yo with us, but we'd tied Dandy and our Border Collie, Buddy, at the barn of a trainer I knew at nearby Jefferson Downs. Finding an apartment for two months with a child and three dogs was never easy.

I'd taken a large hot meal to the dogs at the track and Dandy had practically inhaled his food and lay down and rolled. He got up, eyes widened in pain and panic. He ran off and wouldn't come back. Using a flashlight, I hunted nearly all night. The next morning I found him beside one of the nearby canals. He was dead, his tongue extended, a look of terror still in his eyes. Dismayed and filled with guilt, I hauled his body to the LSU vet school in Baton Rouge, where a necropsy revealed he died of a gastric torsion, a malady that sometimes occurs in large-chested animals such as Dobermans and Thoroughbreds. When Dandy rolled, his full stomach hadn't rolled with him and instead twisted at the top and bottom. He had died an excruciating death. Now the memory comes flooding back.

In the backyard, I put down the full bowl and Jack jogs to it, looking up at me with round, innocent eyes. I sink to my knees, hug him and allow him to lick my face. My eyes fill with tears. I love him. He was my only companion in that lonely Hollywood Park tack room. Why had I hurt him? What in God's name have I become?

I sit at the kitchen table alone in the dark, drinking another three or four beers. Kate finally comes in with Bucky. It's always my chore to feed the dogs, so I get up and start making Bucky his dinner. I ask her where she's been, and she says she's been sitting in her friend's car talking. The friend is a male, much younger than I.

"Is that all that happened?" I ask. "Given your raging hormones, I doubt it."

She sits opposite me, and I notice that the woman who could bottle and sell her effervescence looks worn and haggard. "He's a friend and I need one now. We mostly talked about you."

I put dry food in Bucky's dish and pour in hot water and bacon grease. "Any conclusions?"

"He said you think you're horse dung and everyone else is, too."

"Is that because I got mad at everyone during Thanksgiving dinner last week?"

"You know you overreacted. You decided to take the dogs for a walk at the last minute. We waited a long time before we started without you."

I'd made a scene, telling off a large group of her friends and family. I later apologized to Kate, but all had experienced my anger and it had ruined what should have been a happy day. "This friend, he like your shrink or something?"

"Just a friend. But come to think about it, why not try to see somebody? I'll pay for it."

"You pay for everything anyway. It's your company, your house, your car. You even pick out and buy my clothes."

"I pay you a salary. You've done a good job. We can afford a psychiatrist."

"I've been to a few. All they do is prescribe medication. This stuff I take, I'm tired of it."

With Lithium, I had to go get my blood tested once every two or three months because high levels could cause everything from tremors to blindness. The Paxil made me borderline impotent though my drive was far from eliminated.

I pour hot water on Bucky's food, take it to him and quickly return. I walk over to her chair and hold out a hand. "Look at my hand for God's sake. It's shaking like I have palsy. The Lithium is going to kill me."

"You have to stop drinking. First it was one or two beers, now it's a six-pack every day. And I found an empty fifth of Jim Beam in your drawer. That's making you shake. And you beat Jack tonight and then you pushed me. Eddie, you need some help."

"You drink, too."

"Not every day. Not like you."

"You found the whiskey. What about my pot? You took my grass. Where is it?"

She looks at me a long time, and I can tell she's trying to make up her mind. Usually marijuana cools me out, but we had both smoked some a couple of nights ago and gotten into an argument. About what I couldn't remember.

I glance at the oversized leather purse she's holding in her lap. "You think you're better than me, don't you? I'm just somebody you picked up on the backside of a racetrack. A racetrack bum you brought home and now you own."

I know my voice is rising, but I don't care. "You don't own me, Kate. You'll never own me. Now give me my *#**@&& grass."

I grab for her purse, but she springs from the chair and runs out the kitchen side door, yelling back at me, "Stop it. You're crazy."

I hate the word "crazy," and she knows it. I race after her, stumbling and falling on the cement alcove just beyond the screen door. Suddenly she's back in the kitchen, latching the door with a tiny clasp. She stands there holding the purse, looking defiant.

"I'm moving out," I say. "But first I want my grass. I bought it, and I want it now."

Tears form at the corners of her eyes, something I never expected. Kate is a tough woman, and it's the first time I've seen her cry. "I got to get away from you," I say. "This isn't working."

"A few weeks ago, we were talking about marriage. You told me you loved me for the very first time. Something I said to you every day." Tears run down past the bridge of her nose, and she sniffs loudly.

"You're a fool," I yell. "You thought you could buy me like a new car. Well I'm not for sale, Mommy Dearest."

"You're a good man in a lot of ways. You're just sick. Too sick to even know it." She takes the plastic baggie from her purse, drops it on the floor and walks to our bedroom. The door locks.

I find half of a cinder block, throw it through the screen, unlatch the clasp and scoop up the bag. I don't even feel like smoking. I think of the liquor store down the street, put the bag in my pocket and walk out the front door. I look at my watch, noting I have 10 minutes to make it before the store closes. As I go through the front yard gate, Jack and Bucky stare at my back.

Two Weeks Later

It's dark, but there is moon to light the way as I pass the "No Trespassing" sign. I squint to see each block of upturned concrete before I jump or crawl forward. I'm in a section of San Pedro's Fermin Park that is closed and fenced after it had been ravaged either by an earthquake or seacoast eroding into the sea or both. Its road is reduced to slabs of concrete projecting into the air and others falling away to spaces below. Used by hiding druggies, secret lovers and the homeless, it's a hostile place. At night it's downright dangerous. But what do I care? I've come here to die.

Drunk and unsteady, I took Jack from Kate's nearby backyard a few blocks away. Why, I pause to consider, I don't know. He was with me during a hundred lonely nights in my Hollywood Park tack room. Taking care of him and Bucky for the past two years has given me a purpose outside myself. I just want him with me.

296

It's been two weeks since I moved into a tiny studio apartment two blocks from Kate's house. I'd binged on whiskey and same-sex encounters.

I've never called Kate, and she's never called me. Apparently, she's moved on. She seemed casual about the breakup, treating me like an outfit she wore for a while and then donated to Goodwill. I never told Kate about my secret activities, but I knew she suspected and had insisted on an HIV test when I moved in. How long could I go before I came up positive? I was too proud to talk to Pam, who'd been right about my inability to maintain a relationship.

I stand near the edge and look up at clouds moving across the pale moon, turning the cold Pacific below me into shifting shades of blue-black. I can't make out the beach's jutting black rocks, but I see flashes of white brine and hear the waves roar. My hands tremble, worse than ever. It's been two weeks since I stopped taking Lithium and Paxil, and I am drinking nearly a fifth of Jim Beam each day. I had one contact with a man I found in a magazine who came to my place. I was drunk, nothing happened, and it ended with my yelling at him to leave. The previous night I found myself walking from the city's Cabrillo Beach with no memory of walking there. The old exhilaration returned and I've been awake for over two days. Booze brings me down, but each time I drink I sink a little lower, inch a little farther into that sadly familiar tunnel. Two psyche wards were enough.

It's been eight years since my divorce, and this same-sex attraction took over my life and started its downward spiral. I had washed down 36 Xanax with a pint of Crown Royal and woke up to see a pump suck green bile from my stomach. My life since has been a circle, moving from Louisiana to Dallas to Laguna Beach to Houston and now back to the Los Angeles area. I've moved from my white brick house in Bossier City to a cinder-block room at Hollywood Park. I can run, but I can't hide … from myself. I've been locked up in two psyche wards and become an alcoholic and addicted to crack cocaine. I've gone from an Eclipse Award-winning journalist and TV show host to a groom. I've taken psychotropic medication on and off for nearly the entire time. But none of it has stopped me from having scores of sexual contacts with women and men I never knew, many of the men having faces I never saw.

At the Dallas psyche hospital, the shrink told me many sane persons have same-sex relationships and have no reason to feel guilty. Like heterosexuals, gays can be happy, too. It might be right for them, but not me. I like women, their company, their laughter, their warmth and their bodies. I never actually liked men that way. But I can't stop the contacts. I can never convince myself that it's normal. I can blame that on God. He got me out from between the feds and the Winter Hill Gang. God took away an addiction to crack cocaine. But God hasn't gotten rid of compulsive encounters, and had fixed it so I hate myself because of them. It would be easier had I never believed. I hope God will let me into heaven. I don't want to die. But I want less to live.

I'd left my body after overdosing on THC in that Philadelphia apartment and on the same drug on a Colorado mesa while trying to become a falcon. Could I have demons?

I hate my stepbrother.

For years, I thought I was as much to blame as he was We were close to the same age. I willingly took part. I wasn't forced. But he led. Had he not started me down that road that night we were playing around with our cousins, I don't believe I would have gone down it.

From what I know, he's living a normal life with a job, a wife and children. I don't have the courage to find him and scream into his face. On the back of a Thoroughbred, my rage had an outlet. But when I got down, it had no place else to go so it turned inward. My first divorce triggered memories of my adolescent sexual trauma and, as a way to deal with the pain of the marriage's end, I started acting out the fantasies the boyhood trauma had created. After that, drugs and alcohol became a way to numb the guilt and shame and in the end nothing more than a way to kill myself and enjoy the process.

I step closer to the edge and look down. Am I sure to die instantly? The woman who jumped from here had. I don't want to wind up a paraplegic. God, I'd ridden races nearly 20 years and can still walk. Doing that to myself will be worse than anything. But, of course, I can always try again. A mocking voice inside me taunts, "If you're really a man, you'll jump." Yes, that's right, a real man wouldn't hesitate. I lean forward.

Something black pushes between me and the ledge. It's Jack. I don't want him to fall. I take a step back. He's in front of me, looking up. His eyes are expectant. He still wants me to love him. He still loves me. Something deep in my mind takes over, and it's like I'm coming to after one of my blackouts. My heart melts. I sink to my knees before him and embrace his neck. He licks my face as tears stream down my cheeks.

After a while I get up and stagger back toward Kate's. What I find changes my life.

BATTLING ATTRACTIONS AND ADDICTIONS

ARRESTED AGAIN

42: San Pedro California, Midnight December 8, 1996

I fling open the front gate to Kate's house, noticing an auto parked in front. It must belong to Kate's new boyfriend. Jack runs around the house to the backyard and I follow. The bedroom window is too high to look through. I hear muffled sounds. Kate is with someone. Having sex.

Fighting the urge to bust through the door, I remember there's a key at my place. I run the three blocks and once inside, take a large hit off the Jim Beam, my second fifth in two days. It's been two days and nearly another night of no sleep. Calling Pam crosses my mind. She'd probably pick me up and I'd finally sleep, curled up on her plush couch in front of her fireplace. But I'm drunk and she doesn't tolerate drunks. She's done enough. More than enough. And she'll tell me, "I told you so."

Fear overwhelms me. A fear of myself. My rage is back. Mostly buried deep behind learned layers of civility, it's a glowing, living entity screaming inside my chest. It's heartburn mounted on a blowtorch.

I hate Kate. I hate Debra. I especially hate my first wife, Debbie. These strange leanings and uncontrollable urges were safe inside me until Debbie had an affair. The tiger escaped from its cage and now I can't stop him. It got all twisted in my mind. Now I'm twisted. I can't think. I can only hate.

I fast-walk back to Kate's house, key in hand. I walk in. She's in bed. Alone.

"Who were you with?" I scream. She jumps to her feet in a flannel nightdress.

"I've been here all the time."

"You're lying. You were with your boyfriend. I'm gone a couple of weeks, and you're already in bed with someone."

"You're crazy."

The words bear into my soul. I am crazy. I know it. I just can't help it. I grab her hair and pull, hoping to send her to the floor. She gets loose, screams and runs at me. "You're so dead meat."

I hit her and grab her throat, holding my hands against it for a second. Something clicks inside me and I realize what I'm doing. I throw her to the bed and stand over her, panting. God, what have I done? I run from the house.

That night I drink until I finally pass out. The next morning I call and profusely apologize. I tell her I'm going to get in counseling, meaning it. She's angry but seems rational. I say I'm going to move away from San Pedro. Oddly, she asks me to take her to the airport for a flight to Oregon, where her youngest daughter is about to give birth. She asks if I will feed Bucky while she's gone. I readily agree.

She says her face is swollen and bruised. My remorse is laced with fear. I'm getting worse. That I'm capable of hurting someone physically is scary. What I did is horrible. I have no faith in counseling, but I don't know what else to do about my rage.

The next night I drive her to LAX in her car and wince when I see her eye is black. I keep apologizing. She seems okay, even sad when I say I know the relationship has ended and promise to stay away. At twilight, I return to her home, take Jack and Bucky for a walk and feed them. When I put out the food and return to the kitchen to clean up, I hear a noise.

Behind me are two police officers with stern looks.

I'm arrested for burglary, handcuffed and placed in the back of a police car. Kate had gone to the police, and they had taken photos of her face. I'm also charged with assault with a deadly weapon, my hands.

Inside the patrol car, the police officers tell me I'm going to spend the night in a local jail, be arraigned by video camera the next day. Unless I make bail I'll be booked into the downtown L.A. Twin Towers, a place I'd once heard described as "a zoo." I scoot back into my seat. Thoughts of metal bars and bullies barrel through my mind. I'm 5'4," 140 pounds and 53 years old. But I've been around. I know when to talk and when to keep my mouth shut. I've been a fairly well-known jockey, a newspaper writer and a TV show host. I figure the guys I'll be in with will think I have swag and leave me alone. I heard that some who weren't gay became sissies in jail. Despite my past, I couldn't take it if that happened. Yet will I detest it a week from now if the opportunity arises?

And a lot of people kill themselves in jail. I'm ready to jump off a cliff. Will I get even more serious in jail? My head sinks into my chest, and I clench my eyes shut. I'm going to jail. God only knows for how long. I have no money and few friends. I open my eyes and look out at the streetlights gliding past. In some warped way, I feel safe. I'm out of control. Another week on the streets and I'll either go to jail for something even more serious or some homeless person will be walking at the bottom of the cliff and find my lifeless torso.

BATTLING ATTRACTIONS AND ADDICTIONS

A ROOKIE INMATE

43: Twin Towers Jail, Los Angeles California, December 12, 1996

In a spacious and sterile booking area lined with shiny metal benches, guards have us line up, naked as the day we were born. An overweight guard with rubber gloves walks behind us. "Bend over and spread 'em," he commands. When he reaches me, I comply. All I can think of is a doctor's prostate examination as a finger probes my rectum.

Minutes earlier, I stood before a glass-enclosed clerk, who asked in a monotone, "You on any medications?"

I wasn't sure how to answer. Inside a spacious holding cell minutes earlier, I'd heard some of the guys saying they were going to say they were "hearing voices" so they could get in a special ward with other "crazies." If there, you get medication, including tranquilizers. I'm still in the mindset of hating medications. Yet I realize I'm going to detox from alcohol cold turkey.

"I took some before," I said.

The clerk, a thin man with a mustache I figure is a nurse, nods. He's now interested.

"What kind and when?"

I told him two shrinks had diagnosed me as bipolar and that I took Lithium for seven years, Paxil the last two but decided to stop two weeks earlier.

He scribbled on a form attached to a clipboard. "You hear voices?"

I was stumped. I know hearing voices indicates schizophrenia, and I never had until I stood at the cliff and heard a voice tell me if I were a real man I'd jump. Perhaps that was a demon.

I shook my head, no.

"You taking any illegal medications?"

I wasn't about to admit to any crime. "Just whiskey, a lot of it."

"You gay?"

"I'm not."

He glanced over my shoulder. "Next."

After the inspection, we line up again for our clothes. Nearly everyone in the line gets orange, but I'm given a canary yellow. Guards connect a chain to my wrists and ankles, and I shuffle off to my cell beside an officer who never looks at me. I expect catcalls from cells about fresh meat, but the inmates seem disinterested.

Hundreds on several floors inside this metal building talk loudly. TV and loudspeakers blare. Inmates holler at fellow inmates in other cells who shout back. Sounds from places I can't see, loud, angry and inaudible, flow in a staccato stream from behind rows of iron bars, down hallways and echo off gray metal walls, sounding like a hundred car speakers with too much bass. The noise, deafening and constant, bores into my mind like twisting worms. There's no escape. I know now why they call it "The Crossbar Motel."

I'd spent last night in the San Pedro jail in a cell alone. That morning I was handcuffed and taken to a room where a young woman in a flower dress and lots of makeup says she's a public defender. I was charged with burglary and felony assault with a deadly weapon, my hands. I explained

304

that I had a key to the house, had recently lived there and that the owner had asked me to come in and feed our dogs while she was away.

Later the same day, guards take me to a room with a giant TV where a woman on the screen sits in a black robe. She says she'd dropped the burglary charges and the public defender had pleaded not guilty to felony assault. She sets my bail at $50,000. I have no money for a lawyer, and I know no one with the possible exception of Pam, who is willing to put up $5,000 for bond and risk another $45,000 if I split. I'm going to be in jail for a while, including Christmas. Though I have no "priors," a felony assault conviction can put me in prison for years.

Back at Twin Towers, the guard unshackles me, grasps my shoulder and inserts me inside a cell. Five men greet me with interest and one of them points to a top bunk where I will sleep. The cell is about 8'X10' and has a commode at one end. It's open, and I realize I will use it in front of the others.

We talk briefly, and I tell them I'm a former jockey and newspaper writer, which they seem to think is cool. They ask about my jockey career, and I give them the basics.

"You ever ride in the Derby?" one asks.

I marvel. Even fellow inmates will judge my value as a jockey by the Kentucky Derby.

I consider telling them my sob story about being taken off my Derby mount a few weeks before the race. But this place is filled with sad stories. Besides, my throat is starting to hurt and it's been nearly 24 hours since I had a drink. "I didn't, but I rode a lot at Churchill Downs." I smile. "The most significant thing about my career was I lived through it. I broke 13 bones in the process."

Some nod, showing appreciation. I tell them briefly about the race fixing, how I was in the middle between the Winter Hill Gang and the FBI and how I stood up and didn't testify.

"You know some guys in the Winter Hill Gang?" one asks.

"I know a lot of people," I say boldly.

305

One of them, a shaved-head kid with an 18th Street Gang tattoo on his bare chest, shoots me a grin. He's here for attempted murder after he drove through a barricade to run down a rival gang member. One of the guys is swishy and makes it a point to stand close to another cellmate who says he's in for fraud but says he's innocent and will be released soon. That night sleep comes hard and I wake at three a.m., wanting to use the commode. The man jailed for fraud is in his bunk with the gay guy. I turn over and feign sleep. I never did that kind of sex and my heart beats like it's inside a running jackrabbit.

I'm wide awake, and it's finally quiet. I'm captured. Time has slowed down, and the only thing I can think about is me. Had I stepped over the cliff or had a friend of Debbie's not happened to have a key and come over to find me on the floor with 36 Xanax in my stomach, I wouldn't be going through this. But there are five men in the cell with me, no razors, shoestrings or even plastic bags to put over your head. My life as I know it is over. The race is over. Death will only light the official sign. Sleep doesn't come, and I'm awake when a guard walks down the cell block, shouting, "Rise and shine. Time to get your butts outta bed."

I soon learn that with my "crazy" yellow shirt, I'm likely to be moved to a cell with other crazies and in a cell block with guards who consistently watch the inmates. But my cellmates are friendly, though some try to explore who I know on the outside that might help them. They tell me about the commissary. Someone has to put money on your books before you can buy candy and other goodies. We get to shower every other day but eat inside our cells. Lights are out at 10:00 p.m., and guards wake us at 6:30 a.m. for breakfast. Inmates tell me that on weekends we get to take walks on the roof, though in my time there I never even see the area.

The next day, I hear screaming from a nearby cell. No guards respond. An hour later they show up and escort down the walkway a man bleeding profusely from one of his ears. That evening after dinner, a guard comes with a paper, identifies me and moves me to a cell with one other person. When I ask why, he shrugs his shoulders and tells me only that he has an order to move me. Most of the guards are young, seem to want to make up for a lack of confidence with bluster and are not about to engage in casual conversations with inmates. I later learn that in general LAPD or sheriff's deputies who are recent academy graduates are initially assigned to the jail.

My lone cellmate says he's on his way to state prison and goes to sleep, snoring loudly. I take the time alone to try to use the commode. The next morning I'm put in a cell with five other yellow shirts. Except for one person who sits on his bunk, never talks and constantly chews his lip, they seem less insane than I. It seems they conned their way into the designation so they can get medicated. One thin African-American bends his wrist and waves his fingers at me when I arrive. He is full of information. "When the doctor comes and asks if you hear voices, tell him, 'Yes, sweetie,' and you'll get tranquilizers."

"A whole bottle?" I ask, thinking they might be enough for an effective overdose. I hear my voice squeak and break.

"No silly. You line up each morning after breakfast and take your meds. They make you take it in front of them, and if they think you jiving them, they'll pry open your mouth on the spot. But sometimes we can save them, and when we get a bunch, get high. And there are always people who will buy them."

Anything looks good. My head feels like it's been peeled open, my brain exposed like the nerve endings on a decayed tooth. I can't eat, but I keep throwing up. "My throat's hurting. I think I got strep throat. Think a doctor will see me?"

"You got to put in a request. Might take a week. But tell the guy who comes around that you hear voices, and you'll get to see a nurse right away."

"I thought you said we line up each morning for meds?"

"Deary, you got a lot to learn. And you do look awful gray. Maybe they'll lay some love on you, sweetheart."

I climb into my upper bunk and finger the glands under my ears. They're swollen and when I push it hurts. Maybe I won't have to commit suicide after all. My new friend comes over, glances around to make sure no one sees him and puts in front of my face a striped capsule. I don't know what it is and don't ask. I swallow it. In five minutes, I'm asleep.

Jail is full of lines and each morning guards line up the yellow shirts for meds. The room is a long rectangle with a raised room at the end. There, medical workers and trustees stand behind windows, give the meds and watch as we take them. Just like my cellmate said, several are forced to open their mouths as nurses with wooden depressors move around any suspicious tongues, looking for hoarded pills. After my interview, I'm expecting Paxil or Lithium or perhaps a new psychotropic drugs, or if I'm lucky, tranquilizers or sleeping pills.

When the doctor appears outside my cell and asks if I'm hearing voices, I tell him no but say I have strep throat and need antibiotics. He walks away without a word. I'm sleeping 30 minutes at a time. I'm only drinking water and still throwing up most of that. In the shower, there's a metal mirror, and my skin is the color of slate. I have a fever, sweat perpetually and hear my ears pop and ring. My hands tremble worse than ever. I keep having dreams of being tied down and tortured. I must be close to having DTs.

When my turn finally comes at the meds window, I try to clear the fog from my head as I talk to a busty female nurse who glares at me like I was a dog who just went on her best rug. I give her my name, and she finds a file with my name on it.

"It says here you're bipolar. Is that right?"

I nod, trying my best to avoid talking because it hurts my throat. "You were taking medication before you were arrested."

I tell her about the Lithium and Paxil I had taken for years but had suddenly stopped a few weeks earlier. She twists her thick lips in thought. "Next."

"Ma'am, I have strep throat. Just look at my glands. Can I get antibiotics, an aspirin at least? My head is killing me."

"Next."

"You can die from strep throat. I'm not lying. Just look down my throat."

She moves her glare to a pair of guards standing a few feet from me. She heard my voice, now a raspy squeak, and maybe she thought I was faking. But my swollen glands and throat are impossible to fake.

My eyes are watering. "I'm sick. I'm honestly sick."

"I said, 'next.' If I have to say it again, the guards will haul you out of here, and that won't be pretty, I guarantee it."

I sit down on a plastic chair bolted to the floor and wait until the others get their meds. A guard has me stand, fits me with shackles, and we line up to be led back to our cells, shuffling along in tiny steps. I can't keep from staggering. The guard grabs my upper arm and guides me. He says nothing.

Two of my bunkies help me, and I make it onto the top bunk I'm assigned. At first they're buzzing around, talking about the pills they've taken. One, a young man with shoulder-length hair, has a handful of tranquilizers. He holds them in his hand, and the other four inmates trade cigarettes, candy bars and even dollar bills for them. He says they are Seconals, and I know they are a powerful barbiturate. I also know a lot of famous people from Jimmy Hendrix to Tennessee Williams took Seconals to whack themselves out.

"What you need for five of them?" I wheeze.

"What are you going to do, check out?" he asks, smiling.

"How much?"

"Fifty dollars."

"I can get it. I'm good for it. I can get it."

"Then get it and come back to see me. I got a supply."

"I need them now."

"I need a $300-an-hour lawyer."

He turns away, conversation over. It's Saturday and today and tomorrow is visitors' day. Kate is in Portland, helping her daughter give birth. I call Pam collect. She takes the call and promises to come see me. Maybe Sunday. God I hope. Perhaps I could get the money for the pills. Check out, the man had said. That's a good description. All this has gotten way out in front of me. I close my eyes. I'm stuck, as if I'm sitting on a set of railroad tracks and can't get up. A train called justice is about to roll over me and I can't get up and leave. I'm paralyzed like in one of those awful dreams where your mind is awake but your body is asleep and it won't you're your mind's command to move. Nothing to do but sweat, hurt and throw up. My skinny pillow stinks from my sweat, my whole head is wet, and my throat feels like raw hamburger. I close my eyes again. I'm dehydrated and exhausted from the fever. I drift off in a place that is not real sleep. I hear a roar that turns into cheering. No, I decide, it's actually jeering. It's mocking voices echoing off dark walls, making fun of me, calling me faggot, queer and other names, unprintable. Forms, dark and ugly, move about like gargoyles on speed. They seem to want me to do something. Want me to be close. Want me to be one of them.

I scream. I'm awake. Everyone is looking at me. They look contented. They like my screams. They want me dead. All of them want me dead. My sick body is trapped inside a jail cell with crazy people. But I'm one of them.

I spend the night with dreams of being tortured. A part of me thinks I'm dead. And in brief moments when the fog thins, it dawns on me where I am, and I feel even worse. Years of the same thing could be in front of me. I just can't comprehend what that will be like. Iron bars around me. Every movement controlled by others. Told when to eat food that is determined by someone else. Told when to shower, forced to wear this ridiculous yellow shirt and baggy pants. Moved about in shackles. Knowing I can't leave is the worst.

The next morning a guard comes to the cell with an offer to attend a church service. He says the meds will come later. I decide to go, hoping I have the strength. We're escorted without chains to a different floor in the cavernous building and into a large sterile room with bolted chairs and an altar and cross at the front. The chaplain wears a Catholic priest collar, but his shirt is gray and not black and I don't know his denomination. He serves regular communion, reads from the Bible and speaks. I try hard to block out the pain and listen. At the end, he passes out tiny green Gideon New Testaments, and I take one. Somehow it feels comforting in my hand

We file out amid loud talking and jesting. My throat hurts too much to say anything and my head aches like the migraines I had as a teenager. I was young and riding in Boston, and when my dad came to visit I came down with a migraine and wound up at Mass General, where a doctor punctured the atrium in my nose with a huge needle and used a liquid to flush out my sinus cavities. I got better but thought it strange I only got sick when my father arrived. Maybe his visit brought memories of a past my head couldn't handle. This time I know the pain in my head is part strep throat and part withdrawal from alcohol and perhaps the psychotropic medication I'd taken for years.

That afternoon Pam visits and we sit on opposite sides of thick glass and talk by phone. When I come in and sit down, alarm spreads across her pretty Irish face. She hears my hoarse whisper and grimaces. She cannot help me make bond, but promises to get me a lawyer she knows, a real one and not just a public defender. I tell her I have no date for a trial yet but that a pretrial hearing is in San Pedro the next day and she tells me that's not enough time for her to contact her attorney friend. I explain about putting money on my account so I can buy candy bars from the commissary and she says she'll deposit $30. She mentions Kate and I tell her what I'd done with no fudging. The expected I-told-you-so never comes. I don't know if Kate is going to press charges, but she obviously contacted the police. I don't have a date yet for the trial, but a hearing has been set for the day after Christmas. We're only allowed 20 minutes, which goes too fast. But something inside me changes. I know at least one person on earth cares enough to go to the trouble to visit. And in that lies hope.

In chains again I shuffle back to my cell, as always accompanied by a guard. I need to get some real sleep. I don't have enough money for five Seconals to whack me out for good, but maybe I can barter some of my commissary money for one pill, enough to allow me to sleep. I have to be up at 4:00 a.m. to make the trip to my pretrial hearing in San Pedro. I know it can affect my future. I didn't know how much.

BATTLING ATTRACTIONS AND ADDICTIONS

GOD WINS THE BATTLE

44: Twin Towers Jail, Los Angeles California, December 16, 1996

A guard outside my cell shouts a wake-up call. It's 4:00 a.m., time to get dressed for my day in court. He brings a breakfast of runny eggs I'm too nervous to eat. He comes back, shackles me and takes me downstairs to the first floor area containing giant holding cells. I learn from my cellmates that all of us will be put on buses and taken to various courtrooms in Los Angeles County. At 6:30 a.m. we're shackled hand and foot and to each other then led to a parking lot filled with black and silver Greyhound-like buses. Their engines rumble in the dawn and the place reeks of carbon monoxide. The inmates talk and jive loudly, apparently seeing their trips to court as a break in the boring sameness of a jail cell.

After standing a long time, guards herd us inside. I feel like I'm inside a giant tin can. A metal mesh partition separates the prisoners from the driver and a guard with a shotgun. Metal seats. Another metal mesh partition separates women already in the back. Uniformed guards attach the chain that runs from our handcuffs to the shackles on our legs to a thick chain that runs the length of the bus. An accident and fire and we would cook like burnt toast. I'm placed in a seat next to the darkened window and guards seat a young man beside me.

I notice he's wearing a silver cross and marvel that it's still around his neck because jewelry is normally removed at intake. In minutes we're all in chains and rolling south on the 110 freeway, the L.A. skyline on our left. "How'd you manage to keep your cross?" I ask.

"I just got here yesterday. Guess they missed it when I got booked."

"You a Christian?" I ask.

He explains that he attends church regularly on Catalina Island, where he lives. I tell him my name, and I learn that his is Victor. He's in his twenties with dark black hair and a dark complexion. We briefly swap stories, and I learn he too is facing a long sentence. "I believe we need a miracle," I say.

"Why don't we pray for one?"

I look around. The bus is alive with sounds. Male prisoners are hitting on the women behind us. Some are shouting and hooting at each other. I hear threats and challenges from rival gang members. "I got a Bible," I say, trying to raise enough to get my new green New Testament the chaplain had given me out of my back pocket. That it's even there is a miracle. Guards had patted me down twice but either didn't notice or chose to leave it alone.

Someone in the seat across the aisle shouts, "Where you going, Grandpa? If you got to go, there ain't no bathrooms so you might as well go in your pants."

Others turn to look. If I can twist my body enough, I can get my shackled hands on the Bible. I want it in my hand. I twist hard, turning my backside, and my back to reach it. I try several times and others are laughing, thinking I'm going to go in my pants. I finally turn my hips far enough and with one of my cuffed hands pull out my Bible.

I sit again and hold it with both hands. Victor puts both his shackled hands on it. We bow our heads, and I pray. "Please God, do a miracle for us."

I look out at the passing houses of South Los Angeles and remember standing on the field of Tampa Stadium some 17 years earlier, telling God that if he saved me from the U.S. Marshals and the Winter Hill Gang I would always work to bring Jesus to horse racing. Sam Houston Race Park Chaplain Randy Weaver and his council members had laid hands on me and prayed I would be set free from an addiction to crack cocaine. Then the dark night in the motel across the street from Hollywood Park when I lay on the linoleum floor and read Isaiah 43:19, a verse that cured the addiction. I'd flown out of Boston, the race-fixing trial in the past. The strange woman, Mary Ellen, had walked into my yard in Crystal Beach, Florida. Tapping me on the shoulder as I sat in a full lotus pose with upturned palms resting on my knees, her words rang clear: "God is going to use you in a mighty way one day, son."

Looking outside, I realize Hollywood Park is only a few miles east. God got me through a sentence in one of its cinder-block dorm rooms. I'd broken ribs, but it could have easily been my neck. But I haven't brought Christ to anyone there. Not even to me. As a Christian, I'm a total failure. I can't stop behaviors I hate. God has done a whole series of miracles for me. But they haven't changed me. I'm in jail for assault with a deadly weapon and facing real prison time.

*****

The bus pulls into the basement of the San Pedro Courthouse, a one-story red-brick building that looks like an office building. Other guards get on and use keys to loosen us from the bus' chains. Still in shackles, guards lead us to a large room as we shuffle behind them like penguins looking for food. Inside a holding cell the size of half a tennis court, they remove our shackles and leave. It has cream colored walls and is barren except a seating shelf that lines one side, long enough for most of us to sit on. Others sink to the floor, their backs propped against the wall. The bus has made stops at other courthouses and a dozen of us will have hearings or trials in these courtrooms.

One at a time, guards take prisoners to several courtrooms, where they briefly meet with their lawyers or public defenders and go before a judge. I go early, meet for seconds with a public defender who asks me if I want a speedy trial. I tell her I am going to have a lawyer but need a few days to talk with him. She tells me that unless I make bail, I might be in jail for weeks before coming to trial. I say I want a trial soon.

In handcuffs, I'm led into a section with tiered seating that looks like a place a jury might sit. I'm uncuffed and stand up when the judge enters. He and my public defender talk and they set another hearing for December 26, at which time the witness, Kate, will be present. It's over for now. Unless I die first, I'm going to spend Christmas behind bars. Back inside the holding cell, I walk around, too nervous to sit. In a few hours, all will have appeared inside a courtroom and the silver-and-black bus will head back up the freeway to the Twin Towers. My throat hurts, and the possibility of a long jail sentence hangs in my mind like a guillotine poised to drop. My bail is $50,000, not just a colossal sum but indicative of the crime I committed.

One man, long and lean and in his thirties, walks back into the giant holding cell, sits on the floor and leans his back against the white cinder-block wall. He bows his head and breaks down in sobs. Victor goes over, gets on one knee beside the man and talks to him. The man says he had just been found guilty of a petty theft for stealing a six-pack of beer from a 7-Eleven. He has two felony convictions for selling marijuana. This is his third strike. He's been sentenced to 25 years to life. He says he won't get to see his two young children grow up. There will be no conjugal visits. "My life is over," he cries out. "My freaking life is over."

Victor bows his head, and I know he's silently praying. An African-American in his early sixties walks over. "If you got God," he says, "your life is never over. I know that for sure."

The man explains that he has been clean and sober for 12 years and is a teaching elder in his church. He is only here because he was fishing with his son when a game warden checked his fishing license and learned he had a 12-year-old outstanding warrant. As soon as the man goes before a judge, he is certain to be released. The odds of his even being jailed are long. Perhaps God wants him here, I think.

315

"I'm a new creature in Christ and all of you here can have a new life if you make Christ your savior."

An African-American who looks beefy enough to play tackle for the Rams rises from the floor. "I know Jesus can save your life," he says. "I got saved last year, but I backslid and started selling dope again. Last week a dope freak tried to rob me. He put a pistol to my head and pulled the trigger. The gun didn't go off. Jesus saved me."

I take my New Testament from my pocket and chime in. "I knew Jesus, too. He did a whole series of miracles for me. But I still ran from Him, and I didn't truly believe. I don't want to do that anymore."

The noisy room turns silent. The drug dealer starts again. "We don't have to be captive. We can get set free if we want. If our minds are free, we're free whether we're in jail or on the streets." His voice booms. "I want to get set free. I want to get set free today."

He motions toward the New Testament and I hand it to him. He goes to the first two verses in James. "My brethren, count it all joy when you fall into various trials, knowing that the testing of your faith produces patience. But let patience have its perfect work, that you may be made perfect and complete, lacking nothing."

He stops and looks around. I can't believe what I'm seeing. It's like nothing I've seen before or since. A bluish smoke fills the room, floating down from the ceiling. Within it are thousands of gold flecks, each glistening for a split second, disappearing and reappearing. Its presence is alive.

Time and space cease to exist. A sense of self, who I am and being in a jail cell, dissolves. It's not frightening like the out-of-body experience I had after overdosing on THC in that Philadelphia apartment. This is the exact opposite. I feel the peace of a different dimension, disconnected and separate from any in this world. I feel a need to stand still and let this new space time continuum envelope me. It's as if I can't comprehend the presence in my natural state, so I am being transported to a different place, a place within that bluish cloud with shimmering gold flecks. A place where God resides. I hear singing, thousands or hundreds of thousands of voices singing words I can't understand but somehow know are praising Christ. In this dimension it probably lasts a few seconds yet it seems to go on and on. It's as if God is remaking my heart. Retooling my soul. Rearranging my DNA.

I cry. The misery deep inside me expels along with my tears. Then comes a realization of the pain and sorrow I've brought to so many others. I cry in sorrow. So many have reached out to help. Some, like my oldest sister who prayed for me each day, are no longer alive. They seem to be inside the cloud, telling me they still love me. That they have forgiven me.

I cry tears of joy. I've forgiven my stepbrother.

The cloud still fills the room. Some inmates have their hands raised, praising God. Some are kneeling at the shelf, elbows resting on the top, their hands clasped before them. Others are prostrate on the white cement.

A wailing seems to rise from the floors. They come from men as affected as I. All are crying or moaning. Every eye I see is wet. On my face, tears stream downward in rivers of repentance.

My body fills with light. Not light as in daylight. This light comes in waves. It is as if I've stuck my finger inside a live lamp socket and instead of electricity, light surges into my body. It radiates, pulsates and flows into the essence of my being. As boy, I heard faith healer Oral Roberts pronounce over others, "From the crown of your head to the soles of your feet." It feels like that.

God has forgiven me.

My sins have drowned in the sea of forgetfulness, as far from me as the East is from the West. As the book of James said, I can now count all I had done as joy. The peace of joy floods my every pore, every fiber and cell. I am changed. I am different. Forevermore. I raise my arms to heaven and speak praises. They're in a language not mine. They are words I don't understand but know that God does. I go on, letting the unknown tongue gush from me like a fountain that flows from within me. One that will never be empty. The words have power over the enemy. And while I can lose a skirmish, I know I will never lose the battle. I have a language that God understands.

At some point—I have no idea how long this goes on—we join hands and make a circle in a gesture that is unprompted, natural and organic. Not exact words but sounds like a bubbling brook flow from us and into the cloud. As one, we cry out confessions, pleas for forgiveness and praises. It goes on, not as a disjointed action but as a single stream of multi-layered worship.

And then it is gone. Like a wind that has blown through the room, it passes on. Time and the earthly dimension return. We stop. Some move about. Others are called into court. I clear my throat, marveling that it no longer hurts. I don't want it to end so I sit and lean against the white-washed wall, and in silence ponder what happened.

I later learn that what we experienced is the Shekinah Glory. Perhaps I'll have to wait until heaven to learn if the event changed their lives as drastically as it did mine.

LIFE TODAY

A NEW LIFE

45: Twin Towers Jail, Los Angeles California, Christmas 1996

It's Christmas morning, and guards deliver paper sacks to each prisoner through slots in our cell doors. Inside each package is a card from L.A. County Sheriff Lee Baca wishing us a Merry Christmas along with hard candy, an orange and a box of Animal Crackers. Most of the five others in my cell make jokes, yet we all enjoy the treat. There is a Christmas service in the chapel, and I go. There is a tree with lights, the jail's only obvious decoration. We sing Christmas carols to recorded music, and the chaplain talks about the true meaning of Christmas. For perhaps the first time, I understand the magnitude of Christ's birth and God's gift to mankind.

Kate has started taking my collect calls and Pam has visited again, telling me I will not be able to talk to the attorney she found until the day of the hearing, set for the next day. Kate is not overtly angry, and I genuinely beg her forgiveness and assure her I have changed. I never tell her I want to resume the relationship though I get the feeling that is something she wants to hear. I also tell Pam about the experience. Still I get the feeling neither understands the significance of what happened to me. Why would they? Jailhouse redemption is as common as loneliness.

My throat has totally healed. I no longer seek medication and even turn down a cellmate's offer of a free tranquilizer. I spend all day and most of the night reading my New Testament. Still nagging my thoughts is the possibility of being in jail for a long time. I've never been convicted of anything more than a traffic ticket. Yet assault with a deadly weapon is a Class 1 felony, a crime of violence, and if convicted I could be in jail for years.

After the Christmas service, I get a few moments with the chaplain and tell him about my experience. He nods and smiles, but I see skepticism pinching his eyes and realize he's heard and seen hundreds of jailhouse conversions. However dramatic the conversion, I know the jury—literally and figuratively—is still out.

San Pedro Courthouse

I'm uncuffed, in slacks and a sport coat as I sit at a table beneath a criminal court judge's podium. A few minutes earlier, I spoke with George, the attorney Pam found, and we briefly discussed my case and the small payment he was charging. He seems intelligent, but his clothes are discouraging. He wears a wrinkled suit and a tie under a collar that sticks out over his lapel. Kate is there to testify, and when the prosecutor questions her, she admits that I had hit her but says she never felt in danger. Now sober and thinking more clearly, I realize I never knew that she was with someone else that night and most likely wasn't. When George questions her, she says I had told her that I was stopping my medication and says she had not argued with that decision. She refuses to press charges, though the attorney has gone forward anyway, something my attorney notes to the judge. The prosecuting attorney and George are asked to approach the bench. It is a pretrial hearing, though George told me the matter could possibly be adjudicated here. They stand there for what seems like an eternity, whispering words I can't make out.

George returns and whispers in my ear. I nod, resisting the urge to shout hallelujah. If I plead no contest to misdemeanor simple assault, the judge will sentence me to time served, 16 days, and I will be freed. Of course, I accept.

George states the terms, the prosecutor agrees and it's over. The judge goes on to say to me that I owe George a humongous debt of thanks because he convinced them it was the proper thing to do.

Late that night, I'm processed out of jail. I walk the few blocks to the Metrolink station for a train to Long Beach, where Kate is going to pick me up. The chilling rain that falls from a foggy gray sky can't erase my perpetual grin. Clearly God has performed another miracle for me. I desperately want this one to stick. When I get off the train in Long Beach, Kate is not around. It's midnight and nothing is open. It's raining hard. I spot a bar across the street and figure it will have a pay phone. I call Kate. She's on her way. I hang up and look around.

"What'll it be, buddy?" the bartender asks.

I want a beer. Could taste it already. I've been sober 17 days. One beer won't hurt. "Just give me a Coke, would you please?"

When Kate picks me up, I give her a perfunctory hug and climb in for the ride back to my one-room apartment.

"You've lost some weight, and you're still gray," she says. "I got some supper cooked for you. Get some meat back on your bones."

I want to go back to my place, but I also want to see Jack and it wouldn't be right to be distant to someone who has done so much for me. Kate is a terrific cook, and after jail-house food, a home-cooked meal will be a treat. I visit Jack and Bucky. My lop-eared Doberman is ecstatic. Kate and I eat and chat aimlessly, ignoring the obvious. She asks about my future, and we both agree working for her company is out.

"There is nothing I can do at this point in my life but God's ministry," I say. "I might find a part-time job for now. But I think God fixed it so ministry is all I can do."

"That's a hefty commitment. Sure it won't wear off in a few months?"

"I don't think so. After what happened to me, I don't believe I'll be happy doing anything else."

"How about celibacy? You think you can do celibacy? That's got to be hard for someone like you."

"Like me?"

"Like any of us. I know it's what God wants of all of us who aren't married."

"Jesus never told us it would be easy. Just right. I got right with God in that holding cell. I want to stay right no matter what it takes. Yeah, I was addicted to sex like I was addicted to a lot of things. God got me well. I just don't want to do the things I did before. I read these verses by the Apostle Paul about never looking back and about being a new creation. I'm going to hang on to those words no matter what it takes."

"I know you're going to think it's crazy, but I've been reading the Bible over Christmas. I'm going to try to get right, too."

I bow my head and ask God to help us both. I help clean up the dishes and leave. There was no need to discuss the gorilla in the room. We can possibly remain friends, but we both know the relationship is over.

Within two weeks, I have a job marketing a chain of industrial medical clinics, visiting companies in the nearby Gardena area and trying to convince them to send their injured workers to our clinics. Clear-headed and focused, I make enough money to move into a one-bedroom apartment overlooking the harbor. I attend a lot of churches and visit homeless shelters, making contacts. I join an Assemblies of God church in Lomita and convince Pastor Pruitt to help me organize tent crusades in notorious South Central L.A., including one on Halloween. I hear about an orphanage on the Baja Peninsula, some 150 miles south of San Diego.

I drive down and see shabby camps populated by Oaxaca Indians bused from the mountains 2,000 miles away to work in the fields, starting when they are eight or nine. I arrange for a group from our church to go down and help build bunk beds for Welcome Home Orphanage. There, I meet Joyce, an older woman who also helps them. During one of my trips she prays for me and receives a prophecy. She tells me the Lord said I will go to the Los Angeles Dream Center. At first I think it's a place that cures sleep apnea. But I learn it's a gigantic former Queen of Angeles Hospital turned refuge center for people in need. It houses dozens of different ministries, all loosely joined under one banner.

Two years earlier, famous Assemblies of God Pastor Tommy Barnett ran the some 400 miles from his large church in Phoenix to the Dream Center near downtown Los Angeles to raise the $3.2 million to buy the decaying complex of buildings with 1,640 rooms. I visit the Dream Center to volunteer, but am turned down. Stumped, I decide the Lord must mean at a later time.

Kate and I remain friends. I take Bucky and Jack for regular walks after work and help poop scoop her backyard. One day she calls and says I have to get Jack out of the backyard. I can't have an animal at the apartment I've rented. I'm hard-pressed to figure out what to do. I talk to one of the people at the dog park where I take them to run, and he says he has a friend who has a company that was formerly protected by guard dogs and the dog's quarters are still there. Jack as a guard dog is odd. But I have no choice. I drive him to the place, meet the owner and give him 50 pounds of dog food. I promise to visit and feed Jack each day. Jack has a large area to run in and a house at one end to sleep in. I check it out, and it's clean and looks safe with a massive chain-link fence surrounding it. I've given my landlord notice that I'm moving and started looking for an apartment where Jack could live with me.

Jack doesn't like the place, and I spend a while with him, sitting down and letting him lay his head in my lap while I stroke his slick head, something he loves. It gets dark and time to go. The place is lit, but he follows me to the gate and tries his best to go with me. "You can't go Jack," I say. "You have to live here for a while, but I'll be back every day to visit, I promise. In a little while, we'll have a place together."

He cocks his head and whines. I remember the day I got him from the pound, how he drug me across the street so hard that his tiny leash dug into my hands. How we'd spend lonely nights inside a dim tack room. Throwing a tennis ball he would chase as long as I threw it. Days walking him. The time I stood at the edge of the cliff, almost summoning the courage to step off only to have him bump into my legs and look at me with love in his eyes. He'd forgiven me for beating him and just to think about it makes me tear up. I vowed to never again hit an animal or human and I have not. I scoot out the gate and close it, trying hard not to look back as I get to my car. The next morning at work I get a call from the man who owns the place. Jack has disappeared.

I take off work for the day and drive to the company. I look at the fence and find a place where Jack dug under it and escaped, no doubt to return the seven miles across town to where he lived. A place where he knows he'll see me. I leave my coat at the spot so he'll know I was there. I walk around all day, calling for him. There is a residential area on the way he would go, and I know he will go in that direction. I walk up and down, calling and calling. I drive back and put down my jacket in the field near the fence and put out some dog food so he will know I've been there if he comes back.

In the coming days, I visit every animal shelter, giving workers Jack's photo and my contact information. I get a map and lay out a grid of the area between the company and home. I make up a sign with Jack's picture and a $200 reward and tack it on poles in every area on the grid. Each night, I drive to a grid area, drive and then walk, calling out for Jack and listening in the dark for his bark, something I know as well as a mother knows the cry of her baby. I follow some barks that sound close, but none is Jack's.

I know Kate loves Jack, and she apologizes. We had once taken Jack to the vet for worming and when they put him in a cage, he freaked out and damaged his neck so badly the vet said he might be paralyzed for life. We brought him home and he lay on pads in a protected spot in our backyard without being able to move. We kept diapers under him, fed him by hand and on several nights I slept beside him. It was summer and neighborhood kids came by and fed him popsicles. After weeks he would try to get up but couldn't so I put a blanket under his back end and held it up while he walked with his front legs. We took turns holding him up and he eventually healed, something we celebrated together.

Now, days stretch into weeks and weeks into a month. I don't give up. Workers at animal shelters know me by name. I tell them that even if they collect his body, please call. I talk to at least 100 people living in neighborhoods surrounding the area. None has seen Jack. I begin to think that someone has taken him in, and he is now their dog. He is a beautiful animal, friendly and smart. I talk to police officers who tell me there are groups of roaming wild dogs, and he may have become a part of a homeless pack. I search. I pray. I grieve.

To this day, when I see the hills surrounding San Pedro, I think of Jack and wonder over and over if he had seen them from where I'd left him and tried to use them as a landmark to make his way home.

*****

Perhaps God was preparing me to aid others with similar grief. In April 2011, I was doing spiritual care in Joplin, Missouri, three days after an EF5 tornado wiped out much of the city and killed some 230 people. I was standing outside a destroyed home, listening to the grief and trauma of the family who lived there. Thankful to be alive but saddened by their loss, they spoke about their house that no longer had a roof, the loss of photos and keepsakes, their auto, which lay beneath a gigantic tree, and the loss of several family member's jobs because their employers' buildings no longer existed. But then the mother told me they had to evacuate to a shelter that did not take animals so they placed their dog and cat inside pet-carrying cases inside their intact garage. The family broke down in tears when the mother said they returned to find the pet crates missing.

I never found Jack, and his loss ranks with any I've experienced. I wrestled with the loss theologically. I noted that it came shortly after I had decided to work for God the rest of my earthly life. I never felt God was punishing me, for my concept of a rescuing, ever forgiving and redemptive God was shaped forever in that jail cell. Yet Jesus was clear when he told the man who considered following him but needed time to go bury his father to let the dead bury their dead.

325

However painful, life with Jack is behind me. He'd been there for me when I needed him. For the most part, I'd been there for him. It's love and not relationships that is endless. God is teaching me that after I've prayed and done all I can, there is a time to let it go. Like a butterfly, release it into the air; turn my pain over to Him. God has a new journey for me, one that apparently doesn't include a dog I deeply loved.

*****

A short time later, I'm on a call to Pat Day. He's horse racing's all-time, best-known Christian. We've known each other since we rode together in the early 1970s at Rockingham Park. I feel led to share my new faith. He's happy and encourages me. He also tells me that a mutual friend, former jockey Donald Stover, lives in nearby Long Beach where he works for a Christian ministry, New Life Beginnings. This ministry rescues homeless and battered pregnant women, then helps them give birth. They either raise the babies or have them adopted by loving families. There are several thousand people alive today who would have never drawn their first breath had founder Rebecca Younger not decided to help her first pregnant woman.

I call Donnie, wanting to tell him about my newfound faith. He says he's being "tried in the fire." Facing a 12-year-old charge for cocaine possession, he has to return to the sight of the crime, Amarillo, Texas, a town he was passing through on a bus when arrested. He says he doesn't know a single soul in the city but has to serve two years of probation there. I have one good friend in Amarillo, Dan Fick, then Director of Racing for the American Quarter Horse Association. I call Dan, tell him about Donnie and he readily agrees to do all he can for Stover, something he does indeed live up to.

I take Donnie up on an invitation and the next day we attend an outreach sponsored by a tiny church in notorious Compton. There I see what looks like a bread truck painted by an inner-city muralist. One side breaks down into a stage and on it is a smallish Hispanic pastor whose crew just performed Biblical skits and magic tricks for the children there. Donnie tells me Julian Toriz (Pastor Jay) is a former gangbanger-turned-

326

minister who founded Metro Kidz International, which is based at—where else—The Los Angeles Dream Center, the place my Baja California friend, Joyce prophesied I'd live though they rejected my offer to volunteer.

After he ends and several children pray to know Jesus, I talk to him. A few weeks later he invites me to come live there and work for him. He can only pay $300 a month, though the room and food are free, so I convince my boss at the medical clinic to allow me to work one day a week.

Within two weeks, I trade my harbor-view apartment and marketing job for a single room in the former hospital, one that requires me to walk up five flights. On my room's wall, a former occupant wrote Romans 1:16: "For I am not ashamed of the Gospel of Christ, for it is the power of God unto salvation for everyone who believes ..."

Thus begins a spiritual boot camp of 12 to 15 hours of daily ministry and Bible study that lasts 33 months. I soon quit my job entirely and live on the stipend and free room and board.

For the first time since I was eleven, I become celibate. I use my writing to produce a host of promotional material and grant proposals for Metro Kidz. On Saturdays I wear my red Metro Kitz T-shirt and travel to Nickerson Gardens, one of the poorest and most crime-ridden housing projects in Los Angeles.

I also meet Pastor Clayton Golliher, who founded the Dream Center-based ministry, Hope for Homeless Youth and soon lead one of his teams in late-night forays into Hollywood. Late one evening, my partner and I start talking with two men standing on a dark corner. One says he once attended seminary, planning to become a minister, but stopped believing and dropped out. He raises his toboggan cap to disclose a pentagram tattooed on his forehead and explains he is a card-carrying Satanist. As my partner goes to silent prayer, we talk some more. I tell him about my sexual trauma and conversion in jail, and he says he was sexually abused by his father. After a time I ask if I can pray for him. He nods and I gently reach out to touch his shoulder.

From behind comes a loud crash. I turn to see a car on the sidewalk, a sparking light pole across its dented hood. A few feet away, the auto had run off the road and into a street light. Several people emerge from the auto and race past us. The Satanist and his partner move away, dissolving into the darkness. A few days later we return to the same spot and encounter the Satanist's companion. He tells us his friend overdosed on heroin and died.

He talks and prays with us but refuses to come back and enter the Dream Center's program for men. As we leave, I think about the Satanist and my own story. I could have died so many times. Gratitude sweeps over me. Satan doesn't lose them all.

Kate and I remain friends and friends only. We travel to San Vicente on the Baja Peninsula to deliver over 300 giant baggies filled with Christmas goodies to children who from the age of nine spend 12 hours a day working in lettuce fields. Working with Metro Kidz in South Los Angeles, I come across a small dog whose hair has been eaten away by red mange. Kate keeps it, and we share several hundred dollars in vet bills and then find Elisa Doolittle a home.

I phone and email Dawn and Derek on a regular basis, and they travel to California to see me. We surf and swim in the Pacific, eat together in restaurants, and I hear about them graduating from high school. Derek is going to LSU where he earned a degree in Business. Dawn is on her way to earning a master's in psychology and becoming the hospice social worker she is today. I tell them how sorry I am for missing much of their lives while knowing it's time I can never regain. But they have forgiven me, and I am again part of their lives.

Debbie and I make peace. Today we talk, usually about our children, and she even helped me in remembering details in this book. Gone is my anger and rage, replaced by a peace that transcends logic.

THE SHEKINAH GLORY AGAIN

46: Dream Center, Los Angeles California, October 21, 2000

"Are you sure you want to do this?" Pastor Julian Toriz asks for the third time as we stand outside the door of the tiny chapel at the Los Angeles Dream Center. "Marriage is a big step."

"Yes, Pastor Jay. I am." I stop and search his face. "I've been celibate for the three years I worked for you. You know my heart. God put an incredible woman in front of me, and I know, like so many things in my life, he orchestrated this. Don't you think I'm ready?"

"I know where you two are spiritually. I think I just needed to hear it from you."

Pastor Jay invited me to come to the Dream Center and work for his ministry, Metro Kidz International, three years earlier. I took 17 Berean Bible courses and got an Urban Bible Training Certificate and more than enough credits to obtain a license as an Assemblies of God minister. By now my pay is $600 a month and I'm free-lancing for *Charisma Magazine,* so I use the money to take fundraising classes at UCLA. I raise funds for Metro Kidz, and the Dream Center soon hires me to write the architecture for a $100,000 earmark grant it received from HUD for a job-training program.

But most of my time is spent helping pastors Jay and Clayton in hands-on, in-your-face, rubber-meets-the-road ministry. From the midnight streets of Hollywood to Saturday afternoons in the housing projects to days in nearby Skid Row, I do it all. And love every minute. Someone once said only become a minister if you can never be happy doing anything else and that describes me. And Sandi Steele is another miracle God performed for me

We met in one of the classes, and I noticed she aced every test. She is remarkably pretty, with blond hair and a wide-open Irish face that holds much laughter and confident brown eyes. She had packed and after the last class planned to return to her former home of New Orleans. I was interested but, given my newfound intensity for serving Christ, was not smitten. On the final night, a group of students decided to go to the nearby Rodeo Grill for food and fellowship. I was tired and decided to forego the gathering. I went to my room, sat down, took off my shoes and planted my feet on my tiny bed. Despite my obvious beliefs in the supernatural aspects of Christianity, I'm not one to say that I hear "the voice of God" very often. Yet I heard a voice telling me to go to the restaurant and talk to Sandi. I mentally debated with the Holy Spirit, shook my head and thought about my fatigue. Yet the Holy Spirit won. I put on my shoes, drove to the restaurant, sat beside Sandi and talked. Seven months later, we are marrying.

Pastor Jay, who no longer seems reluctant, shoots me a grin. "Let's pray."

We both do, for the ceremony and the marriage. It's been seven months since I met Sandi in one of the Bible classes. I've been celibate for years and urges I couldn't control are nothing more than bad memories. I love Sandi in more ways than anyone. For the first time in my life, I'm emotionally capable of maintaining a marriage. Like me, her first love is Jesus Christ. That takes away the onus of fulfillment through each other.. I know marriage requires sacrifice. I'm not marrying to get but to give, to minister to a godly woman in all aspects. The Book of Proverbs says he who finds a wife "finds a good thing." The Apostle Paul compares a man's relationship with his wife as Christ's to the church. Christ is the head of the church but as the ultimate servant leader who gave his earthly life for her. That is expected of me. Not just to be willing to fight to the death for her life but sacrifice my flesh each day on behalf of her. My personal relationship with Christ comes first. She's more valuable than my ministry. God, family, ministry. I have my priorities in order. I'm ready.

A few minutes later, we stand at the front of the tiny chapel that was used by nuns who ministered at the former Queen of Angels Hospital. We light candles and then take our first communion together. Sandi is in a white wedding dress, and I have on a tux. Among the some 60 attendees are at least a dozen ministers. Pastor Jay calls them forward. As we kneel, they lay on hands and loudly pray for us.

When Pastor Jay starts to read the verses we've selected and the words we've written, I sense a voice telling me to stand extremely still. Sandi later said she felt the same urging. A beam of light comes through one of the stained-glass windows and falls on us. A smoky, golden-brown haze envelopes us.

Pastor Jay stops speaking. The room is silent and still. It's as if all there have sensed at the same instant the same Holy Spirit prompting to "Be still and know that I am God." Finally, Pastor Jay clears his throat, shakes his head in wonder, looks out over the assembled and announces in a hushed tone, "This is the first time in my life I've seen the Shekinah Glory."

It's understandable. Like mine, Sandi's conversion involved a supernatural event. Her father, a New Orleans police officer, had been killed in the line of duty when she was seven, and her mother was schizophrenic. Named Sandi Steele, she grew up in the city's mean streets, spent time in a Catholic orphanage and was married and had two children by 21. Beautiful and given to performing, she wound up in Hollywood where she met and lived for nine years with actor and comedian Don Knotts. After their breakup, a local group of Satan worshippers tried to enlist her. When unsuccessful, they cut her pet cat and caused a car she was driving to veer into the path of an oncoming car she narrowly avoided hitting. Scared and bewildered, she was in bed in her Hollywood apartment when she felt the urge to pray, got out of bed, and went to her knees. She asked Christ to save her and got back in bed.

"I was lying in my bed looking at a mirror when I started to rise," she once explained. "When I got near the ceiling, I saw a black form leave through the soles of my feet. I think God lowered me to the bed again. I was set free. I knew my life had changed forever."

As we stand in that beam of light shining through one of the chapel's stained-glass windows, I feel something wrapping around us like giant sheets of Holy Ghost bubble packing. The Shekinah Glory.

We move into her studio apartment in Burbank and both of work at the Dream Center as fundraisers. I've completed enough courses and have sufficient endorsement from the Assemblies of God ministers to obtain the church's license to preach. But I have again married, something that violates their written doctrine and makes that goal highly unlikely. The Apostle Paul wrote in Timothy and Titus that an elder must be "a husband of one wife." Though some Bible scholars, including some connected with the Assemblies of God, believe Paul was not speaking about divorce but polygamy, I am disqualified.

Sandi and I still do night outreaches to Skid Row, South Central LA and Hollywood. Pastor Golliher even has me come help him pray for deliverance for a youth who had come in after sleeping in a coffin, having his incisors surgically sharpened and, according to the young man, drinking blood. God has me in serious ministry, licensed or not.

ANOTHER MIRACLE

A NEW MANTLE

47: Los Angeles California, November 1, 2001

I'm sitting in one of the back rows, on a padded scarlet chair in a spacious meeting room on the fifth floor of the International Church of the Foursquare Gospel headquarters, a few blocks from the Dream Center. I tug at my tight-necked white shirt to give me some breathing room and wonder what I'm expected to do. Four years earlier and a few miles away, I was in a jail cell, charged with felony assault with a deadly weapon. That I am about to be commissioned as a Foursquare minister, gaining an international license—the third highest of the four licensing levels—is a miracle only God could orchestrate.

At the room's front, senior Foursquare officials stand on a dais. Speaking is Dr. Rolf McPherson, whose charismatic Mother, Aimee Semple McPherson started the denomination. Today it has 1,800 American churches, another 66,000 around the world and some 7.5 million adherents and members. Looking tan and strong beneath a shock of silver-white hair, the septuagenarian speaks with a soft and solemn voice, addressing the dozen of us about to become ministers.

His mother built Angelus Temple, the historic mother church a block away. She knew such Hollywood legends as Clara Bow and Charlie Chaplin.

Anthony Quinn played the sax in one of her gospel bands, and she's mentioned in the classic "Hooray for Hollywood." She even built her church with a rounded front shaped like a megaphone that faced Tinsel Town. A Canadian country girl whose mother worked for the Salvation Army, she met traveling Irish evangelist Robert Semple at a crusade near her home, came to Christ and married Semple. They traveled to China as missionaries, where both quickly contracted malaria. Robert died. She returned home with their young daughter, Roberta and later married salesman Harold McPherson, who fathered Rolf, the couple's only child. Feeling strongly called by God to preach, she said her resistance made her so ill she nearly died. She relented and started preaching in tents on the East Coast and in Key West. Her husband decided this was not the life for him and returned home.

She continued to preach and she and young Roberta and Rolf traveled up and down the East Coast in her open-air "Gospel Car," camping at night beside the road and using local volunteers to set up her tent so she could preach. While a woman evangelist was considered "from the devil" by many, her dynamic speaking won an enormous following. In 1918, she pointed her odd transportation west and may have been the first woman to drive from the East Coast to Los Angeles. Her 5,300-seat Angelus Temple in Echo Park, Los Angeles, opened on January 1, 1923, packing in overflow crowds. A few years later she became the first woman to own and operate a Christian radio station and the first woman to preach a sermon on radio.

With a God-given gift for healing and straightforward evangelism, she won souls by the tens of thousands. During her Angelus Temple healing services, hundreds left their crutches on the stage, a massive goiter disappeared from one person's neck in front of thousands and several crippled legs straightened to match the other leg. During the Depression, the church fed some 1.5 million persons, likely more than the entire Los Angeles County social service system. Long divorced from McPherson, she married singer and actor David Hutton and on the night of the wedding discovered he was being sued by another woman he had promised to marry. Preaching to crowds around the world, she led a life so interesting the *Los Angeles Times* assigned a writer to cover nothing but Angelus Temple. Despite a life fraught with tragedy, intense media scrutiny and unproven accusations, her faith never wavered and God used her in a truly remarkable way. God gave her a vision for Foursquare: Jesus as Savior, Healer, Baptizer in the Holy Spirit and Soon Coming King. It's one I embrace.

I sit and wait to be commissioned in the denomination she founded, realizing that it's never too late for any of us to change and Christ always uses the flawed because that's all he has to work with. On stage, Dr. McPherson calls Dream Center pastor Matthew Barnett to the dais. As the young man stands beside the old, Rolf talks about the church's history, something he knows intimately not because of genetics but because he led the denomination as president for several decades. At last, he walks to Matthew's front, places both hands on his shoulders, prays with a quiet intensity and turns to say to all there, "Whatever mantle that has been passed on to me I pass on to you."

Matthew Barnett is a man without guile. With Dr. McPherson's words, goose bumps rise on my forearms. A warm shiver flows through me as if I've had an injection of new blood. My eyes water. After all I'd done, how could I have arrived here? If my life were a train, I'd be tons of twisted metal, smoking and hissing in a dark of night desert. That I am even alive is a miracle. How can all this happen in such a short time? I once jockeyed Revelation's pale horse from Hades and now will one day ride Christ's white horse from heaven.

From the pit to the pulpit. From crack cocaine to Christian crusader. From same-sex promiscuity to sanctification. From an obsession with self to a consuming love for Christ. Ignatius of Loyola, who founded the Jesuits, coined the phrase "infused contemplation," meaning a moment when the grace of God enters and totally takes over. That is what I felt in that courtroom holding cell and what I feel at this moment. My future path may have speed bumps, wrong turns and restless searches along my spiritual road map. But Jesus has already allowed for them. There will be no turning back.

God hadn't caused my death-filled childhood, sibling sexual trauma, same-sex promiscuity, greed, crack cocaine addiction, suicide attempt, stays in two psyche wards and incarceration. They were products of Satan in possession of a fallen world until Christ returns. God kept me alive even while I turned my back and walked the other way. Just as Jesus was literally resurrected from death, so was I. The crowd gathered in Jerusalem on the day Jesus was crucified could have saved him but selected the criminal Barabbas to be set free. But Jesus loved Barabbas so much he willingly died in his place. He did the same for this criminal.

While others have successfully used different paths to recovery, recovery for me is a reason and not a road. That reason is God the Father sending his only Son, in the form of a carpenter from Nazareth named Jesus, to live without sin and die rejected and shamed by the world as the sole sacrifice for my sins. That's the reason I'm redeemed, bought back with a price I can never repay. It's a gift I only have to accept. Christ's love is beyond reason. It transcends human understanding. It broke my bondage of self hate, freed me of earthly ambition and turned me loose in a hate-filled world armed with the soul penetrating power of the Holy Spirit working within me to reproduce Christ's love. It is a weapon for which Satan has no defense. That radical love released will make the devil dig for his cell phone and dial 911.

I did many things I regret. I hope fans and workers in horse racing will forgive me for the times I cheated. Yet I cannot change the past. I can only ask for God's and their forgiveness and move on with a sincere urgency to do better. The fourth step in AA is to make a "searching moral inventory of ourselves," and that is what this book represents. I also promised I'd always work to bring Christ to horse racing. Through the grace of God and the leading of the Holy Spirit, I believe this book will help do that.

I often hear skeptics say God's power to answer prayer, inspire the Bible and perform miracles are sheer conjecture. Yet, the power of God

336

can be measured by changes in my life and many like me. What I've done since God healed me in that jail cell is living, breathing, measurable proof of the existence of God. Can anyone who reads this book think I could change so radically without the direct intervention of God?

What happened to me since that supernatural jail house event had nothing to do with me. I didn't decide to become a minister and chaplain and give up my destructive habits. God's love performed a healing miracle on my behalf so definitive my rage, the root cause of my habits, vanished. After Christ's love overwhelmed me, there was nothing else I could do and be fulfilled. After his resurrection, Jesus physically left earth, leaving behind the Holy Spirit who healed me, is healing me and will continue to heal me.

I felt Christ's loving grace when I carried a cross through the midnight streets of Hollywood, fed the homeless in Skid Row and prayed out demons at a bus stop. I did nothing more than share that same grace when I helped give transsexuals and runaways, sexually abused youth and pregnant teens the opportunity to come back to the Dream Center, hit the tilt button and reset their frantic pinball lives. Today, I feel that same healing love when I join the journey of those bent by grief, jolted by trauma and enter the intimate, sacred space of the dying.

At the commissioning, other Foursquare officials lay hands on Matthew and pray, some in tongues. Dr. McPherson asks those about to be commissioned to stand. I do as I raise my hands to the Lord and close my eyes, not caring if others notice my Holy Spirit tears. He reads from Matthew 28:18 with Jesus saying in his resurrected body shortly before he ascended into heaven, ". . . All authority has been given me in heaven and on earth. . ." He adds John 20:21 where Jesus also in his resurrected state says to his disciples, ". . . Peace to you. As the Father has sent Me, I also send you."

Dr. McPherson straightens and looks at us with a confidence that makes my soul soar. "Thus, I declare each of you as one sent by God, with the full authority given by God the Father to Christ himself."

And it's over. I'm a licensed minister. It's not that anyone needs a piece of plastic in their wallet to do ministry. Actually, some of the most devout of God's servants have no title and seek none. To me the license represents trust, trust that a large, well-known denomination determined I was worthy of their sanction. I already knew I'd serve the Lord the remainder of my life and trust in him to fill my needs. Ministry in the Bible's Greek means "helps." I don't want to sound pious, but more than anything I want to spend the rest of my life helping others. Exactly how God wishes me to do that is still being revealed. Right now, being a Saturday night chaplain in a Level II Trauma Center is like remembering to tuck and roll when a mount collapsed beneath me. I'm not finished. I'm on an exciting adventure.

If you haven't already, you're welcome to start your own journey with Jesus this very instant.

The End

Made in the USA
Middletown, DE
17 August 2019